# NATIONALISM AND DEMOCRATISATION

# Nationalism and Democratisation
## Politics of Slovakia and Slovenia

Erika Harris
*University of Leeds*

**Ashgate**

Published by
Ashgate Publishing Limited
Gower House
Croft Road
Aldershot
Hampshire GU11 3HR
England

Ashgate Publishing Company
131 Main Street
Burlington, VT 05401-5600 USA

Ashgate website: http://www.ashgate.com

**British Library Cataloguing in Publication Data**
Harris, Erika
  Nationalism and democratisation : politics of Slovakia and
  Slovenia
  1. Nationalism - Slovakia 2.Nationalism - Slovenia
  3. Democratization - Slovakia 4. Democratization - Slovenia
  5. Slovakia - Politics and government -1993 - 6. Slovenia -
  Politics and government - 1990 -
  I. Title
  320.9 ' 4373 ' 09049

**Library of Congress Control Number** 2001098449

ISBN 0 7546 1890 0 ✓

Printed and bound by Athenaeum Press, Ltd.,
Gateshead, Tyne & Wear.

# Contents

# List of Tables

# Acknowledgements

I wish to express my gratitude to the numerous individuals and the Economic and Social Research Council who supported me through the development of my PhD. thesis on which this book is based.

I wish to thank in particular to prof. David Beetham whose guidance, knowledge and advice have been invaluable to me in all my academic endeavours thus far, and to Dr. John Schwarzmantel for his constant support, practical and intellectual insight and encouragement which made the writing of this book a less arduous process. I extend a note of thanks to the Department of Politics at University of Leeds and all my colleagues there for providing a supporting working environment.

My appreciation goes to prof. Rudi Rizman and Alenka Krašovec for making my research in Ljubljana more pleasant and for keeping me up to date on Slovene politics when I could not be there personally. I wish to pay special tribute to the Institute of Philosophy at the Slovak Academy of Sciences in Bratislava for their incredible hospitality. I am deeply indebted to its Director Doc.PhDr.Tibor Pichler, to Doc.PhDr. Tatiana Sedová, Dr. Karol Kollár and Ing.Egon Gál and many others there for their friendship, and for helping me to rediscover the country I left many years ago. I also want to extend a note of thanks to prof. Oren Yiftachel for keeping the debate about nationalism going and to Dr. Kieran Williams for his much appreciated comments.

Finally, my deepest gratitude goes to my husband Julian, for his patience and unwavering faith in me. It is to him that this book is dedicated.

# List of Abbreviations

| | |
|---|---|
| ANO | Alliance of New citizen |
| DS | Democratic party (Slovakia and Slovenia) |
| DÚ | Democratic Union |
| ECE | Eastern Central Europe |
| Együttéllés | Coexistence |
| CSCE | Conference on Security and Cooperation in Europe |
| ČSSR | Czechoslovak Socialist Republic |
| ČSFR | Czecho-Slovak Federal Republic |
| DEMOS | Democratic Opposition of Slovenia |
| DeSUS | Democratic Party of Retired People |
| EU | European Union |
| HSLS | Hlinka's Slovak People's Party |
| HzDS | Movement for Democratic Slovakia |
| IMF | International Monetary Fund |
| JNA | Yugoslav National Army |
| KDH | Christian Democratic Movement |
| KSČ | Communist Party of Czechoslovakia |
| KSS | Communist Party of Slovakia |
| KVP | Košice Government programme |
| LCS | League of Communists of Slovenia |
| LCY | League of Communists of Yugoslavia |
| LDS | Liberal Democratic party |
| MK | Hungarian Coalition |
| MKDH | Hungarian Christian Democratic Movement |
| NATO | North Atlantic Treaty Organisation |
| NC SR | National Council of the Slovak Republic |
| NSi | New Slovenia |
| ODS | Civic Democratic Party |
| OSCE | Organisation for Security and Cooperation in Europe |
| SMER | Direction |
| SMS | Party of Young people of Slovenia |

# Introduction

The year 1989 marked a turning point in world history. The rigid division of Europe into East and West, the bipolarity and the predictability of the Cold War system and the merciless suppression of political changes in the region which lasted for nearly half of the century disintegrated within two years. By 1991 communism as a political system was dismantled, the Eastern Central European countries have liberated themselves from Soviet tutelage and the three multinational communist federations, the Soviet Union, Yugoslavia and Czechoslovakia, have been dissolved. The subsequent establishment of democratic structures in all successor states, for all its modernising and emancipating efforts, was accompanied by many ethnic and national conflicts.

A decade later three things are clear: first, postcommunism became synonymous with democratisation, second, postcommunist transitions to democracy produced greatly divergent outcomes and third, democratisation was inseparable from the issues of the nation. It is the conjunction of those three issues, postcommunism, democratisation and the nation which constitutes the realm of the following study, whilst the subject of the analysis is the link between them. Most of academic endeavour into postcommunism has been consumed by the exploration of political, economic and social transformation which as challenging as it was, nevertheless, proved less problematic than the transformation of national and ethnic identities commanded by the magnitude of political changes. This book will diverge from the more conventional accounts of postcommunism and seek to explain the transition from communism to democracy by magnifying one major element of the transition process - the nation and its identity.

## Objectives

The book is concerned with the relationship between nationalism and democracy in a particular setting: the larger framework is postcommunist Eastern and Central Europe, the focus is on newly independent democracies, explored through the case studies of Slovakia and Slovenia.

1

The purpose is to seek an answer to two related questions about what is the role of nationalism in the democratisation process, and under what conditions nationalism is less or more compatible with the democratisation process. The complex dynamics that characterise the relationship between nationalism and democracy will be discussed at length throughout, but the first point to convey is that the role of nationalism in the democratisation process cannot be generalised and constitutes a complex process in itself, conditioned by the political context of the society undergoing the transition to democracy. The political context will be viewed as an aggregate of factors contributing to and determining the equilibrium between nationalism and democracy: the stage of national development, the conditions and circumstances surrounding the achievement of independent statehood, the previous regime and the period prior to that, the formation of transitional elites and the stage in the transition, and finally, the issues of ethnic composition and harmony within the state. The broad range of factors taken into consideration indicates that this book adopts if not a sympathetic, but an objective attitude to nationalism which it views, for better or worse, as an integral part of the turbulent and all-encompassing changes in new states, seeking a direction, for the first time under democratic conditions.

Identity and democratisation are intimately linked and the compatibility of nationalism and democracy depends on how compatible their objectives are. It is those objectives that change, depending on the politics of the time and so does the role of nationalism in the democratisation process. All findings of this study suggest that nationalism aided the political change in ex-communist countries, it provided the populations of these countries with a sense of purpose and identity, and in the newly independent democracies it assisted the state-creation - all conducive to democratisation. Clearly, nationalism's role at the beginning of the democratisation process can be relatively positive; the debate here is about the limits to nationalism's capacity to remain positive.

## Definitions

The study of nationalism inhabits an area of individual and collective identities and their psychological and cultural interpretations. As such the concepts used in studies of nationalism are often contested. The conceptual controversy, however, does not obscure the fact that the study of nationalism is essentially about its political causes and consequences[1].

I take nationalism to be a form of politics[2] which focuses on the articulation and the promotion of political aims in the name of and on behalf of a nation, or national group. Nationalism refers to aspirations to political sovereignty, or a degree of it within a given territory; hence, nationalism is not limited to actions or policies of a nation whose name the state carries, but could be policies and actions of other national groups living within the territory of the state. 'The nation' stands for a large social group integrated by a combination of objective relationships, such as territory, politics, economy, language, history and culture, and their subjective reflection in collective consciousness[3]. By national identity is meant the identity that derives from the membership in a nation[4].

Ethnicity refers to a social bond based on the belonging to an ethnic group, defined as a particular collectivity based on real or putative common ancestry and memories of shared historical past and cultural focus on one or more elements defined as the epitome of their peoplehood[5]. The distinction between the nation and the ethnic group lies in the fact that ethnicity is strictly a cultural trait in which binding issue is primarily the common ancestry and not loyalty to a legal structure of the state (at least not necessarily the state of citizenship).

The state is a legal concept, it describes a definite territory and denotes the aggregation of political and administrative institution. The term 'nation-state' should thus mean a state populated by one national group. As is apparent most states comprise of more than one national group, hence the distinction between the dominant nation and minority. The term 'dominant', far from numerical dominance or territorial extension, signifies merely a national group who has the pre-eminent authority to distribute rewards and values in the state; in contrast, a minority is a national/ethnic group which defines itself (or is defined) as a separate cultural entity from the assumed official culture of the state.

Related to these working definitions, and rather importantly for this study, is the distinction between 'nation-building' and 'state-building'. Nation-building stresses cultural homogeneity, its policies are rooted in a deliberate effort to construct an overarching collective identity based on a putative common national sentiment, mostly ethnic sentiment. State-building stands for a complementary project, but aims at social solidarity rooted in loyalty to the state, its institutions and its interests[6].

## Structure of the book

The book is divided into eight chapters. The first chapter establishes the parameters of the study. It focuses on contemporary nationalism in Eastern and Central Europe at this specific historical conjuncture - the end of communist rule. The chapter explores politics inspired by democratisation and what appeared to be its concomitant - nationalism, and the evolving dynamics between them. It advances various propositions as to the salience of nationalism and concludes that nationalism is inspired by a multiplicity of factors, ranging from historically predetermined conditions to factors deriving from politics of the transitions to democracy. I was convinced from the beginning, that to understand particular nationalism and its contemporary manifestations requires a journey throughout its historical development; hence, historical legacy and the transitional project form a consistent theme throughout this book and the case studies of Slovakia and Slovenia are divided in the same way.

The second chapter locates the relationship between nationalism and democracy in theoretical discourse. It consists of two main sections: first, critical examination of the relationship between nationalism and democracy, their compatibilities and contradictions; second, introduces the case studies and illustrates the use of theoretical arguments. The core theme here is the clash between two overlapping, but conceptually different processes: the culturally pre-occupied nation-building and administratively and politically orientated state-building. The chapter draws a clear distinction between ethnic solidarity, national identity and the identity of a political community. It also draws attention to a political unit as the precondition of democracy and the role of national self-determination in the formation of such a unit.

The following four chapters are devoted to the case studies. Each case study is divided chronologically into two sequential chapters. In both cases, the first chapter explores firstly, the national and political development within the former multiethnic states, and secondly, the politics of transition to independence and democracy. This is then followed by the subsequent chapter dealing with an analysis of socio-political and cultural conditions in independent Slovakia and Slovenia. Those chapters both contain: an analysis of the political structure and electoral behaviour, the exploration of the political tradition and the evaluation of respective ethnic policies.

Thus, the third chapter follows the Slovak development within Czechoslovakia. It focuses on the failure of the common Czechoslovak state to establish a united political nation, which it is argued here, was the main reason for the break-up of the state. Another reason was the divergent levels of political and national development between the Czechs and Slovaks. The disintegration of Czechoslovakia, with hindsight rather inevitable, was not really desired by the populations of the Czech and Slovak republics. This had serious consequences for the formation of political elites in independent Slovakia. The fourth chapter finds independent Slovakia, politically and ethnically divided, the new nationhood and democracy both suffering from the lack of conviction and direction, resulting in the considerable rise of nationalism, particularly towards the Hungarian minority. Since the 1998 elections the identity-related domination of Slovak politics appears to be waning and the chances for Slovakia to join the first wave of the EU's Eastern enlargement are increasing.

The negative role of nationalism in the democratisation process in Slovakia is contrasted with the situation in Slovenia. The fifth chapter provides a detailed account of the Yugoslav system and Slovenia's development within the Yugoslav federation. The question of the rising national awareness in combination with the divergent levels of economic, political and cultural developments within a federal state, comparable to Czechoslovakia, is also at the heart of this chapter. This is done in order to evaluate how the previous regime affected the democratisation process in Slovenia. The sixth chapter, after a closer examination of the actual process of Slovene independence concentrates on its central theme, consensus on the issues of national interest and the legitimacy of the democratisation process.

The seventh chapter addresses the international environment post-Cold War. It centres on European integration and the role of the nation in the era of globalisation. Subsequently, it offers theoretical and empirical discussion about the interrelationship between national identity and foreign policy-making, generally, and in Slovakia and Slovenia particularly. The conclusion draws together the principal issues raised in this book and offers concluding thoughts about postcommunism, nationalism, democracy and integration. In order to assess the findings of this study within a wider perspective of theories of democracy and nationalism, the following points are stressed. First, the nationalist challenge to democracy comes from ethnic politics which are a result of (re)assertion of ethnic or national identity in order to readjust or strengthen the position of its group. We must therefore assume that nationalism will remain a permanent feature of our world for foreseeable future. Second, the classical theories of nationalism do not account adequately for nationalism in the new postcommunist democracies. The new element of contemporary nationalism is the synchronisation of nation-building, state-building and international integration compressed into one process - the democratisation process. Third, the relationship between democracy and nationalism vacillates between a partnership and challenge. As much as nationalism can be mobilised, it can be reduced and this is where democracy comes to play the most important role.

# Notes

[1]   M.Hechter *Containing Nationalism* Oxford, Oxford University Press 2000.

[2]   J.Breuilly *Nationalism and the State* Manchester, Manchester University Press 1993.

[3]   M.Hroch 'From national movements to the fully–fledged nation' *New Left Review* 198 April 1993 pp.3-20.

[4]   L.Greenfeld *Nationalism* Cambridge (MA), Harvard University Press 1992  p.7.

[5]   R.Schermerhoorn 'Ethnicity and Minority Groups' in J.Hutchinson and A.D.Smith *Ethnicity* Oxford, Oxford University Press 1996.

[6]   O.Yiftachel 'Nation-Building or Ethnic Fragmentation? Frontier Settlement and Collective Identities in Israel' *Space and Polity* 1:2 1997 pp.149-169.

# 1 The End of Communism and the Crisis of Identity

The beginning of the 1990s enters history as the end of communism[1], but also as a period of an intense ethnic and national reawakening, often with dramatic consequences. Years of postcommunism have made it clear that the transition to democracy was inseparable from the issues of the nation and that political pluralism entailed an upsurge of ethnically based politics. The map of Eastern/Central Europe (henceforth ECE)[2] was profoundly changed by a number of new states, whilst domestic politics of nearly all states in the region involve seeking a solution to demands from minorities. The essay on nationalism and democracy by Ghia Nodia states boldly that 'nationalism is the historical force that has provided the political units for democratic governments'[3]. It further argues that if Ernest Gellner says that 'nationalism engenders nations'[4], then it is equally true that "democratic transitions engender nations"[5]. It cannot be denied that some 28 new states[6] born out of the disintegration of the ex-Soviet Union, Yugoslavia and Czechoslovakia, give credibility to Nodia's view that 'democracy never exists without nationalism'[7]. The degree to which this is true is one of the questions this book attempts to answer.

There is no doubting a link between nationalism and democracy, but that link is not teleological - not all nationalism leads to emancipation, not all national emancipation ends in democracy, and not all transitions to democracy will end as democracies. The 'revolutions' of 1989 in ECE were 'nationalist' only in the sense that they sought national sovereignty out of the Soviet Empire, but it cannot be argued that newly independent ECE states emerging as a consequence of the postcommunist democratisation ever developed any authentic separatist movement prior to their independence[8]. It also pays to remember that we do not know whether the earlier attempts at liberalisation (e.g. the Prague Spring 1968 and the Hungarian uprising of 1956), might have possibly led to further democratisation without nationalist mobilisation[9] if they had happened in another geopolitical space and without interventions by the Soviet Union. National solidarity energized the 1989 revolutions and created the context within which these transitions became so euphoric, but it was also nationalism that eliminated much of that euphoria and finally killed it in the Balkans.

All that can be asked is why was it democratisation that engendered nationalism of the 'old' kind, the ethnically based nationalism of blood-language-religion-culture mixture, which paradoxically is often referred to as 'new'[10]. The 'new' context of this latest wave of nationalism in ECE - the integration into transnational structures, the requirements of the international community for the provisions for the protection of minorities and the possibility of democracy itself - are precisely the ones that make its resurgence seem so anachronistic.

While recognising the strength of Nodia's argument, the fact is that only a few of the new states in ECE are true nation-states, that is that only very few consist largely of one national group (and that is indeed where the transition seems to have progressed faster)[11], and that democratising and nation-building simultaneously are fraught with contradictions. What is clear is that nationalism, certainly for the first few years of the transition process, was central to politics in the new states of the region. Neither the glorification of its effects on democracy, nor the more traditional dismissal and underestimation of the nationalist phenomenon, are helpful in solving this question.

The task of this chapter is to examine more closely the conditions under which contemporary nationalism spreads in the new states and to seek an answer to two questions: one, why has there been an intensification of nationalism in postcommunist societies and two, is nationalism an 'indispensable element' of democracy in general[12], or is it merely a necessary and logical concomitant of postcommunist transitions? The discussion in pages to follow is divided into three parts: 1. the particular features of the 1989 revolutions which inaugurated democracy in the region and how these processes differed from other transitions from other authoritarian regimes; 2. what is meant by nationalism in the context of this book; 3. analysis of the various factors, often mutually reinforcing, that contribute to the salience of nationalism in the region.

The principal argument is that democratisation itself has contributed to nationalist mobilisation. However, the intensity of nationalism varies in line with the particular histories of those countries, including the very recent history of the end of the communist regime and where applicable, the extrication from the former communist federations. In answer to the second question, the conclusion argues that nationalism is the logical concomitant of transition to democracy in postcommunist societies, not because democracy has to go hand-in-hand with nationalism, but because the weakness of these states and their democratic institutions allows nationalism to take up a position of the great unifier, mobiliser and legitimiser in all tasks that a newly independent democracy needs to perform.


## Revolutions of 1989

In the first years of post-1989 revolutions in ECE many comparisons were made between the French Revolution (1789)[13] and the '1989 revolutions', which started with the toppling of the Berlin Wall and led to the end of communist rule in the whole region. To compare the inglorious end of the communist parties' monopoly of state power to the execution of Louis XVI might appear farfetched. However, the comparison is relevant, for we must agree that there are certain events whose consequences have profound implications for human existence and therefore merit to be called historic - the French Revolution, the Bolshevik Revolution (1917) and the '1989 revolutions' were such events[14].

If the great revolutions of the past claimed to be a beginning of a new era and indeed carried history forward, regardless of what we might think a better alternative would have been, the 1989 revolutions position in history is not so clear. Depending on one's point of view, the year 1989 marks either the conclusion of the era which started with the Bolshevik Revolution[15], or the extension of democracy, heralded by the French Revolution, to Eastern Europe, therefore a final stage in the European revolutionary tradition. Somehow the year 1989 is associated rather with 'the end'[16], than with 'the beginning'. The reason for this perceived lack of novelty[17] is occasioned by the often expressed idea of 'return', to either independence, common European home (Gorbachev), or democracy - all of which claims are open to questioning. For one, hardly any newly independent postcommunist democracies can claim to have been independent or democratic prior to the Second World War and the subsequent imposition of the Soviet rule.

Moreover, there was nothing new about the values or ideas that these 'revolutions' brought; the new order was even older than socialism. A plural political system, market economy and open society were already established values in the West. So, where does this leave the comparison with the French Revolution? The analogy can be made with the end of apathy, spontaneous mass action, the refusal to carry on in the same old undignified way and indeed the inauguration of a new social order, even if the values and norms were not new. These were 'political revolutions'[18] and they transformed the existing order decisively and it would appear irreversibly. There is reason to doubt whether all new democracies will become stable functioning liberal democracies, but at the same time there is also enough evidence to be certain that the Leninist system based on ideological uniformity, coercion and suppression has been dismantled for a long time to come, if not for ever. The fact that these revolutions have been followed by ethnic strife, nationalist upsurge, rampant corruption, the rise of illiberal parties and a degree of nostalgia for the old regime does not take away the most important message of these revolutions - freedom of choice for all people.

## The End of Communism and Democracy

The bankruptcy of state socialism seems to have given an almost undisputed credibility to liberal-democracy, to the point of its most famous adherent Francis Fukuyama's claim of 'the end of history'. A disproportionate amount of attention has been given to Fukuyama's thesis possibly because it reflects, without any regard for the lessons learned by history and other similar claims of the 'end point of mankind's ideological evolution'[19], what could be called a general assessment of the revolutions of 1989.

There are several implications to this 'end of history' interpretation of the end of communism which bear directly on the transition to democracy.

1. It neglects the historical evidence that the attempt to establish liberal democracy in conjunction with the formation of new states is also not new in the region - a similar situation arose after 1918[20]. Yet none of the new states emerging from the Paris Peace treaties remained democratic for longer than a decade with the exception of Czechoslovakia.

2. Jeffrey C. Isaac argues that whilst he believes that 'there is much merit to this liberal interpretation'[21], it is politically and morally flawed. Politically because it ignores important forms of politics practiced by democratic oppositions that are not adequately covered by liberalism; morally because it marginalizes the importance of non-electoral, antiparliamentary forms of political activity ('forum' politics[22]) that played an important role in the ending of communism and at the same time constitute a more grass-roots type of participatory democracy.

    The strategy for political action was more rooted in the resistance to the system than in direct achievement of political power. Secondly, was the appeal to internationalism. To Eastern European dissidents national independence was a condition for social reform and social decency, but this was clearly distinguishable from nationalism that elevates the importance of belonging to one particular nation and brings the pursuit of maximal conditions for that particular nation into politics. The initial anti-Communist struggle in Czechoslovakia did not seek self-determination for either the Czech or Slovak nation - that came later. Equally, the democratisation of Slovenia was followed by independence, but independence was not the intended goal behind the tentative democratising reforms sparked off by civic movements throughout the 1980s. Finally, the alliances formed were extremely broad, embracing liberals and the Orthodox Church, democrats and nationalists, socialists and conservatives, as well as workers and intelligentsia. They aimed at a new type of society, a self-managing civil society, or rather a civilized society, based on active citizenship, human rights and non-violence. One of the reasons for the quick end of 'forum politics' was that it was an idealistic vision at a time when the end of communism seemed too remote to contemplate, thus the actual government under these policies and with such unlikely alliances did not need to be scrutinised for its feasibility.

As much as 'living in truth'[23] was an admirable aspiration and struggle, it was not a daily practice of politics - this was democracy that could not be criticised or blamed, devoid of competition, ambitious politicians and decisions about mundane issues of allocation and taxes. C.S.Maier warns against the 'feeling of anticlimax', that succeeded the initial euphoria of 1989, a collective sense of disillusion which leads to 'heightened xenophobia' characterised by appeals to ethnic exclusiveness and the desire to 'reinvigorate the national unit'[24].

The Yugoslavian tragedy certainly warrants such pessimism. On the other hand it appears that the situation of the early 1990s, when the transition in ECE countries seemed to be completely overshadowed by the dangers of ethnic nationalism, has changed recently and nationalist pressures seem to be waning. Nevertheless it is clear that one of the forces that can divert democracy into more extremist path of politics is nationalism. This book attempts to shed light on how and why the best intentions of 1989 politics, once transferred out of opposition into parties, governments and parliaments, joined forces with nationalist ideologues and ended up, in many cases, in opposition to all that democratic reforms stood for.

3.  Notwithstanding the above, the fact is that no matter how troubled the transitions to democracy in ex-communist countries are, and however legitimate the doubts about the sustainability of that project may be, we must concede that they all are or at least wish to be transitions to democracy. The populations and political leaders declare their countries to be liberal democracies, they wish to be accepted as such, their potential admission into the European Union is based on the

assessment of their democratic credentials. Moreover, even the less democratically inclined political leaderships claim the devotion to democracy and recognise that it is possibly the only system capable of giving legitimacy to the effort of an often difficult and always tumultuous transition. Chapter 4 will guide us through all pitfalls of postcommunism in Slovakia, but will end with the general elections of 1998 which were a confirmation that even the troubled transition in Slovakia was ultimately a transition to democracy. The government of Vladimir Mečiar, the leader of the HzDS (Hnutie za Demokratické Slovensko/ Movement for Democratic Slovakia), aided by the right-wing nationalist party and a populist leftist movement, marked by nationalism and authoritarian tendencies and the main political force since (and behind) the independence in 1993, was defeated by the combination of democratic forces. The most meaningful factor about these elections in the present context, was the difference from 1989. If 1989 can be assessed as a victory of anticommunism rather than a victory of democracy (as the subsequent evolution of Slovak politics demonstrated), after nearly a decade of political turmoil, the elections showed that the society itself had enough resources to bring about the changes[25], without any external influences and against many obstacles created by Mečiar's administration.

## Postcommunist Transitions and Nationalism

As a consequence of this last point, there is a burgeoning literature[26] which argues about the relevance of comparison between postcommunist transitions and other transitions to democracy, mainly in Southern Europe and Latin America. I shall refrain from reviewing this literature, but for a few comments which are relevant to the relationship between nationalism and democracy.

The main point is not whether there are differences between transitions from communism and other authoritarian regimes; of course there are, but that does not make the comparison irrelevant, on the contrary, comparison sharpens the discussion about the problems transitions encounter. The point is that the differences might be too great, which begs the question of how useful and meaningful such comparisons can be. When it comes to democratisation, one could argue that all comparisons are valid and should not be confined to democratisation since the 1970s, amounting to what S.Huntington called a 'third wave'[27]. There are many good reasons why including postcommunist transitions in the 'third wave' may not deepen our understanding of the post-1989 developments in the ECE countries. Firstly, there were no signs of democratisation in those countries during the 1970s;

equally difficult is to argue that there was much interconnectedness between postcommunist transitions and the transitions in Asia (i.e. Philippines, South Korea and Taiwan in the latter half of 1980s). Secondly, one is well advised to consider the considerable differences in the international environment after the end of the Cold War, when the integration of new postcommunist democracies into the existing Western political, economic and security structures is, at the end of bipolar competition, perceived to be less urgent, and is thus much slower than was the integration of the Southern European states (i.e. Spain and Portugal) in the 1980s. On the other hand, the developments in the Soviet Union in the late 1980s cannot be divorced – in fact they were of decisive importance - from the subsequent developments in the rest of the Communist Europe. Hence, the 'wave' of transitions from communism is better viewed as a distinct phenomenon; if not a 'fourth wave'[28] then certainly a particular pattern of transitions within a chronological 'third wave'.

Based on the supposition that communism was a unique type of authoritarianism and that postcommunist transitions are therefore a specific type of transitions, there are two main differences compared with transitions from other authoritarian regimes.

The by now a well accepted point that the communist transitions mean the dual track transition to pluralist democracy and a market economy has further implications. The transition is not merely a change of regime, but the creation of a whole new social order, including the formation of new middle classes and a transition from a relatively socially equal society to a system of an increased social inequality[29]. The communist parties' political monopoly and the complete penetration into the private sphere affected society in the most profound way, including the definition of private and political interests. Democracy means in this case a redefinition of society, that is its identity and interests at individual and group levels and the re-definition of the range of possibilities of attaining those interests. This particular feature of postcommunist transitions, when people were uncertain about their place in the new society and about who was to represent their interests and even about how those interests were to be defined can partly be responsible for the ensuing prevalence and strength of ethnic cleavages[30].

Related to this point is the increased significance of nationalism when compared to earlier transitions, particularly the Latin American ones. In contrast, nearly all Eastern European transitions were at the same time movements for national liberation - either from an oppressive regime, or from Soviet tutelage, and mostly from both. In this sense the inauguration of democracy in the region amounts to the creation of new sovereign states, a fact that has many implications for democracy and its consolidation.

The most distinguishing characteristic of postcommunist transitions is the fact that popular sovereignty and national sovereignty merged into one process[31], similar to 1848 and 1918, reaffirming the idea that the nation-state is the best framework for democracy. If we accept that democracy is the most valuable form of government, then national self-determination became one of the consequences of postcommunism. The disintegration of all multinational states in the region meant that a number of new states are involved in nation- and state-building at the same time. There is a considerable difference in transition processes between well-established states (i.e. Poland, Hungary) and new states (i.e. Slovakia and Slovenia). In the latter 'democratisation' does not fully describe the political situation, because not only the character of the state was changing, but its very boundaries, its position in the international community and the decisions about who are 'the people' who constitute the state were all undergoing redefinition.

The preoccupation with building the nation-state in the region where most states are not ethnically homogenous can work against democracy, as we have seen in the interwar period and recently in Yugoslavia and less dramatically in Slovakia. The fact that the least successful transitions are in the ethnically less homogenous countries suggests that there is an obvious correlation between the success of transition and ethnic/national homogeneity. Such a conclusion would lead to an absurd claim, that ethnic 'homogeneity is a prerequisite for democracy'[32]. This argument is morally indefensible, and politically flawed: ethnic homogeneity in the region is attainable only through unacceptable methods, such as population transfer, an imposed assimilation, or ethnic cleansing - all these methods have been employed at some point in the history of the region and the consequences do not need to be repeated here; it ignores political strategies, such as consociationalism, federation, collective rights and regional autonomy as a way of establishing multicultural politics. The exemplary protection of minorities in Slovenia, the progress concerning the Hungarian minority in Romania, the inclusion of the Hungarian ethnic parties in the new Slovak government illustrate that a political solution is possible, even if difficult at times.

Post-1989 development in ECE is a complex and at times a dramatic transformation to the new capitalist society which combines new elements of political change with the acceptance of old principles of Western societies. It was in this rapidly changing environment that liberal democracy was if not overwhelmed, then at best had to compete with nationalism. Adam Michnik had pithily observed that 'nationalism is the last word of communism'[33].

*Ethnic Politics - the Main Argument*

Postcommunist transition is a particular type of democratisation, more than 'a transitional stage', rather a condition 'showing its own dynamic'[34]. The argument that runs throughout this book is that two main characteristics of that condition are the position of nationalism at the centre of the political stage, and the fact that the very process of democratisation has itself contributed to the increased role of nationalism. As became apparent fairly soon after the collapse of communism, the transition to democracy would involve more than the transition in political, social and economic spheres. This 'triple transition'[35] needs to be supplemented by a fourth one[36], nation-building. This was not only because the end of the Soviet external empire meant the restoration of national sovereignty, but also because in many cases it led to the actual establishment of new national states, with new borders and new international status - often the culmination of delayed national development, due to historical factors. It can be argued that national revival and the subsequent conflicts between majorities and minorities involved a self-perpetuating dynamic leading to an increase in nationalist mobilisation. This revealed fully the unique and unprecedented nature of postcommunist transitions, whilst the surprise at the vehemence of these conflictual processes uncovered gaps in the understanding of these particular types of democratic transitions.

The newly expanded political arena, newly acquired political resources (i.e. the right to form political parties, free elections and the freedom of the media) and the competition emerging from it provided a fertile ground for ethnic-nationalist mobilisation on two important levels. Firstly, the collapse of the existing state power left an ideological and identificational vacuum that was easily filled by one identity, which appeared more fixed and coherent - national identity.

Secondly, nationalism functions as an effective instrument for old and new elites to retain or gain power by offering the 'nation' as a refuge for those who seek scapegoats for the injustices of the past, but mostly uncertainties of the present. Such mobilisation rests on a certain rhetoric steeped in emphasis on insecurities and fear based on historical injustice perpetrated against 'the nation' and projected to the future. In the ECE region it is often a neighbouring state whose ethnic kin is usually a minority in the new state. Consequent distrust and possible hostility among various ethic groups are in turn an impediment to liberal democracy and its basic principle of equal political status of all citizens. This paradox is well summed up in the statement that 'democracy is good for ethnic mobilisation, but not so vice versa'[37]. On a more positive side, there is of course the question of the promotion of loyalty towards the national project connected to cultural, economic and political developments, which new governments have to pursue. The use of nationalist ideology for cementing popular support, either for the new state or for competing elites, is not unique to postcommunism.

*Politicisation of ethnicity* There are many definitions of nationalism, but contrary to many complaints about the ambiguity of the concept the scholarly literature on the whole concurs in at least two of its characteristics: collective and political. Hence, nationalism in this book is viewed as a form of politics and limited to 'articulating and promoting political aims in the name of and on behalf of a nation, or national group'[38]. When such promotion takes a form of the politicisation of ethnicity for the purposes of political gain of one ethnic group over others, we are talking of ethnic politics and that is where the challenge to democracy in connection with nationalism lies.

By ethnic politics is meant a form of nationalism which mobilises an ethnic group into a movement, striving for the autonomy and identity of the group. Such a movement generally relies on kin relations, collective memories, language or culture. It is therefore not restricted to nationalism of the state and its sovereignty, but could be that of minority or a national group within a state, e.g. the Hungarian minority in Slovakia, the Slovak national movement within Czechoslovakia, Slovenes in Yugoslavia. Ethnic politics then refers to the conflictual claims of different ethnic groups, either vis-à-vis each other, or vis-à-vis the state, which can take the form of politics of irreconcilable ends, but more often involves a struggle to maximise the influence and conditions for one's own national group. Throughout the following discussion nationalising and homogenising policies of the new nation-state (i.e. new constitution, language laws, state education, citizenship laws, immigration policies, the provision for minorities, land reforms etc.), are seen also in the light of ethnic politics, for invariably they entail the promotion of interests by one ethnic group, which has acquired nationhood - the dominant nationality.

When the focus of identity becomes ethnic identity and when the definition of group interests becomes dominated by ethnic affiliation, invariably it leads to an exaggerated preference of one group over another, often to the point of belittling (or even hostility) of others. The policies of the state or minority inspired by such a preference of one group over another lead to ethnic politics, a precondition of which is ethnic nationalism. The distinction between ethnic and civic nationalism informs many theories of nationalism and the question of its compatibility with democracy, and will be discussed in the second chapter. Here it is sufficient to say that this binary classification rests on the assumption that ethnic nationalism poses a considerable challenge to democracy by its inherently collectivist, thus illiberal, definition of the nation as a community of descent. Civic nationalism then is antithetical in character, inclined towards an inclusive definition of the nation as a community of equal citizens.

Obviously such a strict distinction does not reflect the complexities of nationalism and its historical and political processes nor does it mean that ethnic or civic nationalisms are unchanging in their character as if written in stone. In the nineteenth century when some nations (e.g. Slovaks, Croats, Czechs, Slovenes, Serbs) tried to liberate themselves from the autocratic empires, the overwhelming group identity was the ethnic identity, but nationalism which drove that revolutionary struggle did not carry the same negative notion of oppression that we now associate with ethnic nationalism.

The difference is that what we are now witnessing in ECE is the establishment of political pluralism, but accompanied by an upsurge of ethnically based politics, which leads to unrest among majorities and minorities, whilst civic identities are dissolving into ethnic ones, often to the detriment of the democratisation process. Ethnicity may have a legitimate role to play in defining identity and contributing to the formation of communities, but when it comes to the establishment of democratic rules and political mechanisms, in order to ensure the equality of all citizens before the law, ethnicity offers little contribution.

## Historical Legacy and the Transitional Project: Salience of Nationalism in Postcommunist Societies

It is a truism to say that the present and the future are determined by the past. However, when it comes to postcommunist societies the past encompasses at least three different pasts exercising a different influence on the present: the pre-communist past, which could be that of an independent state, a federation or a multinational kingdom; the communist period which varied in the intensity of the regimes; and the very immediate past of the extrication from the communist regime, followed in many cases by the dissolution of the existing states.

In the introduction to this chapter I have proposed a question as to why has there been such an intensification of nationalism in the postcommunist societies. The pages to follow concentrate on a number of factors that derive from those national pasts and that can be generalised, and also to show how and to what extent they have shaped the role of nationalism and identity politics in the region. These are:

1. historical animosities;
2. communist nationality policies;
3. communist ideology;
4. elite competition; and
5. the issue of minorities in new democracies.

They are not mutually exclusive, on the contrary they are compatible and emphasise the causal influence of the past, remote and very recent, on the transition from communism to democracy.

## *From 'Ancient Hatred' to Contemporary Nationalism*

In the early days of postcommunism the most common (and the most oversimplified) explanation for the rise of nationalism in ECE countries became the story of 'ancient hatreds'[39], long suppressed by communist party rule and released by the end of it in all their viciousness.

There are many reasons why the 'ancient hatred' view should be contested as a wholesale assessment of the rise of nationalism in ECE countries. The obvious reasons are factual. Let us take the Yugoslav conflict first. Contrary to the popular and often even scholarly claim the Serb-Croat dispute is not 'ancient' - Serbs and Croats had not fought until the beginning of the 20th century[40], which hardly even at the beginning of this new century justifies the term 'ancient'.

Secondly, such views are too reminiscent of Cold War rhetoric, when the whole region was treated as a monolith, always slightly suspect and backward, which having first fallen under the aberration of communism, is now returning to its backward attitudes. That is equally untrue. The historical animosity between Slovaks and Hungarians never resulted in violence, the expectations of wide spread violence in Russia were not realised, the traditionally difficult relationship between Turks and Bulgarians in Bulgaria actually improved after 1989 and Poles and Lithuanians have also avoided conflicts despite historical animosities.

Thirdly, even if it were true that the region is a victim of history, there is an alternative view of history which to my mind sheds a more reflective light on the historical causes of nationalist mobilisation and separatism in the region. My concern here is to show the link between historical developments and nationalism, the exploitation of history, and the effects of recent developments, all of which add to a mobilising potential that 'ancient animosities' can generate in modern politics.

The first consideration is the relationship between the state and nationalism. The state is seen as an indispensable provider of economic and physical security, and it appears that contemporary nationalism has flared up when and where the old states collapsed and new ones are deficient in providing the security the populations are seeking. Despite the often propagated view that the nation-state has sacrificed its predominance to global economic interdependence and transnational networks, the recent developments in ECE do not bear this notion out; on the contrary they confirm the significance of the state and its link with nationalism.

Both the state and the population seek reassurance, the former appeals to loyalty, the latter to privileges of the nation the state is supposed to protect in return for political loyalty. Legitimacy of the state depends on much more than its performance. All aspects of government, how the state is governed and by whom, are in flux and exacerbated by an extra dimension - who is governed is also open to challenge. Political entrepreneurs enter a political stage where there is a lot to gain (or maintain) and where the rules are not established. The extent to which the elites are willing to manipulate 'ancient' history in order to fill the legitimacy gap, is exemplified by the extreme case of the Serbia-Kosovo conflict in which Serbian nationalist elites used events from 600 years ago to legitimise the oppression of ethnic Albanians in Kosovo[41].

There are three further points, linking the state, society, history and nationalism, involving a significant distinction between Eastern and Western Europe. First, is the matter of 'sequence'[42]- what comes first, the state or nationalism. When at the beginning of the 19th century, under the impact of the French Revolution and industrialisation, nationhood became a paramount basis for political organisation and group identification, Eastern Europe did not comprise one indigenous state, but was divided between the Romanov, Ottoman and Habsburg empires. In contrast, some West European state structures were already in place and state-building continued, reinforced by nationalism. The statehood aspirations of Eastern Europeans were crushed time after time by the hostile empires, who often responded with more oppression (e.g. Hungary towards Slovaks after 1848). The emergence of nation-states in the East was and remains a long, belated and painful process, associated with conflicts between national communities.

This particular facet of Eastern and Central European history adds a further complication bearing directly on the contemporary politics. The dominant nationalities of these former hostile empires constitute often a minority in a new state, usually geographically concentrated on the border between their ethnic homeland and the new state (e.g. Hungarians in Slovakia and Romania). The consequence of this cannot be underestimated. The perception of the minority becomes that of an historical enemy and all its demands (particularly any mention of territorial autonomy, or collective rights) are thus treated with a degree of suspicion. Consequently, the minority issue is taken out of its normal realm of democratic politics into the realm of state security[43] of a state still in the process of (re)establishing its own identity.

The problem with the newly re-established national identity, reinforced by independent statehood and further legitimised as a restoration of historical justice, is that its definition is more ethnically determined, for the states that previously inspired civic identity are broken up along ethnic lines. Re-establishment and re-definition by one national group demands re-definition of identity by all other groups, connected by history and geography. Consequently, the creation of new states requires redefinition of identity by minorities who often find themselves in a new state without having wished for it - the thus described process perpetuates the use of history, often in order to adjust to a new situation.

Secondly and related to the belated nation-building process were the conflicts between imperial power and local elites, which were often translated into national conflicts[44]. The local and nation-building elites of non-ruling nationalities (in the absence of indigenous bourgeoisie, mostly intelligentsia, and clergy), fighting for representative rights, sought the support in 'the nation' and the preservation of its interests against the imperial enemy and thus had to present their own demands in more 'national' terms, rather than in political terms (i.e. liberal). Social progress in ECE is thus traditionally associated with 'national' struggle.

M.Hroch argues that in contrast to the superficiality of 'ancient hatreds' explanation of the 'new nationalism' in ECE, it is much more plausible to see this nationalism as analogous with 19th century national movements. Considerable similarity lies mostly in the rapid change in the ruling elite (even if in some cases the elite remains the same, the form in which it competes for a constituency is different), and the formation of the nation-state simultaneously with the new capitalist order. Adding democratisation to this process these national movements resemble the kind of accelerated 1848 revolutions. Also striking are the demands of a linguistic and cultural nature as in all national demands. Language has once again become the expression of independence (Croat as fully independent from Serb, Slovak guarded by language law, Moldavia has reclaimed the Latin alphabet, the Baltic Republics have made the issue of language the pre-condition of citizenship etc.), which clashes considerably with similar developments by minorities who are equally demanding of their cultural and linguistic rights.

Thirdly, national identity is 'situational'[45]. People in their daily lives, under normal circumstances identify themselves by their occupation, their religion, their gender, their locality or by their membership of an association, or any other combination of identities which they consider to be a relevant and meaningful reflection of their existence. At different times a different identity may come to the fore, but generally people go about their business juggling the multiplicity of allegiances and identities with or without much conflict and usually without many considerations about 'the nation'. There is nothing about national identity that should be in conflict with one's profession, one's gender, one's religion or political orientation - under normal circumstances.

As soon as national identity includes elements that require allegiance and commitment that are in conflict with other loyalties, conflict is inevitable. We must concede that there are situations when the focus on identity is altered and the collective identity overrides all other identities. Such situation can be a war, or some other collective trauma. That is true of Western Europe too, but the difference with the ECE is that particularly in this century the wars, due to the specific geopolitical and historical developments, were not only frequent, but accompanied by major shifts in borders and populations[46].

Individuals and collectives were often not given the opportunity to be in charge of their destiny, nor their identity. This led to nearly permanent feelings of insecurity, increased the perception of threats and so radicalised politics. It does not take much imagination to see why in ECE freedom and national independence are often considered one, and seen to be best secured in an independent state. Thus, history matters, however it is not necessarily 'ancient' history, but rather the recent one. When the change in political circumstances makes the exploitation of history feasible, in order to increase nationalist mobilisation, all history merges into one 'living history'[47] and 'ancient hatreds' become a part of political discourse.

*Communist Nationality Policies*

One must agree that the collapse of the Soviet Union, and the disintegration of Yugoslavia and Czechoslovakia, testify to the prevalence of nationalist sentiments and tendency toward separatism in all multiethnic Soviet-type societies[48]. The question here is whether this evident fact can be seen as a logical outcome of communist nationality policies.

The system designed to withstand the national cleavages and dedicated to internationalism seems to have inadvertently created and fostered policies which made an independent nation the obvious option after communism. Yet it cannot be said that communism intensified nationalist passions; the majority of dissidents during 'party' rule were protesting against the practices of the party, not against its national policies. They wanted liberation, but not necessarily a national one, and if they were labelled as nationalists it was for another reason altogether. For example, when Tito removed the Croat reformist leadership (1971), who sought to loosen the command system in politics and economy, he justified the action by accusing them of divisive nationalism[49] and counter-revolution against the Party, without which, he claimed, Yugoslavia would fall apart. The point is that everything that failed to fall within the framework of the party dictate was seen as divisive, therefore nationalistic.

If it was the national banner that replaced the banner of 'brotherhood and unity', the question is why and what were the theoretical assumptions, institutional arrangements and practices which regulated national policies in multiethnic communist states. Their assumptions originated in the Soviet Union but were later applied with some modifications to Yugoslavia and Czechoslovakia. It can be argued that not national policies, but the system to which these policies were subordinated and which they were meant to support was responsible for the subsequent break-down of these states, with disastrous consequences in the case of Yugoslavia.

The communist federations (Czechoslovakia became a federation only after 1968) were built on the principle of national-territorial autonomy. It is not an exaggeration to say that Soviet Russia under Lenin became 'the first modern state to place the national principle at the base of its federal structure'[50]. However, it was not national-territorial autonomy as such that was at the heart of federal arrangement, but the internal stability of an omnipotent unitary state and later its outer empire (the Soviet Union and Czechoslovakia). Yugoslavia on the other hand, claimed that a strong unitary state was a necessity against the threat of inclusion into the Soviet empire. One could question the validity of a federation without democracy and all three cases, regardless of the motivation, demonstrate that such a federation is unsustainable in the long term and that it provides the basis for nationalism.

The theoretical assumptions behind Soviet national policy are to be found in Marxist theory which, it must be contended, had never been put into practice by Marx, but by Lenin who faced a much more complex set of circumstances than the 19th century author could possibly envisage. The communist revolution did not happen as a result of capitalism's collapse under the weight of the inner contradictions, as predicted by Marx, but through an imposition of a Marxist ideal onto a pre-capitalist Russia[51] - in reality a Leninist project. Lenin, faced with the choice between the Bolshevik victory, or fidelity to the Marxist denial of people's identification with the nation, he combined the two. The continuing rhetoric of communist ideology aimed at the elimination of national antagonisms, even if the reality throughout the Soviet history showed that running a country of such an enormous ethnic, cultural, economic and social diversity would have to compromise the ideology based on such a grandiose ambition.

The fundamental principle of federalism under communist rule was the 'linkage'[52] of ethnicity, territory and political administration. Immediately it is obvious that such an arrangement misses political autonomy only, in order to fulfil the characteristic of a sovereign state. Ethnicity was institutionalised on a group level by the federal governments, which were governed by indigenous elites and on a personal level by passports that stated the citizenship and nationality separately. The institutionalising of ethnicity on both individual and group levels was implemented with very few modifications in Yugoslavia and Czechoslovakia (e.g. in Czechoslovakia: citizenship - Czechoslovak, nationality - Slovak, or Magyar etc.). In sum, nations under communism were given the chance to enhance their national consciousness through education and the development of indigenous elites (of which more below). In fact one could hardly forget one's nationality having been reminded of it through the extensive bureaucracy with every minor document.

It adds to the ironies of the end of communism that the highly centralised states relied on indigenous elites to contain any national grievances and so to maintain the integrity of their rule, yet when the rule weakened it was these national elites which were able to seize power. In the system of permanent shortages, relentless competition for dwindling resources in the centre and the resulting corruption (which communism increasingly had become), the role of elites must be seen as highly instrumental in ethnic mobilisation. The case of Slovenia and Croatia which directly affected the break-up of Yugoslavia, suggests that in the course of development of the communist system elites became powerful, less reliant on the centre and confident about the support of their populations (see chapters 5 and 6). What made the break-up of these federations easier was that for administrative purposes, the successor states effectively already existed as federal units under the previous regime.

It is essential to all considerations about nationality policies in communist Eastern Europe that behind federalism hid a totalitarian state (in the case of Yugoslavia an authoritarian state with a degree of private ownership, but still centralised rule by the communist party), employing various methods, mainly 'divide and rule' in order to maintain its grip. The case of Slovakia is an interesting one in this context. The 1968 invasion of Czechoslovakia was justified by that ultimate doctrine of the Soviet hegemony and the disregard for the sovereignty of nations under its command - the Brezhnev doctrine which asserts that 'the sovereignty of independent socialist countries can not be set against the interests of world socialism and the world revolutionary movement'[53].

Yet, after the invasion, when the new period ironically called 'normalisation', brought the new constitution of Czechoslovakia, Slovakia and her post-Dubček leadership, seen as a more trustworthy partner in 'the world revolutionary movement', was rewarded with the status of an equal national state. Article 2 states that 'the basis of the Czechoslovak Socialist Republic is the voluntary union of equal nations, the Czech nation and the Slovak nation, based on the right self-determination for each'[54]. The 1968 invasion interrupted the liberalisation and enabled the conservative forces to regain power under the leadership of Husák who expressed his view on the old 'Slovak question' already as in 1967: 'all experience leads to the conclusion that the co-existence of peoples in one state unavoidably creates the desire for a situation of equality of these peoples'[55].

The Federation Law was based on divided sovereignty, which would suggest power from below, but the system remained pyramidal[56], called 'democratic centralism' and had all to do with centralism and nothing with democracy. However, even under those conditions the federal government in Bratislava contributed to the formation of more confident and experienced national elites and thus strengthened the chances for independent statehood later. When the federation came under pressure, under the strained conditions of post-communism and transition, it was those already existing institutional and administrative structures which enabled the break-up of Czechoslovakia to take place so quickly and effortlessly (see Chapter 3).

It is not the case that communist national policies - the institutionalisation of ethnonational principle - led inevitably to the disintegration of the Soviet Union, Yugoslavia and Czechoslovakia. Those policies were designed originally to assist the Bolshevik victory and maintained later in order to serve the Party in its control of the unitary state. Thus, the outcome could be seen as paradoxical in view of the aim those policies were to serve, but logical in view of what they entailed - namely territorial federal organisational units, thus 'ready made republics'[57] to take over once the rule finished. Democracy needs a constituency and it is hard to imagine how a state discredited as those communist states had become could carry out far-reaching reforms which were only undermining their legitimacy further. How otherwise was the new order to be crafted, if not in those national units? Having nurtured their cultural autonomy, having grown their own elites, having been industrialized, educated and modernised, the political autonomy unachievable under communism, for good and ill, became the logical conclusion to democratisation.

*Nationalism as a 'Replacement' Ideology After Communism*

Whilst exploring the communist period and its influence on postcommunist nationalism, this section focuses on the socio-psychological developments in postcommunist societies. It argues that the homogenising elements contained in communism and nationalism made these societies more susceptible to ethnic mobilisation.

Because the communist experience affected the society also in ways in which identities were defined and relationships constructed[58], the postcommunist 'condition' involves two other aspects relevant to this study. First is the search for a 'moral community', which results in either idealised discourses of nation or democracy, or both. This leads to a situation conducive to demagoguery, thus impeding the democratic resolution of everyday problems, which contrary to simplistic idealised notions of politics requires a complex set of rules, values and procedures. The second point, bearing directly on the issues of minorities, concerns the earlier communist definition of society as a homogenous whole, always in relation to 'others' (i.e. non-communist etc.), which created a society preconditioned to identify itself in relation to something else.

Communist parties pursued policies of social and economic equality. However, political equality was not an issue open to discussion. What political equality entailed would have undermined the system, which had evolved into a coercive apparatus, penetrating every aspect of people's private and public life. Moreover, the system's justification was a guarantee of social equality. Thus, equality had to be achieved by measures which were visible and tangible such as negligible differences in official income, forced collectivisation of the land (with exception of Yugoslavia and Poland), uniform housing and education, no gender discrimination and attempted assimilation of groups such as the Romany. This is not to say that all of these policies are to be criticised, but that the main purpose was to create 'social homogeneity'[59], in order to minimise the differentiation and articulation of social and political interests and a society where everyone was dependent on the state.

These policies were presented as 'moral imperatives'[60], which brought morality as a replacement for political interests into the political arena and made it the basis of political community. The Party as the guardian of that morality was then justified in its claim to represent the society as a whole; a notable difference to liberal-democracy, where a political party is meant to represent the interests of a specific group subscribing to its manifesto. The main consequence of presenting society as 'one' is that, similar to ethnic politics, it is claimed that 'there could not be other divisions than that between people and its enemies'[61]. Enemies were class enemies, revanchist Germany, the capitalist West, the dissidents, to name but a few examples.

Whilst communism and nationalism are not thought of as the same in this discussion, there are similarities. They both involve a tendency to define community by 'sameness' - a particular collective identity founded on ideologically inscribed values, always in relation to others who are often by implication seen as less worthy. Both ideologies engage in presenting a belief or an idea as a reality and an absolute truth. The step to populist rhetoric of simple solutions on behalf of the populace as a whole, as we have seen it in some ECE countries (i.e. Vladimír Mečiar in Slovakia, Slobodan Milošević in Serbia, nationalist opposition nearly everywhere) is a small one, particularly in societies where the tolerance of differences was often seen as lacking in conviction and principles, thus morally unacceptable. I am suggesting that the collectivist and ideological character of communism has left its mark on public consciousness and discourse and survived its fall[62] by migrating into another form of collective consciousness - the nation, or ethnic group.

The dichotomisation of society under communism influenced other areas of society, which bear directly on democratic transition. I shall point out: the role of dissidents and the idealised vision of politics they brought with their struggle; the role of the 'nation' in communism; and social independence[63].

Václav Havel, the epitome of a dissident, describes in his essay 'The power of the powerless' the communist system and its ideology as based on the principle that 'the centre of power is identical with the centre of truth'[64]. In such an ideologically structured system, dissidents represented the other side of the coin; if society was living a lie (Havel), they represented the truth. Their struggle was also in the name of morality, and the interests of society as a whole against the betrayal of the Party. Again there is an issue of morality as a basis of the community, defined in relation to the 'other' and a discourse full of abstract, intellectualised arguments, which do not provide solutions to the daily struggle in the new insecure environment of democratisation. The ideal version of democracy, presented as freedom (in ex-communist countries freedom was often synonymous with the West and an immediate access to Western prosperity), does not resemble the situation now.

Petr Pithart, one of the founding members of the Czech Civic Forum, which disintegrated soon after the object of their opposition did, wrote:

> I admit that we did not have enough imagination and political experience to find a symbolic solution which would result in catharsis, a feeling of purification and a loss of the need to look for objects of aggression[65].

Pithart's article, at the heart of which is disappointment - disappointment of ex-dissidents with the 'sluggishness of transformation'[66] and disillusion in the public - concludes with the warning that mass disappointment results in mass movements and that today's 'new nationalism is one of those movements'[67].

This might appear too dramatic a statement, but there is an explanation for the elevation of the nation in ex-communist countries. Nations are undergoing a re-identification, through two mutually reinforcing processes. On one hand there is a process of 'rebirth' a recovery of national myths, symbols, history, literature, all of which was either suspended, suppressed or lost during the communist era. On the other hand there is the process of 'purging the nation'[68] of a period now considered alien. The Russian population cannot fully enjoy such luxury, but in the rest of the communist bloc, communist regimes are associated with the Soviet Union's imposition of their rule. The question how such regimes could survive for such a long time is a painful one, with which the public has to reconcile itself. One of the ways of doing so is again a search for something 'morally pure', an unrealistic desire for a clear cut disengagement from that past, when everyone knows that communism was an integral part of their past. If communism was an imposition of foreign rule, an occupation aided by corruption and terror, then the nation 'remained uncontaminated'[69], it eventually resisted and appears now as a new heroic myth.

The last point I would like to make is the identity of 'self', which is also undergoing a redefinition on various levels. Everyone who has lived under the Soviet-type of communism recognises the 'social schizophrenia'[70] that went hand in hand with the regime and became a way of life - the difference in public and private discourse, a gap between reality and rhetoric. There was a public self, careful about expressing opinions in public, and private 'self', reserved for home and friends one could trust, where one discussed what 'they'(and all East Europeans became adept in this, with the exception of a few), were doing. 'They' were the enemy.

The definition of one's self was based on an enemy, which stopped one doing as one pleased, achieving, travelling, whatever image one had of one's self was always blurred; either there really was an obstacle, or one could imagine one - in any case there was always someone to blame. Personal responsibility and initiative, those two integral elements of freedom, were not encouraged and people got too used to the comfort of having an enemy. This phenomenon (described in various permutations by numerous, mostly East European authors, of which only a few are mentioned here) is the most damaging legacy bequeathed by communism to those societies. In the words of J.Šiklová:

> For so many years we have nurtured illusions concerning our abilities and denied possibilities. Now, the time has come to prove our valour.... What if we fail? Should we expose ourselves to possible injury?[71]

The question that follows from this is whether the new individual, in charge of his/her actions, now without the protection of a collective identity (as 'we', under communism) will search for another enemy. The general sense of insecurity during the transition does lead to anti-democratic rhetoric of passing the blame to other groups, being ex-communists, Jews, gypsies, minorities, foreigners, new entrepreneurs etc.

In conclusion, the above suggests that communism as practised in the Soviet-type of societies, where the interests of the people were expressed in moral terms, but at the same time the very pursuit of their real interests was blocked by an oppressive regime, created a society of individuals in search of a new identity. In the absence of unifying values, such as tolerance, trust and cooperation and in the face of cynicism created by the system's chasm between reality and rhetoric, the identification with institutions and law is weak. If as a consequence the emphasis on identity becomes overtly national or ethnic, one of the explanations can be sought firstly in the lack of civic values, and secondly, in the absence of other possible identification markers (i.e. political parties). In the new and insecure environment, when all other identities (i.e. political, personal, professional, etc.) are in flux, ethnic identity is easily invoked and seems to function as a replacement for all other identities, which have temporarily lost their meaning.

## *Elite Competition and the Intensification of Ethnic Politics*

So far the discussion has focused on the reasons for the salience of nationalism in ECE at the end of communist rule and the possible obstacles it thus poses to democratisation through examining the past and the communist period. The remainder of this chapter focuses on the present and emphasises how the transition project has become a stimulus to the evident increase of nationalism. R.Brubaker tells us that:

> far from solving the region's national question the most recent nationalising reconfiguration of political space has only reframed the national question, recast it in a new form[72].

Nationalism will now be looked at not only as a result of historical processes and the previous regime, not merely as state-seeking politics, but as politics within and between already existing states - nationalising policies of the newly nationalising states[73]. These new states are nation-states of and for particular ethnocultural nations, whose elites conceive of them as such, but in reality they are 'incomplete'[74], in the sense that many of their populations belong to another ethnocultural group, or nation often across the border. This is a situation which can lead to attempts by elites to remedy this deficiency in 'national' composition, or to rectify the past or present real and perceived discrimination by promoting their 'nation'. Such remedy takes the form of politics seeking linguistic, economic, cultural, demographic and political benefits for their national group - all of which stands for ethnic politics.

In the newly independent states, where (the) nationhood is a new experience and democracy is still only an aspiration, but an aspiration that at the same time offers an opportunity to articulate many new national demands, previously beyond the possibility of achievement, the two can find themselves pulling in opposite directions. The logic of experiencing nationhood and all its manifestations is quite different from the logic of democratic politics, the former appealing to collective identity by descent, the latter to individual choice and free association. Ideally, both individual choice and descent should not be exclusive of each other, but for the moment the pages to follow concentrate on the novelty of democracy and nationhood and how this experience affects competition among elites and thus, intensifies ethnic politics.

By elites I mean political decision makers, making decisions about action and allocation of resources, human or material, on behalf of a group, here defined as an ethnic group - in short, who rules, who decides and who gets what. Democratising politics of the region can be characterised by the dominance of elites for various reasons:

1.  The end of communist rule produced a political vacuum and at the same time created a possibility for very swift careers, as the new ruling class started taking shape. The new elites came from three main sources: ex-dissidents and other individuals who were not directly linked to the communist regime); new entrepreneurs; the third group were veterans, by which I mean the communists, who recast themselves under different political names, mostly with a more left-centre slant. In this group could also be included the managers of large former state enterprises and/or political managers and leaders of previous trade unions, in short the ex-nomenklatura.

    It is important to realize that these were the only elites with actual experience in politics and with the necessary networks at home and abroad, either in a commercial or political sense. As such they were instrumental in the initial stages of democratisation. When these ex-communist elites formed new political parties, they counted on their already existing membership, which they could successfully put into use in a new political system. This could account for their success, particularly in Slovenia (see chapter 5 and 6), where there was practically no change in elite structure and in Hungary, where the regime was 'transformed', meaning that elites in power initiated democratisation. In the Czech Republic and Slovakia, where democracy was brought about by a 'replacement'[75] of old elites by the opposition, initially it appeared that communists had been totally discredited, but not for long. Mečiar and his political supporters' domination of Slovakia's political scene between 1992-1998 illustrates clearly the successful 'recasting' of some members of ex-second echelons elites into the new leadership.

2.  The point to emphasize when discussing the role of elites in post-communist transitions is the lack of a blueprint for such transition. The fact remains that however impressive the record of dissident 'civil society' prior to 1989 was, the end of communist rule came with reforms in the ex-Soviet Union. The communist regime became a spent force when it started reforming itself. Gorbachev is synonymous with the 'revolution from the top'[76], which created the conditions necessary for reforms to succeed and for 'revolutions' from the bottom to take place, on its heels, in the rest of the region.

3.  The most conspicuous characteristic of these recent revolutions is the lack of premeditation and the speed with which decisions had to be taken, with the consequence that it was never clear who was to carry out which actions and what the consequent results would be. The very simultaneity of transition processes affecting nationhood, political constitution and the allocation of economic resources generated the atmosphere of mobilisation because everything, including political and economic power was within grasp.

Elites were more than representatives of state authority, they were the true shapers of societal consciousness in these transitions. Generally, it can be stated fairly convincingly that in postcommunist countries the change of system did not bring a radical change in elites[77]. One of the paradoxes of postcommunism is the continuity of elites in a discontinued system and the perpetuity of old values and outdated methods which seem to have survived the radical change of the system. Much of the nationalist rhetoric comes precisely from these 'recycled' elites who use it in order to bridge the credibility and legitimacy gap between themselves and the population.

Any exercise of democracy needs a popular base. Politicians need a constituency for two reasons: to attain power in order to fulfil other goals and to maximize their power in order to secure the fulfilment of those goals. No elite can rule without support, and the existence of ethnic diversity means that ethnic identity is an easy way to find a politician's constituency. In ECE, where constituency is often a new nation, or a minority group, ethnicity is a successful glue to bind support and identify interests. However, the increased political competition by itself is not a sufficient reason for the identification of parties on ethnic lines.

The added dimension in the region lies in the fact that once the opposition to the communist regime ceased to be a mobilizing factor for the whole society, the other interests were not clear. Definition of interests was clearer whilst society defined itself against a totalising power, but once that disappeared the re-definition of interests was difficult in politically inexperienced societies. The political vacuum created by the end of communism is often blamed for the rise of nationalism and even if one would be well advised not to explain all of nationalism by this 'vacuum' hypothesis, it remains a valid consideration when it comes to political identification. The Left-Right spectrum - the usual political identification of parties in the West - made little sense in societies that considered themselves to be classless, therefore economic and other interests were often voiced more in national than individual terms.

The break-up of Czechoslovakia could be counted as an example of the extreme role of elites in postcommunism; the populations of the Czech Republic and Slovakia, even given the increasingly acrimonious atmosphere in the state, were not given the chance to decide on the separation, nor the continuation of the common state in a referendum, and the state was dissolved mainly through the efforts of V.Klaus and V.Mečiar as the winners of the 1992 elections, for which they did not have a mandate. The ruling elites, Czech and Slovak, could not count on enough support to allow a referendum and it must be argued that the creation of independent Czech and Slovak states was more a result of the post-communist confusion, exploited by ambitious politicians, than the reflection of inherent Slovak nationalism[78] (see chapter 3). If the break-up of Czechoslovakia is viewed as an example of the important role elites play in postcommunist transitions, it is also necessary to note that 'separatists' had material to work with, by which I mean that elites cannot manipulate in a vacuum and that their rhetoric relies on the assumed consent of their population. The dissolution of Czechoslovakia will be argued precisely on those two points, the role of political elites and the exploitation of the existing national grievances in the federal state which became translated into a national question.

Two considerations arise from the above. Elites, competing for influence, particularly in the transitional stage where democratic focus lies more in procedures than in values, are not always scrupulous in the methods they employ. Secondly, in order for elites to succeed, their claims must find a degree of resonance in the population itself. What we see is the exploitation of ethnicity for the purpose of securing a large popular base, which can lead to the alienation of other ethnic groups, whose elites then engage in the same strategy leading to potential demands for autonomy, or secession.

### The New State, the Minority and the 'External' Homeland.

The last factor contributing to the salience of nationalism in postcommuis addresses these newly restructured national questions. It argues that the disintegration of multinational states intensifies the insecurity among various ethnic groups and that this situation is further exacerbated by triple nationalism, that of nationalising states, minorities and their 'external' homelands[79].

The break-up of Czechoslovakia seemed baffling because there appeared to be no support for independence and no violence whatsoever; the initiative came from the obviously weaker partner, Slovakia and at a time when one could have assumed that the defeat of totalitarianism would have brought the two nations closer together. At the same time it is reasonable to argue that if there was no popular demand for independence, there was also a considerable lack of support for the continuation of the federation. It is obvious that despite the high degree of uncertainty and insecurity in Slovakia, elite mobilisation is only a part of the story.

One approach could be to view the split of Czechoslovakia as the culmination of the disintegration of the Austro-Hungarian Empire, the process which started before the First World War and was interrupted by the Cold War division. From this perspective the disintegration was inevitable and desirable, giving Slovakia, now educationally, economically and technologically more advanced, an equal chance to participate in European integration. This however would not explain the break-up of the Soviet Union, nor the extreme violence of the Yugoslav conflict, and leaves the issues of minorities unanswered. Another approach is to seek an answer to the Czecho-Slovak split in ethnic politics in conditions of extreme uncertainty, which is a more convincing line of inquiry and explains the disintegration of the remaining multinational states in ECE better. This approach is maintained throughout this book and its empirical validity will be tested in the following chapters.

Another question begs to be asked. Why did the Czechs let Slovakia go so easily[80] and what are the dynamics of the difficult relationship between Slovaks and the substantial (11%) Hungarian minority? The explanation for the peaceful dissolution of Czechoslovakia is rooted in the Czech acquiescence to and even encouragement of Slovakia's secession, in contrast to, for example, the Serbo-Croat conflict. One of the answers could be that the number of Czechs living in Slovakia was small, thus the Czech politicians were not pressured into protecting their ethnic kin[81]. The same can be argued about the less peaceful, but relatively quick separation of Slovenia from the Yugoslav federation. However it is a simplistic answer in the Czech case. The Czech view of Slovakia as an obstacle to a quick problemless integration into Western Europe was more relevant as was the Slovak resentment of not being in full control of their situation - a resentment easily invoked in Slovak national consciousness.

The situation of the Hungarian minority in Slovakia is different. The intolerance claimed by both sides is a result of a dynamic, which Brubaker calls a "triadic nexus involving three distinct and mutually antagonistic nationalisms" - that of a minority and the newly nationalising state where they live and the external national homeland to which they belong[82]. Although Brubaker does not deal with the Hungarian minorities in this context, it seems to me that the role of the external homeland is well exemplified by Hungary, which has some 3 million of their ethnic kin spread all over the neighbouring territories, namely Slovakia (600 000) and Romania (2 million) as a result of the disintegration of the Austro-Hungarian empire after the First World War. The issue to explore is that of dual affiliations, civic and ethnic, and the situation when they conflict; when a minority feels more loyalty to the 'external' homeland, or is perceived not to attach enough loyalty to the state of residence and citizenship.

The issue of dual affiliations is particularly sensitive and potentially explosive in newly independent states. The new state has to undergo certain processes such as writing a new constitution, establishing criteria for citizenship, recasting some institutions and filling them with new personnel (often as rewards for the support of new nationalising elites), carving out a new position in the international community and seeking to homogenise around the ideal of this new state. All of these processes, as much as they are a necessary concomitant of nation-building and state-formation, can be perceived as threatening by minorities, particularly when the dominant nationality treats the new state as if owned by them without enough consideration given to issues which are important to minorities and constitutional provisions for them.

*Minority and 'external homeland' as political actors* When do we speak of a minority? This is a political issue, not simply an issue of a different language and the adherence to different customs from that of dominant nationality. A minority, which enters a political arena is characterised by three elements:

1. the public claim to membership of an ethnocultural nation, different from the dominant one;
2. the demand for state recognition as a minority group; and
3. the assertion of rights based on such recognition, which involves certain collective rights, cultural and/or political[83].

In sum, a minority is not a given by virtue of existing, but by virtue of a decision to represent itself as such and this is where dual affiliation comes to be viewed as a threat to a nationalising state or vice versa. Minority nationalism then works on two levels; it has to adopt a political agenda vis-à-vis the nationalising state, in order to formulate its demands, but at the same time it has to sustain a certain vision of that state as a threatening one - otherwise the rationale behind the mobilisation is less credible[84].

This is not to say that all is in perception. Slovakia's Language Law (1995, changed 1999, see chapter 4), required the safeguarding of the purity of the Slovak language used in all spheres, which could in theory have jeopardised a whole range of job opportunities for Hungarians - an example of a nationalising project which is more than a perception and hence becomes a serious political issue. It is also an example of nationalising rather than democratising, a short sighted policy using state power against a national minority, which has a strong affiliation with an historically oppressive nation, in order to demonstrate the intention to remedy the past.

The challenge already existing between a nationalising state and a minority is exacerbated by the 'external national homeland'[85], also to be seen in political, not geographic terms. A state becomes an external homeland, when political and cultural elites chose to define ethnic kin in another state as members of their nation, thus monitor and protect their interests. Such a stance is well exemplified by the speaker of the Hungarian parliament: 'we feel inevitable responsibility for our compatriots whose places of birth were carried by the storms of history to within the borders of other countries'[86]. Even more so by the law recently adopted by the Hungarian Parliament which concerns financial and other support to ethnic Hungarians living in the neighbouring countries[87]. If it is easy to see the nationalising projects of new states, it is also easy to see how a minority gets accused of disloyalty and the external homeland of illegitimate interference. Interwar Europe provided many examples of homeland politics, resulting in 'revision' of the Hungarian borders into Eastern Czechoslovakia (Ruthenia) and the annexation of Bohemia by Germany who claimed to protect their ethnic kin.

The approach to contemporary nationalism in the region through the interplay of a minority, the nationalising state and an external homeland by emphasizing the relational character of those three actors gives a more realistic picture of conflicts than the traditional studies of state-seeking nationalism. A fitting example is former Yugoslavia. Whilst Slovenia's secession was more in line with the traditional view of secession in the face of Serbia's aggressive push for hegemonic control of Yugoslavia, Croatia's secession was a result of a more complex 'triadic' dynamic.

The all-Yugoslav election of 1990 was a triumph for nationalists, among them Croatia's Franjo Tudjman, who began to employ every symbol of Croatian nationalism, including those from the fascist Ustaše regime and embarked on a series of nationalising policies. These included the removal of Croat Serbs from the key cultural and political positions in favour of Croats and the new constitution which claimed Croatia to be the 'historical right of Croatian nation' so removing the Croat Serbs from the co-ownership of the country.

The situation was made worse by the exaggerated and often fabricated rhetoric of Serbian politicians in Croatia, which portrayed Croatia as a physically threatening nationalising state. It was the Serb minority that was equally politically irresponsible and participated actively in creating a situation where the present and the future were seen in the sinister light of the Croatian fascist past. The increasingly more mobilised and fearful Serb minority in an increasingly nationalising and independent Croatia was very destabilizing and further exacerbated by Serbian homeland nationalism. The Serbian minority in Croatia was encouraged to be an intransigent opposition to the new regime by an openly propagated alteration of Serbian territory from Belgrade, which led to the more uncompromising politics of Croatia and eventually war.

However, notwithstanding the correctness of Brubaker's account there is an important and compelling argument, missing from his analysis - the political system and its absolute importance for the relationship between minorities (their external homelands) and nationalising states. The creation of a nation-state based on the ownership of that state by one particular ethnic nation has been a part of the democratisation processes in ECE, but a deliberate exclusion of minority from the affairs of the state is not compatible with democracy. The ethnic affiliation of the minority can move towards a more civic affiliation and vice-versa, all depending on the politics within the state - minority and majority relationship is not unchanging in its ethnic meaning, but that depends on the degree of priority given to either nationalism or democracy in the politics of the state. The coexistence of nationalism and democratisation does not mean that there is an inevitable parallelism between them - if certain policies and rhetoric can mobilise nationalism, it means that a different rhetoric and different policies can reduce nationalism, or even eradicate it, just as democracy can stagnate, reverse or progress.

**Conclusion**

One might ask whether the tenth year of new regimes in ECE is too soon to make any meaningful assertions about the state of democracy in these countries[88]; however, it is not too soon to say something about the state of transition. An inescapable observation seems to be the spread of national sentiments throughout the region and the prominence of ethnic politics as an integral part of the transition process in the newly independent states. An argument advanced in this chapter was that democratisation itself contributed to this salience of identity-based politics, which at the same time can pose significant obstacles to further democratisation.

With the above in mind three points worth noting emerge in conclusion to this chapter:

1. One common feature between all postcommunist countries is that democratisation projects have to contend with various legacies of the past, whether the remote past or as recent as the actual fall of the communist regime and the immediate period after. These varied histories affect the contemporary project of transition in different ways. It is the differentiation rather than the commonalities between these countries that define the course of their postcommunist transitions.
2. Related to the first point is that all identified factors or a combination of them are contributory to the rise of nationalism, but depending on their intensity and relevance they lead to varied consequences. As the case studies will demonstrate, the accumulation of factors conducive to nationalist mobilisation was higher in Slovakia than in Slovenia. Slovakia also counts among 'difficult'[89] cases of postcommunist transitions, particularly in connection to nationalism. A further consideration arises from this. If nationalism is inspired by the multiplicity of factors which derive from countries' varied histories, it would indicate that the nationalist phenomenon at this particular point in history should be a subject of a much more sophisticated 'multifactorial theory'[90], than theories of nationalism or transition to democracy provide at the moment.
3. The last point concerns the relationship between state, nationalism and democracy - a theme that lies at the basis of this book. The remaining question to be answered in this introductory overview of the postcommunist national landscape is whether nationalism is a logical concomitant of democratic transitions in postcommunist countries.

There are at least three issues in need of clarification here. Firstly, transition to democracy is not merely a challenge to the non-democratic regime, which would suggest that with democracy a new legitimate system is established. In the case of some countries the transition challenged the very boundaries of political community, or simply who should constitute the state, thus the very legitimacy of the state - it was the answer to this challenge that resulted in the disintegration of multinational states.

Secondly, is the issue of a sovereign state as a prerequisite for a modern democracy. There cannot be a democracy without a sovereign state - no amount of democratic developments can substitute for the lack of sovereignty. Hence, going back to the introduction of this chapter and Nodia's statement that 'democratic transitions engender nations', I would say that post-communist transitions to democracy engendered new sovereign states. Engendering nations is not the same as engendering sovereign states - the building of a nation is a different process to the building of a democratic state, which is at the heart of democratic transition. What we are observing are those two processes happening simultaneously.

Thirdly, is the legitimacy of the state, a point which I want to emphasise. The question of the legitimacy of the state is central to democracy; however, in new states, often multiethnic states, still in the process of consolidating the new nationhood and statehood, the legitimacy of that state is also at the centre of nationalist mobilisation. Thus, nationalism is perhaps an indispensable element of postcommunist democratisation processes, certainly at their beginning, which is not the same as Nodia's claim that democracy cannot exist without nationalism.

Postcommunist politics produced an overwhelming manifestation of the 'nation' and a strongly 'nationally' orientated democratisation process. This political reality of postcommunism gives rise to certain problems for democracy which are the subject of the following chapter.

## Notes

[1] By the end of communism I refer to the end of communism in the Eastern and Central Europe only. I describe the state of affairs in ECE countries as postcommunism. J.J.Linz and A.Stepan, in *Problems of Democratic Transition and Consolidation* Baltimore and London, The Johns Hopkins University Press 1996, refer to them as post-totalitarian (p.44), which according to their definitions of totalitarianism is a convincing distinction, however in my opinion post-totalitarianism only denotes the communist system, which has become less 'revolutionary', but has not changed its ideology and the main characteristics of the communist regime remained. These were mainly: a) supreme authority and the unchallenged hegemony of the Communist Party; b) a high degree of centralisation and discipline within that organisation with hardly any space given to intra-party debate; c) state ownership of the means of production (with some exceptions made for agricultural, but not industrial production in some countries, i.e. Poland, Hungary and

Yugoslavia). See also A.Brown 'Transitional Influences in the Transition from Communism' *Post Soviet Affairs* 16 April/June 2000 pp. 177-200.

[2] By Eastern/Central Europe are meant the following countries: Poland, Hungary, the Czech Republic, Slovakia, Croatia and Slovenia. This distinction is not strictly geographical, for Central Europe should include Austria and if one was to conceive of Central Europe strictly as a region between Russia and Germany, then Ukraine, Belarus and the Baltic States would fit the north-south parameters as much as one could include Bosnia-Herzegovina, Macedonia and even Greece. ECE therefore denotes a geographical-historical region with certain cultural traits, such as the common tradition of the Habsburg Empire, a more advanced political and economic development and closer links with the West prior to 1945. For a more in-depth discussion see A.Hyde-Pryce *The International Politics of East/Central Europe* Manchester, Manchester University Press 1996 and A.Ágh *The Politics of Central Europe* London, Sage 1998.

[3] G.Nodia 'Nationalism and Democracy' in L.Diamond and M.F.Plattner ed. *Nationalism, Ethnic Conflict, and Democracy* Baltimore and London, The Johns Hopkins University Press 1994.

[4] G.Nodia p.7 and p.9 respectively. The latter statement is from E.Gellner's influential work on 'modernity' of nation *Nations and Nationalism* Oxford, Blackwell 1983 p.55.

[5] Nodia p.9. Here I agree with Fukuyama's comment on Nodia's chapter, in the same book, concerning the logic of this statement. E.Gellner's argument is that industrialisation created the conditions conducive to nationalist ideas. Gellner does not mentions democracy; his preoccupation was not with nationalism as a movement for liberation, but as a corollary of industrialisation, which of course does not exclude the fact that democracy was born during the same historical process, but so were liberalism and socialism. For more in-depth exploration of Gellner's theory of nationalism and its connection to democracy see J.Hall *The State of the Nation* Cambridge, Cambridge University Press 1998.

[6] A.Brown 'Transnational Influences in Transitions from Communism'.

[7] G.Nodia p.4.

[8] For example the SNS (Slovenská Národná Strana-Slovak National Party), the first party to advocate full Slovak independence was formed in 1990. V.Mečiar who negotiated Slovak independence and became its first Prime Minister was never a member of any separatist movement.

[9] Point also stressed by J.J.Linz and A.Stepan, *Problems of Democratic Transition and Consolidation,* note 7. For speculation what might have happened in Czechoslovakia, see H.Gordon Skilling *Czechoslovakia's Interrupted Revolution* Princeton, Princeton University Press 1976 and for more 'nationalist' explanation of the 'Prague Spring', as set in motion by the Slovak efforts to decentralise the Communist Party, see G.Golan *The Czechoslovak Reform Movement* Cambridge, Cambridge University Press 1971 and V.Kusin *The Intellectual Origins of the Prague Spring* Cambridge, Cambridge University Press 1971.

[10] R.Brubaker 'National Minorities, Nationalizing States, and External National Homelands in the New Europe' in *Daedalus 121* Summer 1991 pp.107-132 p.107 talks of nationalism being recast in a new form.

[11] E.g. Poland 97.8% homogenous, Hungary 91.35%, Czech Republic 94.5% J.Bugajski, *Ethnic Politics in Eastern Europe* Armonk, London, M.E.Sharpe 1995.

[12] F.Fukuyama 'Comments on Nationalism and Democracy' in L.Diamond and M.Plattner *Nationalism, Ethnic Conflict, and Democracy* p.28.

[13] R.Blackburn ed. *After the Fall* London, Verso 1991, particularly essays by J.Habermas and E.Hobsbawm; Jeffrey C. Isaac 'The Meanings of 1989' *Social Research* 63:2

Summer 1996 pp.291-344; P.Pithart 'Intellectuals in Politics: Double Dissent in the Past, Double Disappointment Today' *Social Research* 60:4 Winter 1993 pp.752-761; A. Smolar 'From Opposition to Atomization' *Journal of Democracy* 7:1 January 1996 pp.24-38.

[14] F.Halliday *Revolution and World Politics* London, Macmillan 1999 p.21, defines revolution as 'a major political and social transformation in the context of a contradictory modernity involving mass participation and the aspiration to establish a radically different society'.

[15] E.Hobsbawm 'Goodbye to all that' p.115 in R.Blackburn *After the fall.*

[16] In this instance I am not referring to the article by F.Fukuyama 'The End of History?' *National Interest* Summer 1989 pp.3-18. The term 'the end,' in the context of postcommunism has been in a sense appropriated by this article, which is regrettable.

[17] Best expressed by: 'theirs was not a revolution of total innovation, but rather the shuckling off of a failed experiment in favour of an already existing model'. G.Stokes *The Walls Came Tumbling Down: The Collapse of Communism in Eastern Europe*, cited in J.C.Isaac 'The meanings of 1989' p.302 and 295.

[18] V.Tismaneanu 'Reassessing the revolutions of 1989' *Journal of Democracy* 10:1 January 1999 pp.69-73 p.72.

[19] F.Fukuyama 'The end of History?'(also the book by the same author *The End of History and the Last Man* New York, Free Press 1992). His thesis can be summed up by: 'What we may be witnessing is not just the end of the Cold War, but the end of history as such: that is, the end point of mankind's ideological evolution and the universalisation of Western liberal democracy as the final form of human government' p.4.

[20] See also J.Rupnik 'Eastern Europe: the International Context' *Journal of Democracy* 11:2 April 2000 pp.115-129.

[21] J.C.Isaac 'The Meanings of 1989' p. 293.

[22] N.Ascherson in J.Dunn *Democracy the Unfinished Journey* Oxford, Oxford University Press 1992 p. 245.

[23] V.Havel *Living in Truth* J.Vladislav ed. London, Faber and Faber 1989.

[24] C.S.Maier 'Democracy and Its Discontent' *Foreign Affairs* 73:4 July/August 1994 pp.48-65 p.54 – 62.

[25] M.Bútora Z.Bútorová 'Slovakia's Democratic Awakening' *Journal of Democracy*10:1 January 1999 pp.80-94 p.83.

[26] Against the comparison see mainly V.Bunce 'Should Transitologists Be Grounded' *Slavic Review* 54:1 pp.111-127 and 'Comparing East and South' *Journal of Democracy* 6:3 July 1995 pp.87-99; G.Nodia 'How Different Are Postcommunist Transitions' as above; S.Meiklejohn Terry 'Thinking About Postcommunist Transitions: How Different Are They?' *Slavic Review* 52:2 Summer 1992 pp.333-337. For comparing mainly, Philipp C.Schmitter and Terry L.Karl 'The Conceptual Travels of Transitologists and Consolidologists: How Far To The East Should They Attempt to Go?' *Slavic Review* 53:1 Spring 1994 pp.173-185; Juan J.Linz and A.Stepan *Problems of Democractic Transition and Consolidation.*

[27] S.Huntington *The Third Wave* Norman OK, University of Oklahoma Press 1993.

[28] A.Brown 'Transnational Influences in the Transition from Communism' p.182.

[29] For the relevance of economic factors in transition see: C.Offe 'Capitalism by Democratic Design?' *Social Research* 58:4 Winter 1991pp.865-892 and A.Przeworski, M.Alvarez, J.A.Cheibub and L.Limongi 'What Makes Democracies Endure' *Journal of Democracy* 7:1 January 1996 pp.39-55.

[30] J.Elster, C.Offe and U.Preuss *Institutional Design in Post-communist Societies* Cambridge, Cambridge University Press 1998. The authors argue that 'amorphous nature

of socioeconomic conflict lines' in post-communist countries provides the strongest argument for expecting very different trajectories and outcomes in this region compared with the Latin American and Southern European transitions. p.248.

[31] J.Rupnik 'The Postcommunist Divide' *Journal of Democracy* 10:1 January 1999 pp.57-63 p.61.

[32] J.Rupnik 'The Postcommunist Divide' p. 61

[33] A. Michnik 'Nationalism' *Social Research* 58:4 Winter 1991 p.757-763 p.759.

[34] G.Schöpflin 'The Problems of Democratic Construction' in *Daedalus* 123:3 Summer 1994 pp.127-141 p.127.

[35] C.Offe 'Capitalism by Democratic Design? in *Social Research* 58:4 Winter 1991 pp.865-892.

[36] A.Ágh p.77.

[37] J.Elster, C.Offe and U.Preuss *Institutional Design in Post-communist Societies* p.254.

[38] I.Bernik and B.Molnar 'Ethism, Nationalism and State-Building:The case of Slovenia' Paper presented at the Congress of the International Political Association, Seoul, August 1997.

[39] Also often referred to as 'deep-freezer' thesis, the pressure cooker, etc. all invoking the same image - that of potential suppressed violence waiting to happen. See K.Verdery 'Nationalism and National Sentiments in Post-Socialist Romania' *Slavic Review* 52:2 Summer 1993 pp.179-203 p.179; J.Snyder 'Nationalism and the Crisis of the Post-Soviet State' *Survival* 35:1 Spring 1993 pp.5-27 p.5; I.Banac 'The Fearful Asymetry of War: The Causes and Consequences of Yugoslavia's Demise' *Daedalus* 121 Spring 1992 pp.141-173 p.142; S.Holmes 'Cultural Legacies or State Collapse' in M. Mandelbaum *Postcommunism* p.28.

[40] For the history of the Balkan nationalism and Serbo-Croat relationship in particular, see mainly, L.J.Cohen *Broken Bonds* Oxford, Westview Press 1993 and M.Glenny *The Balkans 1804-1999* London, Granta Books 1999.

[41] It is important to add that Serbia is a special case and that as much as the disintegration of former Yugoslavia fits the postcommunist correlation, the conflict between Serbia and Kosovo is different. Serbia under Milošević's rule was hardly a democracy, its conduct was that of a repressive undemocratic state trying to maintain the regime and as such should not be compared to developments in other postcommunist states.

[42] A.Leibich 'Nations, States, Minorities: Why is Eastern Europe different?' in *Dissent* Summer 1995 pp.307-313 p.313.

[43] For this point I am grateful to W.Kymlicka who expressed a similar argument in his lecture at the York University 29 May 2001.

[44] See the illuminating article of M.Hroch 'From National Movement to the Fully-Formed Nation' *New Left Review* 198, March/April 1993 pp.3-20. Also, by the same author, *The Social Preconditions of National Revival in Europe* Cambridge, Cambridge University Press 1985.

[45] A.D.Smith 'The Ethnic Sources of Nationalism' in *Survival* 35:1 Spring 1993 pp.48-63 p.48.

[46] The Versailles treaty 'rewarded' the victors and the dynastic empires were replaced by 'successor' states, which were actually smaller versions of the empires they seceded from, incorporating 'beneficiaries' of the new order (i.e. Czechs), somewhat reluctant nationalities (i.e. Slovaks, Croats), and other apprehensive minorities of the 'disadvantaged'(i.e. Hungarians and Germans). Hungary lost 2/3 of its territory to Czechoslovakia, Croatia and Romania, which led to an attempt for a territorial recovery during the Second World War and the annexation of the Subcarpathian region of Czechoslovakia. Stalin's and Hitler's rule meant another major geopolitical shift

accompanied by the brutal methods of genocide and expulsions. Czechoslovakia lost Subcarpathia to the USSR (80 000 people), 140 000 Jews were killed and 3 million Germans and Hungarians expelled. Poland lost nearly all of its Jewish population and approximately 3 million people were involved in repatriations between the USSR and Germany.

[47] L.Deák *Hungary's Game for Slovakia* Bratislava, Veda 1996 introduction.

[48] A.Motyl ed. *The Post-Soviet Nations* New York, Columbia Press 1992, in which particularly the essays by G.Gleason, R.J.Hill, N.Harding Walker Connor and M.Beissinger. For the idea of nation-building in the Soviet Union see the work of R. Suny 'The Revenge of the Past: Socialism and Ethnic Conflict in Transcaucasia' in *New Left Review* 184 November/December 1990 pp.5-37.

[49] I.Banac 'The Fearful Asymetry of War: The Causes and Consequences of Yugoslavia's Demise' p.157.

[50] R.Pipes *The Formation of the Soviet Union, Communism and Nationalism*, cited in V.Zaslavsky 'Nationalism and Democratic Transition in Postcommunist Societies' *Daedalus* 121 Spring 1992 pp.97-121 p.99.

[51] For a comprehensive treatment of national question and Marxist theory see W.Connor *The National Question in Marxist-Leninist Theory and Strategy* Princeton, Princeton University Press 1984.

[52] V.Zaslavsky 'Nationalism and Democratic Transition' *Daedalus* 121 Spring 1992 pp.97-121 p.99.

[53] Quotation from M.Kramer note 4 p.236 in J.J.Linz and A.Stepan *The Problems of Democratic Transition and Consolidation.*

[54] V. Žák 'The Velvet Divorce - Institutional Foundations' in J.Musil ed. *The end of Czechoslovakia* Budapest, Central European University Press 1995.

[55] G.Golan *The Czechoslovak Reform Movement* p.197.

[56] J.Rychlik 'From Autonomy to Federation 1938-68' J.Musil ed. *The End of Czechoslovakia.*

[57] For the institutionalisation of nationality as a fundamental social category and the consequences for the disintegration of the Soviet Union see R.Brubaker *Nationalism Reframed* Cambridge, Cambridge University Press 1996.

[58] G.Schöpflin 'The problems of democratic Construction' in *Daedalus* 123:3 Summer 1994 pp.127-141 p.128.

[59] K.Verdery 'Nationalism and National Sentiment in Post-socialist Romania' p.191. For the rest of this section I refer to Verdery (1993) in distinction to another similar article by the author 'Nationalism, Postsocialism, and Space in Eastern Europe' in *Social Research* 63:1 Spring 1996 pp.77-95, henceforth Verdery (1996).

[60] Verdery (1993) p.191.

[61] C.Lefort cited in Verdery (1993) p.191.

[62] For a similar argument see N.Dimitrijević 'Words and Death: Serbian Nationalist Intellectuals' in A.Božóki *Intellectuals and Politics in Central Europe* Budapest, Central European University Press 1999.

[63] J.Musil 'Czechoslovakia in the Middle of Transition' *Daedalus* 121 Spring 1992 pp.175-195 p.190.

[64] V.Havel et al. *The power of Powerless* p.25.

[65] P.Pithart 'Intellectuals in Politics: Double Dissent in the Past, Double Disappointment Today' in *Social Research* 60:4 Winter 1993 pp 751-761 p.755.

[66] P.Pithart p.760.

[67] P.Pithart p.761.

[68] M.Urban 'The Politics of Identity in Russia's Postcommunist transition: The nation against Itself' *Slavic Review* 53:3 Fall 1994 pp.733-765, refers to these processes as 'positive' or 'negative', respectively. One could argue that both processes involve a great deal of myth and falsification and therefore do not merit this description.

[69] A.Smolar 'Revolutionary Spectacle and Peaceful Transition' in *Social Research* 63:2 Summer 1996 pp.439-464 p.449.

[70] Verdery (1993) p.193.

[71] J.Šiklová 'What Did We Lose?'*Social Research* 63:2 Summer 1996 pp.531-564 p.535.

[72] R.Brubaker *Nationalism Reframed*  p.4.

[73] I am not suggesting that the term 'nationalising' refers strictly to postcommunist states; nearly all European states at some point in their history have engaged in policies that can be described as 'nationalising', that is in pursuing the policies with the aim to homogenise the whole population according to the dominant culture. The degree to which the states are 'nationalising' is the question of democracy which is at the heart of this book. My preoccupation at this point is merely with the salience of nationalism in the region and not with comparisons between established and new democracies. For that discussion see T.Kuzio 'Nationalising states or nation-building? A critical review of the theoretical literature and empirical evidence' *Nations and Nationalism* 7:2 April 2001 pp.135-154.

[74] R.Brubaker *Nationalism Reframed* p.9.

[75] For 'transplacement', 'transformation' and 'replacement' see S.Huntington *Third Wave* pp.113-114.

[76] C.Offe 'Capitalism by Democratic Design? Democratic Theory Facing the Triple Transition in East Central Europe' in *Social Research* 58:4 Winter 1991 pp.865-892 p.866.

[77] See I.Szelényi and S.Szelényi 'Circulation or Reproduction of Elites During the Postcommunist Transformation of Eastern Europe' in *Theory and Practice* 24:5 1995 pp.615-638.

[78] In view of the long history of Slovak efforts at self-assertion, there was a widespread tendency by Western journalists to depict the break-up of the state as a result of Slovak separatism. See also C.Skalnik Leff *The Czech and Slovak Republics* Boulder, Westview Press 1997 p.126-144.

[79] This section draws on the work of R.Brubaker *Nationalism Reframed* Cambridge, Cambridge University Press 1996, forewith indicated Brubaker (1996), particuarly the chapter 3 'National Minorities, Nationalizing States, and External National Homelands in the new Europe'. Under the same title *Daedalus* 124:2 Spring 1995, forewith Brubaker (1995). For an account of the contemporary international situation concerning ethnic groups and their security (societal security) see O.Waever, B.Buzan, M.Kelstrup and P.Lemaitre *Identity, Migration and the New Security Agenda in Europe* London, Pinter Publishers Ltd.1993.

[80] S.Saideman 'The Dual Dynamics of Disintegration' *Nationalism and Ethnic Politics* 2:1 Spring 1996 pp.18-43 p.36.

[81] S.Saideman 'The Dual Dynamics of Disintegration' p.36. The argument about the protection of ethnic kin can be questioned. Slovak politicians did not appear to be concerned about a considerably larger number of ethnic kin living in the Czech lands (500 000, as opposed to 40 000 Czechs living in Slovakia, *RFE/RL* 3:27 8 July 1994 'Czech - Slovak Relations' pp. 9-17 p. 17).

[82] Brubaker (1996) p.4.

[83] Brubaker (1995) p.112.

[84] Brubaker (1995) p.115.

[85] Brubaker (1996) p.5.

[86] Z.Gál Summary of world broadcasts BBC EE/2388 22 August 1995.

[87] According to this law, to come into operation in 2002, the Hungarian government offers cultural subsidies, work and education opportunities in Hungary, travel etc. to ethnic Hungarians who are citizens of neighbouring countries. It has been criticised by Slovakia, Romania and the EU, who expressed concern that such support would discriminate against non-Hungarian citizens in mixed regions. Hungary has rejected this accusation and claims that the main purpose is to avoid mass immigration into Hungary, after it joins the EU. *Sme* 20 June 2001.

[88] According to A.Lijphart, 'a political system can be called democratic' when it is reasonably responsive to the citizens' wishes 'over a long period of time' - this criterion was defined as 'at least thirty or thirty-five years'. Cited in M.Kaldor and I.Vejvoda 'Democratization in East and Central European countries' p.61.

[89] J.Elster, K.Offe and U.Preuss in *Institutional Design in Post-communist Societies,* whilst comparing Czech Republic, Hungary, Slovakia and Bulgaria, called the first two 'easy' and the latter two 'difficult' p.268.

[90] The expression is borrowed from J.Musil *The End of Czechoslovakia* p.92, used in context of the dissolution of Czechoslovakia.

# 2 How Compatible are Nationalism and Democracy?

One cannot get away from the fact that nationalism is in a state of constant tension with democracy and their compatibility remains a subject of continuing debate. If the main theme of this book is to clarify the role of nationalism in the democratisation process, the aim of this chapter is to explore the relationship between nationalism and democracy. First, on a theoretical level and following the clarification of its principal concepts - nationalism and democracy, the chapter endeavours to contribute to the ongoing debate about compatibilities and contradictions inherent in their relationship from the time of their historical inception in the French Revolution to the current wave of postcommunist transitions. Secondly, on an empirical level, it illustrates the theoretical arguments by introducing the case studies of Slovakia and Slovenia and the framework within which these will be explored in the following chapters.

The heart of the argument is that democracy presupposes a political unit (state), whilst the unit is usually a nation-state which came into existence as a result of national self-determination of one dominant culturally determined 'nation'. Nevertheless, most states include minorities within their territories and consequently, the democratisation process in the newly independent multinational democracies faces the clash between two overlapping, but conceptually different processes: the culturally preoccupied nation-building on the one hand and administratively and politically orientated state-building on the other.

Nationalism's role in the democratisation process is complex and cannot be generalised - it depends on the extent to which it can contribute towards democratic state-building. The proposition here is that such a contribution requires nationalism to shift its emphasis from cultural and ethnic affiliation to the unity of political community. Nationalism's capacity to do so depends on many variables; the introduction to case studies in this chapter will outline the framework within which these different conditions will be explored in detail in chapters 3-6.

45

## Nationalism and Democracy: Theoretical Concepts

Both ideologies share their historical and ideological origins in the French Revolution. Both are associated with popular sovereignty and participation from below meaning rights, beliefs, expectations and interests, in short both are rooted in the idea that all political authority stems from the people. The most obvious manifestation of the link between people (nation) and political power is Article 3 of the French Revolution's Declaration of the Rights of Man and Citizen:

> The principle of sovereignty resides essentially in the Nation. No body, no individual can exercise any authority which does not explicitly emanate from it[1].

There is however a crucial difference. Democracy is a system of rule whose legitimacy relies on explicitly defined political principles about participation, inclusion and political equality, in order to achieve a just rule. Nationalism on the other hand bases its legitimacy on one principle - the rule of 'the people' who constitute its nation. Vesting political legitimacy in 'the people' is the basic premise of nationalism and democracy, but the definition of 'the people' is precisely where nationalism and democracy can challenge each other. Thus, the focus of the analysis below is on the rudiments of democracy - its forms and norms - and on the ideas of nationalism in order to highlight the contradictions and ambiguities between them.

### *Democracy: Attainment and Progress*[2]

Democracy, in some form or another, says Philippe Schmitter, 'may well be the only legitimate and stable form of government in the contemporary world'[3], yet despite the high legitimacy that democracy enjoys, sustaining it seems at least as problematic as establishing it. The experience of the most recent wave of transitions to democracy suggests that the preservation of a democratic regime is arguably more difficult than its establishment, precisely because the premise of a just rule means different things to different people who all expect their interests to be served adequately by democratic rule. The body of this book explores the trajectory of democratic transitions in two countries: in Slovenia, a linear gradual process of democratisation from the establishment of pluralism towards increasingly more democratic order; in Slovakia on the other hand, a somewhat circular transition, from the establishment of democratic structures through various 'derailments' to a new (it will be argued a third attempt) beginning of the transition to democracy. Clearly, the term democracy is used very loosely, yet the principles of democracy are specific and definite and that is where the next section turns to.

*From rules to substance* First, I ought to defend the word 'transition' from the accusation of teleology. The term is used throughout this book with a view that the aim of the process of the transition to democracy is a progress towards more democracy, that is more freedom, equality, growth in individual opportunity and autonomy of institutions, security and accountability. The new ECE democracies and their political systems are judged (for the purposes of the European integration or by their own electorates) on how far that process has progressed whilst the end point is assumed to be a reasonably stable democratic regime (usually compared to Western European model). However, such an outcome, whilst aspired to, is not an assumption that transition will necessarily mean a progress in that direction. Thus, the word 'transition' means exactly that, a process of change that is heading towards a goal - in the distance and sometimes vaguely outlined - but a process that can be sidelined or reversed and ultimately fail to reach the goal it set out for itself. Similar considerations apply to the term democratic consolidation, of which more below[4].

In its core meaning democracy is the implementation of the idea of popular sovereignty, that is the notion that the will of the people should prevail. This is done through certain procedures, that is, a system is deemed democratic, when 'most powerful decision-makers are selected through fair, honest and periodic elections in which candidates freely compete for votes, and in which virtually all the adult population is eligible to vote'[5]. Thus, the democratic principle of legitimacy is that of consent and participation, which means that all laws and obligations are considered legitimate only when people have consented to them, in our times through their representatives. Democracy here is used as a 'shorthand' for liberal democracy, which consists of two distinct components:

1. The protection of a people from tyranny, that is liberal constitutionalism, which concerns itself with legal and structural mechanisms against the arbitrary exercise of power; and
2. The implementation of popular rule, which is democracy per se.

As Sartori explains, if constitutional mechanisms are about 'how' decisions are taken, then the popular will is about 'what' is decided[6]. Whilst mechanisms can be imposed and structures erected nearly anywhere, 'the people' and their decisions are less predictable and influenced by socio-economic and cultural factors, and nationalism constitutes one such very important factor.

For democracy to be assessed there must be some objective criteria. So, when it is said that in ECE democratic structures are sufficiently in place to call them democracies, that means that nearly all formal qualifications necessary for a regime to be called democratic are functioning, obviously with varying degrees of success. Those are:

1. Inclusive citizenship for all people living in the territory of the state;
2. Rule of law, whereby the government must respect the law, with individuals and minorities protected from the 'tyranny of the majority';
3. Legislature, executive and judiciary must be separate and the judiciary sufficiently independent to be able to uphold the law;
4. Power holders must be elected in free elections;
5. Freedom of expression, sources of information and associational autonomy must exist and be protected by law; and
6. The armed forces and police should be politically neutral and independent[7].

On a moment's reflection it is obvious that the above criteria should be regarded as minimal, or rather 'formal'[8] conditions of democracy - procedures are necessary conditions for democracy, but never sufficient. Clear-cut definitions and formally fulfilled procedures still raise considerable questions about the actual performance of democracy. There is a more substantive component to democracy, concerned less with institutional practices and more with the substance, that is the degree to which democratic institutions can be implemented and yet, undemocratic practices persist (or a problem of new democracies whereby old embedded practices function within the newly emergent system). This substantive element of the democratic process remains 'unfinished'[9] and should be continuously re-examined, so that individuals are always in position to influence the conditions in which they live and decisions that affect their lives. Democracy then can be best defined as: 'a mode of decision-making about collectively binding rules and policies over which the people exercise control', hence the most democratic arrangement is that:

> where all members of the collectivity enjoy effective equal rights to take part in such decision-making directly - one that is to say which realizes to the greatest conceivable degree the principles of popular control and political equality in its exercise[10].

In that respect, democracy is not a static state of affairs, 'there are no final democracies'[11], only more or less established ones, nearer or further away from the 'ideal', which remains elusive. All democracies, including the long established ones must renew and restructure according to the changing socio-economic developments, thus all democracies must be engaged in the continuous process of democratisation. The dichotomy of democracy and authoritarianism might have always been too simplistic, but the latest 'third wave' of transitions, including those of Eastern Europe and Asia, illustrate the shortcomings of such a distinction. There are many forms of democracies on the continuum between the minimal-formalist (free and fair elections and inclusive citizenship are the two conditions beyond any discussion, for in the absence of those principles one cannot talk of even minimal democracy) and more substantive democracies, whereby all the above criteria would be in place to such an extent that economic and societal cleavages are minimal.

So what about democratic consolidation? The first thing to mention is that this discussion concentrates on liberal democracy, thus a regime such as Slovakia in the period 1992-1998, described as a 'semi' or 'electoral'[12] democracy is somewhere between an authoritarian regime and liberal democracy. Even among these 'electoral' democracies there are differences[13]. Slovakia for all its semi-democratic characteristics was hardly Milošević's Serbia which could, at a stretch, count as an electoral democracy. In Slovakia, in that particular period an elected parliamentary majority party proceeded to remove the opposition not only from parliamentary procedures, but reduce all competition in political (and social) life, thus the legitimately elected leadership descended into a kind of 'tyranny', with Mečiar assuming the role of 'saviour' of the Slovak nation. A similar type of politics could be observed in Croatia and Belarus and in attempts of the nationalist-conservative coalition in Hungary between 1990-1994, an observation which brings to the fore one of the problems faced by nascent democracies - what is often being consolidated is not a liberal-democracy, but a regime with fewer or more democratic features.

The change of government in such democracies does not mean democratic consolidation; if a semi-democratic type of regime is defeated by a more democratic one, the change constitutes a progress towards the establishment of a fully democratic regime, not its consolidation. One could argue that in the context of new democracies there are only more or less 'consolidated' transitions; hence, by the term 'consolidated democracy' should be meant a regime whose demise is less likely and that is expected to continue without challenges to its basic principles and norms.

*Democracy and National Self-determination*

There are many challenges to democracy, but the main concern of this book is on one major challenge - nationalism. It derives from democracy's most fundamental prerequisite: the existence of clear boundaries to state territory and its political community. Any exercise of democracy requires a prior legitimate political unit, because no competition or cooperation can take place without a clear definition of who is in the game and where the physical boundaries of the 'playing field'[14] are. The predominant principle for defining those boundaries in modern times is 'nationality', which provides the criteria for who 'the players'(people) are who determine their political destiny[15], thus the decision about who and what constitutes the 'nation' is an integral part of democratisation, hence the crucial role of nationalism in transition. Where the issue of boundaries and identities were either not settled properly before, or have changed as the result of the transition, nationalism is as much a challenge to democracy as it is its precondition.

Whilst democracy comes in a variety of forms, but with determined principles, the principle for determining 'nationality' is open to many interpretations - herein lies one significant point of ambiguity between nationalism and democracy (see below). Democratic theory makes clear that political rights, are vested in the 'nation', but there are at least two interpretations to how the national unit is defined. As remarked before, the 'nation' can be an aggregation of citizens in the state, united by the attachment to that state and the legitimacy of their regime (in this case a democratic one), or the 'nation' can claim to be a political expression of an ethnic group. In the latter case the ethnic group can be the dominant nationality of the state, or it may be a minority. Despite the clarity of such a classification, it is worth reiterating that these are ideal types and that the majority of nation-states are a combination of the two principles (ethnic and civic) and moreover, a combination of various ethnic groups with varying degrees of political consciousness at different times. The establishment of states, the prevalence of either 'ethnic' or 'civic' principles for the definition of the 'nation', is characterized by a degree of historical contingency and open to interpretation, to which democratic theory offers no solution.

National self-determination is a principle that holds that any self-differentiating people has the right, should it so desire, to rule itself[16] and thus can make ethnicity the ultimate measure of political legitimacy. If the essential meaning of democracy is popular control and the key to democracy is the autonomy and self-determination of people, the overlap between 'demos' (the polity) and 'ethnos', the 'self-determining people' can leave, and usually does, some residual people who are left out of what is considered 'the nation'. Fundamental to democracy are equal political rights, that in principle are guaranteed by citizenship, yet the organizing principle of ethnicity can prevent some members of the polity from inclusion (e.g. ethnic Russians in Estonia, Arabs from occupied territories in Israel, the 'guest' workers in Germany) in the decision-making processes by being denied the citizenship of the country of residence.

Immediately it is important to note that awarding citizenship is one of the essential democratic criteria, yet citizenship is not a guarantee of full inclusion and participation. When Slovakia under Mečiar's government was viewed as a state with ethnic conflict, the problems faced by the Hungarian minority and the Romany was not about being denied citizenship. The former felt that they were denied an equal political status and a share in the governance of the state of which they were citizens, whilst the problems of Romany continue to be about exclusion, social conditions and the lack of protection from discrimination by the state authorities.

## *Nationalism: Defining the Nation, the State, Ethnic Group and Minority*

'Nations are formed and are kept alive by the fact that they have a programme for tomorrow', said Jose Ortega y Gasset[17] and nationalism should be viewed as such a programme. The idea of nationalism is as follows: the principal object is the nation, the objective is the future of the nation, the strategy is the promotion and protection of the nation and its interests. Under interests are understood: the identity, the unity, the recognition and dignity of the members of the nation, best safeguarded through the attainment and maintenance of a sovereign rule, or a degree of autonomy, the lack of which carries a permanent threat of national demise. Accordingly, nationalism is best seen as a 'collective action designed to render the boundaries of the nation congruent with those of its governance unit'[18]. The basic message of nationalism is the conviction that belonging to a national group, its existence and survival are of supreme importance to its members and the right they all share as members of humanity. Thus, all nationalisms, whether the state-seeking nationalism, the hegemony-pursuing nationalism of a majority, an autonomy-seeking minority nationalism, the homogenising nationalism of a newly independent state, nationalist movements for devolution or other reorganisation within a multinational state, all share these basic ideas and pursue them with a varying degree of intensity.

The all-encompassing object of nationalist endeavour - the nation - can be defined as a large social group integrated by a combination of objective relationships (economic, territorial, political, linguistic, historical and cultural) and their subjective reflection in collective consciousness[19].

The idea of 'the nation' however stands for more then just a large social group integrated by many subjective and objective relationships; 'the nation' and the membership in it are infused with sentiments of dignity and recognition, with historical memories, with the politics of the present and expectations for the future, all of which add to one's identity and thus national identity constitutes a potent force in an individual's identity. There may be many terminological inconsistencies surrounding the terms nation, ethnic group, the state, the nation-state and minority, but all refer to larger social groups with high degree of solidarity and emotional investment.

Ethnicity refers strictly to the belonging to an ethnic group, a particular collectivity based on 'real or putative common ancestry and memories of shared historical past and cultural focus on one or more symbolic elements defined as the epitome of their peoplehood'[20]. Ethnicity stresses the importance of subjective perception of identity, thus the distinction between the nation and the ethnic group can be summed up by saying that the latter is a similar concept, but narrower in that the binding issue is common ancestry and not the loyalty to a legal structure of the state.

Ethnicity is a cultural trait, it is not defined by state borders, but can transcend them, which explains the strength of ethnic affiliation in migrant communities and among minorities across borders and continents. Naturally, ethnicity is associated with a specific territory[21] - ethnic homeland - around which ethnic identity is framed and reproduced throughout time and which is seen as a 'cradle' of the ethnic/national group. Without the symbolic value given to 'land' we could not explain Milošević's success in mobilizing Serbian nationalism against Kosovo, considered by Serbs to be the 'cradle' of their nation. Without the notion of 'homeland' there would not be the Zionist movement and its culmination, the state of Israel, as there would not be that powerful concept 'motherland' (fatherland).

Notwithstanding the fact that it is ethnic solidarity which sets in motion a more political process of nation-formation, thus nationalism, ethnic identity in itself does not make a nation. Equating ethnic solidarity with national identity and that with the state is precisely where the problem of nationalism and democracy in a multicultural state lies, for the state is even less an expression of ethnicity than is nationalism. The state is a legal concept, it describes a definite territory (occupied by one or more ethnic groups/nations), political institutions and an official government, whilst the nation describes a cultural heritage which may or may not be institutionalised in the common state institutions and a group with a sense of homogeneity.

It can be argued that the legal concept of the state which emerged from the Peace of Westphalia (1648) predates nations as political entities. This Westphalian state and its legitimacy has only later been enhanced by the principle of popular sovereignty and by the doctrine of national self-determination, both of which have provided as it were the moral principles for a political state, thus creating the nation-state. To some early political thinkers, such as John Stuart Mill (1806-1873), the nation-state and its cultural homogeneity were a precondition for democracy, well demonstrated by the claim that members of the same nationality (e.g. language, literature) should be united under the same government, 'and a government to themselves apart' and more resolutely by the well-known dictum 'that free institutions are next to impossible in a country made up of different nationalities'[22]. Thus, it must be noted that the legitimacy of the nation-state has always been entangled with two contradictory principles: civic (democracy) and ethnic/national (self-determination). This fact gives nationalism a different character depending on which of the two principles it pursues more actively; nationalism has an integrative quality, which can contribute towards a more civic (democratic) character of its state, or it limits its integrational effort to only one ethnic group, in which case its democratic potential and that of its state remains limited too.

The nation-state is not the universal reality, quite on the contrary, most states are multinational; hence, the pursuit of state-culture congruence (nation-building) is not the same as seeking to establish a united political community (state-building)[23]. The sentiment of belonging to a culture transcends borders and does not have to be attached to a nation-state, as the conflicts between minorities and majorities in the world today amply illustrate. Ethnic groups, which define themselves as a separate cultural entity from the assumed official culture of the state, are minorities, particularly when across the border is a nation-state whose dominant culture has been erected out of the same ethnic origin.

This book distinguishes between an ethnic group as a minority and dominant nation, to avoid the confusion between the often conflictual demands of each vis-à-vis each other. There is a tendency to call ethnic groups with specific claims a minority, as there is a tendency to call large ethnic groups with already established territorial boundaries within multinational states nations (Scots; Welsh; Czechs and Slovaks within Czechoslovakia; Serbs, Croats, Slovenes within Yugoslavia; and all republics within the Soviet Union).

Therefore, multiethnic, multinational and multicultural state, all describe a state with different cultures, which strictly speaking would mean that all states are multicultural. However, not all states declare themselves as such, as not all ethnic groups seek a political arrangement to reflect their separate status - a multinational state is not one that comprises different nations, but one that declares itself as such[24], and more importantly, responds accordingly. That means a normative readjustment to the fact that minority cultures constitute an integral part of the state's culture which in policy terms would imply that there are no privileged groups.

When it comes to equality between national groups, nationalism and democracy often find themselves pursuing a different agenda. Nevertheless, two points should be stressed: first, decoupling of nationalism from democratisation processes reduces the understanding of all current revivals of ethnic self-determination round the world (including the postcommunist transitions); second, nationalism's glorification of national independence does not necessarily spell inequality, on the contrary the principle of national self-determination recognizes the equality of people and nations. The descent of nationalism from defence of liberty and culture to oppression of others (and often its own people), belongs to the study of nationalism, but is not a definition of it.

### Civic or Ethnic Nationalism? Modern or Ancient Nation?

In conclusion to these introductory clarifications of concepts that monopolise studies of nationalism I want to stress the position of this book on two important issues: the well established distinction between ethnic and civic nationalism and the debate about the modernity versus 'ancientness' of the nation[25].

*Civic/ethnic distinction*   The literature on nationalism is replete with the distinction between ethnic and civic nationalisms, and suggestions that ethnic nationalism by defining its nation as a community of descent is inherently collectivist, illiberal and contradictory to inclusive citizenship, thus a considerable challenge to democracy. Civic nationalism then is antithetical in character, inclined towards an inclusive definition of the nation as a community of equal citizens, hence its benign character, providing it maintains this inclusive quality it can be complementary to democracy. In other words, whatever the objectives of ethnic nationalism may be (improvement of political or cultural conditions, or dominance in the state), their achievement seeks to accommodate only one particular group, whose membership is defined by their ethnicity and not open to 'others', whereas civic nationalism can extend the membership of the group to all people inhabiting a given territory.

This binary classification informs many theories of nationalism and its compatibility with democracy, and takes on different forms of description, always with a more positive evaluation given to civic nationalism rather than ethnic[26]. Leah Greenfeld[27] makes the distinction clear by saying that the idea of the nation, which originally implied sovereignty of the people, originally emerged as individualistic, but later emphasized the people's uniqueness. She suggests that 'these two dissimilar interpretations of popular sovereignty' (individualistic - libertarian versus collectivistic - authoritarian) underlie the basic types of nationalism, which may be either 'civic' (voluntaristic), that is identical with citizenship, or 'ethnic', which implies particularism and is necessarily collectivistic and collectivistic ideologies are inherently authoritarian.

It is important to stress that this is a hypothetical discussion because awarding citizenship to foreigners is subject to strict laws in all countries of the world and mostly based on the exclusion from the country of application rather than inclusion. Moreover, in ECE post-1989 nationalism and democracy stimulated and inspired each other and demands were ethnic and civic at the same time. The problem with such confusion is that democratisation requires civic values, whilst they are not available, because being rather a result of democracy, it is difficult to be a prerequisite at the same time.

I prefer to view the above distinction as an 'ideal' type and refer to it because of its well established meaning. By 'civic' I mean an attachment to the state of citizenship, by 'civic tradition' a tradition of stateness and political institutions, whilst 'ethnic' refers strictly to cultural traits. In the contemporary world, where so many ethnic communities fight for recognition, ethnic nationalism can no longer be portrayed merely as the oppression of majority over minority. The ethnic/civic distinction might be useful as an academic tool to distinguish between different forms of nationalisms, but we must concede that it is not an adequate tool for assessment of nationalism in the new states of ECE, which encompasses both ethnic and civic elements at the same time, as the following chapters will show.

*Modernists and primordialist* Nearly all writing on nationalism touches upon the discussion about the modernity versus 'ancientness'[28] of the nation. Here I shall omit this discussion which in my opinion adds very little to the purpose of this book. Both approaches primordial and modernist[29] have something relevant to say. The relevance lies however not in the argument about 'what came first, nations (primordial) or nationalism (modernist)', but elsewhere. Primordialism's continued relevance lies in its emphasis on 'perception in guiding human action'[30]. The importance of modernism on the other hand is not so much in its common belief in the modernity of the nation (in the wake of the French Revolution), but rather in the number of theories that can be brought under the modernist umbrella.

There are various strands in the modernist school, each emphasizing a different factor in its account of nationalism: e.g. the economically determined approach stressing the material side of the history[31] over the last two centuries; nationalism driven by modern communication to fabricate 'imagined communities'[32]; nationalism as an active and powerful actor in the politics of the state[33] (much of the case study of Slovak nationalism is informed by this approach); and finally, the ideological approach that sees nationalism as a doctrine that by some terrible mistake has entered history with terrible consequences[34].

Nationalism in this book is viewed as a modern political force, that uses its easily invoked connection to the 'ancientness' of the nation. It creates a modern national identity which nevertheless defines itself through symbols of historical defeats and victories (perceived or real is irrelevant), and by its strongly ideological basis it regularly rivals all other ideologies. What the above approaches to nationalism do not adequately account for is the supreme mobilizing potential of nationalism in today's world - a world torn by its excesses, where the force declared regularly to be waning revives with such regularity and vigour and whose myths are longer lasting than other myths of collective identity (e.g. the myth of the proletariat).

It is my contention that the reason for this is not the lack of understanding of nationalism, but the underestimation of its role as an integral part of any democratisation process. The preoccupation with 'real or constructed' identity that nationalism creates overshadows the very identity of nationalism itself that cannot be reduced to any one aspect of socio-political development. In fact the one single factor that characterizes nationalism is the multiplicity of appeals through which it addresses its potential constituency and as such nationalism is a potent form of collective allegiance and its significance remains rooted in its capacity to represent the people and their collective will.

## Nationalism and Democracy: Ambiguous Relationship

As signalled thus far - the relationship between nationalism and democracy is inherently ambiguous. This ambiguity is rooted in the fact that politics instigated by nationalism and democracy both claim to answer to 'the will of the people'. The undesirable consequences of nationalism have been amply demonstrated over the course of this century[35], nevertheless democracy is linked to a sovereign political unit and that to a modern state. The creation of that state has most likely been preceded by a struggle for national self-determination in an attempt to secure rights for its national group. Each national struggle carries within itself two ideas: more rights and recognition of a given territory and a distinctive group sharing certain ethnic and /or political characteristics. In each case the idea is simultaneously democratic and prone to an undemocratic practice, because the definition of a territory, its group and its corresponding rights can and usually does generate a definition of 'the other' who may then be excluded, politically or even physically from the unit that has thus acquired a new political status. Hence, the compatibility of nationalism and democracy travels a very thin line, for every positive side there is a glimmer of the negative side, which does not mean to say that the relationship must fail, merely that it is a difficult one to manage. Nevertheless, in the next few pages I shall focus on the positive elements of national identity whilst pointing out the potential negative characteristics and discuss the contradictory logic of nation-building and state-building.

## National Identity and Self-determination

The three main pillars on which nationalism rests are national self-determination principle, its ontological key element - national identity and the interests of the national group. The idea of national self-determination stands for the establishment of the preferred form of government, whether it is a component of a multinational state, a federation or as an independent state[36]. What are the arguments for national self-determination, that is for the boundaries of political units (states or federal units) to coincide with national (cultural) boundaries?

The underlying assumption is that the nation is an important source of personal identity[37], which provides one with a place in the world and hence exercises a considerable influence over one's opportunities and choices in life. Obviously, one's life is largely influenced by more immediate groupings and relationships than 'the nation', but national culture provides an important moral and practical resource in an individual's existence. The main reason for favouring national self-determination derives from the above assumption that national cultures are worth protecting. Moreover, each community feels that the distribution and management of their resources and decisions about the future of their community is best served by more autonomy.

Why it is a national state that is considered best equipped to protect a group's culture and autonomy has to be sought in real or imagined national experiences. Historically there are many instances when a multinational state has tried to assimilate weaker groups by force (e.g. Magyarisation in the nineteenth century), or economically exploit a more successful national group (e.g. the Yugoslav federation versus Slovenia), or simply dominate the state's policy by numerical preponderance (e.g. the Czechs in

Czechoslovakia), so that empirically there is enough evidence to assume that the best protection against the erosion of one's culture and resources is to share decisions with like-minded people, thus keep it within one's own state. That however does not stop a particular political or economic grouping from the exploitation of its co-nationals, so strictly speaking national self-determination implies the correspondence of the popular will and state borders[38]. Herein is the connection between democracy and national self-determination. In principle only a democratic state would be able to ensure that the national self-determination truly reflects the will of "the people" and therefore, in theory, national self-determination is linked to democratic consent and citizenship and the development of a modern state, itself the guarantor of the nation.

In the context of postcommunist transitions nationalism must be viewed, at least partially, as a positive force. The idea of the nation provided the populations of the ECE countries with an identity and self-esteem when both were rendered hollow by communist regimes. By the same token, the idea of national self-determination in the East European context, contributed to the legitimacy and coherence of the new-born states and helped their citizens to endure the initial hardship of the transition. The problem however is that the idea of the national self-determination, which can be interpreted as the right to democratic government, does not necessarily guarantee the existence of a democratic regime.

One reason is the above-mentioned fact that under democracy we understand liberal-democracy and that the logics of liberalism and democracy, even if now merged, are quite different. Liberalism focuses on individual and human rights, democracy locates the power in the people; liberalism places limits on the power of governments, even democratic ones, whilst democracy grants power to the people, whether the result is democratic or not. So, it would be stretching the concept of national self-determination too far to claim that it requires or guarantees democracy.

It is clear that national self-determination has lost its good name due to the violence with which it is often pursued and because national self-determination once achieved does not guarantee a democratic regime in the name of which the process legitimised itself in the first place. The problem is magnified in a multinational setting - a priority given to compatriots of the dominant nationality, thus overriding obligations to minorities and the use of state apparatus to these ends means that aggrieved minorities have little choice, but to make appeals to their own self-determination (which might include secession) and so the process of societal fragmentation is set in motion.

The individual's relation to his or her nation can be compared to the individual's relation to any other group of which he/she is a member - that means that identity is linked to recognition, to dignity and self-esteem, status, safety and prestige[39]. It is important to stress that generating an identity is a psychological necessity and a part of human nature. How this necessity has come to be associated with national identity has to be sought in the role of the nation-state. Our social reality is inconceivable without nations (therefore states) and the specificity of national identity is that it distinguishes national from any other types of identity. Hence, 'national identity derives from a membership in "a people" defined as a nation, which implies that national population is perceived as homogenous'[40] - in this context any other types of stratification, such as status, gender or class are secondary. A more cynical view would be that it is one identity, among the many an individual has, that is awarded without a personal effort; it is attached to the membership rather than an achievement and allows for an individual to play a part in history which in most cases would not otherwise happen. Humiliation of the nation, its defence and future are in a similar way all entangled with one's identity.

Nationalism's emotive power rests on that fundamental human need for identity[41], recognition and dignity in the world that divides people into nations. Daily we are confronted with the plight of refugees round the world and what makes their situation so problematic is not just the lack of shelter and food, but because we all instinctively understand the humiliation that denial of one's identity carries. To claim that nationalism is therefore politics of identity only, would be to rescue the primordialist argument through the back door, which is not my intention. Identity being such an important facet of human existence, is open to manipulation and misinterpretation, to exploitation and the pursuit of self-interest and hence to politics. These are facets of nationalism's own identity and the main reason behind its political success.

## The Contradictory Logic of Nation-building and State-building

Nationalism is a political movement - it has to engender action and political solidarity among a significant proportion of the population and imbue them with a common goal. As has been stressed above national self-determination is not limited to the establishment of independent statehood. Nationalist mobilisation of the political will continues whenever grievances, real or putative, are belittled and no political or administrative solution has been found, or when nationalist elites create a sense of dissatisfaction in order to seek a remedy for their waning legitimacy. In Slovakia nationalist mobilisation gathered momentum after independence; the political elite in order to camouflage the growing political cleavages concentrated on the ethnic ones. One could identify this kind of nationalism as 'post-independence', so nationalism of the newly independent states is the type of nationalism that affects the transition to democracy directly and is the subject of this study.

If nationalism was only about intellectuals writing stories about ancient heroes and states declaring citizenship and language laws, without encountering opposition from other national groups, we would not be considering the impact of nationalism on democracy and there would be nothing controversial about nationalism. The emphasis upon culture and identity is possibly useful in understanding a type of nationalist development or the mechanisms it uses in a particular country. However, too much focus on the particularity of nationalism is to neglect the fact that the controversy comes from nationalism's innate tendency towards the appropriation of the state's authority and the exercise of power. Power, despite the much-propagated view that the state has sacrificed its predominance to global economic interdependence (see chapter 7), is still about significant control of the national state.

Here we face a major dilemma of the nationalism-democracy relationship. Nation-building and state-building are overlapping, but two conceptually (and historically) different processes. The well-established idea of seeing a nation as 'a people' in possession of a state might be the ideal of nationalism, but a nation, seen as a cultural community, can exist without a state as much as a state does not need one such 'people' to exist; what a democratising state needs is a unified nation in a political, not a cultural sense. In other words, democracies require a sense of identification with the political community which in terms of identity means that being a citizen should rate as an important component of who they are. To Dunkwart Rustow one single background condition for transition to democracy is national unity, meaning 'that the vast majority of citizens in a democracy to be must have no doubt or mental reservations as to which political community they belong to'[42]. The point to underscore is that a political community is not determined by culture or common heritage, membership is not a given, but can be acquired or chosen, so that strictly speaking nation-building should mean the integration and harmonisation of the whole society and all citizens in it.

It is the state, however, that controls the territory and has the supreme authority to impose rules and forms of behaviour and demand taxes; in short, a nation and its leaders cannot impose any desired rules or behaviour without the significant control of the state. In the process of nation-state consolidation, state power plays a fundamental role, also because it holds the key to the major element of cultural homogenisation of state's population: the education system. The state in order to increase, or maintain its legitimacy has a vested interest in creating and reinforcing the nation - it must justify the purpose of its existence, which besides the physical protection of its citizens and their welfare, is also the guardianship of the national culture.

In newly independent states, both the state and the nation are engaged in the process of strengthening their position; the main resource that the nation has for acquiring political power stems from the unity provided by the psychological identification of its members. Nationalism is thus conducive to nation-building process - a deliberate effort to construct an overarching collective identity, which is usually based on a 'putative common national (ethnic) sentiment, culture and heritage'[43] in an effort to create a sense of purpose that a state needs in order to function effectively. State-building then is in principle a complementary project, aiming at the establishment of a political community of citizens and at forging social solidarity and loyalty to state institutions. The compatibility of those two processes is however dependent on whether the state and its leaders who pursue nation-building policies perceive the state to be of and for the dominant nation. The clash between the administrative and the political emphasis of democratising policies on the one hand and the culturally preoccupied nation-building process on the other hand aiming at the consolidation of the nation is less relevant if there is a congruence between the polity (demos) and culturally conscious nation (ethnos), which is not the reality of most states in ECE.

In multinational (multiethnic or multicultural) states those two processes can be conflicting, mostly due to the assumption by the dominant nation and its nation-building elites that the state is their own nation-state which implies the exclusion of other ethnic groups from the ownership of the state. In the case of newly independent multinational states the problem is further magnified by the tension about the order of preference given to either state-building or nation-building.

When it comes to democratisation, the legitimacy of the democratisation process, as will be argued throughout, is central to politics, but in new multinational democracies that are still in the process of consolidating the nation which the state embodies, legitimacy of that state is also at the heart of nationalist mobilisation. The disintegration of the postcommunist Czechoslovakia is a good example. The legitimacy of transition and the common state was challenged by the Slovak claim that the state consisted of two peoples, each of which had the right to decide the fate of its nation (the pace and type of transition), thus, the building of a common state lost to the challenge of nation-building from one of its constituent parts[44].

Paradoxically, civic identity tends to lose out as soon as there is a disagreement about state-building policies. Ethnic nationalism is as much a consequence of unsuccessful state-building as it is its cause, for the disintegration of the state, the loss of its legitimacy, diminishes civic affiliation and leaves the field open to ethnic mobilisation. The disintegration of Czechoslovakia changed the civic identity of the Hungarian minority, who found themselves citizens of a new state they did not want. Consequently, the Hungarian minority was faced with strong nationalising policies of new Slovakia, inspired by historical animosity against Hungary and the minority's lack of enthusiasm for independent Slovakia. Therefore their identity became narrower, in the sense that they became defined as 'the Hungarians' and without the protection of more neutral and historically less hostile Prague. Similarly, the mobilisation of Slovaks within Czechoslovakia could not be done on the basis of civic identity, for the state that should have inspired that identity was being questioned - in both cases state-building failed to create a political nation and lost to an ethnic one.

*National Identity and Democracy*

Within the above pages my concern has been to point out dilemmas that arise from the theory and practice of nationalism and democracy generally. This thus sets out the theoretical foundations on which the exploration of nationalism and democracy rests for the remainder of this book. It can be reduced to the following three points:

1. The intrinsic link between nationalism and the formation of the political unit, from which derives the significance of nationalism in the transition to democracy;
2. The compatibility of the self-determination principle with democratisation, but the contradictory logic of their extension to nation-building and state-building; and
3. Nationalism's evident capacity to offer a group identity, allegiance, representation and recognition, which accounts for nationalism's capacity to mobilise and legitimise - the reverse side of this capacity is nationalism's proneness to the appropriation of political power.

In order to conclude this question of the compatibility between nationalism and democracy which is crucial in deciding the role of nationalism in the democratisation process of a particular state, the last link to explore is whether whatever national/ethnic identity has to offer is conducive to democracy, and how it is different from nationalism.

The political importance national identity carries can be summed up as a feeling of cohesion and purpose in achieving a common goal which despite many divisions inside the state can be surmounted, in return for safety and belonging. In short, national identity makes the complexities of life and politics simpler, by offering a clearer definition of interests and choices and some guidelines in the formation of relationships with others[45].

Democracy does not offer this comfort. It is a system of certain principles and procedures and uncertain outcomes[46]. It arrives at collective decisions through controversies and many compromises - at best it is a decision which is perceived as 'good enough' by the majority of people. One of the many sources of making sure that there is a general sense of satisfaction with the outcome is national identity. At the beginning of the transition process, when open state institutions already function, but the nascent democracy suffers from not yet clearly established rules of competition for power, when not enough time has passed for the population to settle into the new regime and experience its benefits, in such an environment the claims of nationalist demagogues can become very persuasive for obvious reasons.

First, the very quality of democracy - choice, uncertainty and complexity - makes nationalism appealing, because by defining national community in less political and more ethnic, therefore homogenous terms, it makes the definition of interests easier to grasp and thus appears to simplify the political landscape that has become too complex. Secondly, democracy allows for nationalist politicians to promote their ideas. But, let us not forget what those ideas can be. Nationalism's strength lies in the elevation of one national group's identity and solidarity, therefore by implication in the exclusion of others from all advantages that belonging brings. This is not the kind of solidarity that democracy seeks. Hence, national identity in a democratic nation should mean the loyalty to a political community of the whole citizenry, held together by common efforts to realize the common project - democracy and justice.

But, as has been pointed out by Dimitrije Djordjević, 'it is easier to be an emotional nationalist than a rational democrat'[47], so the question is whether nationalism and democracy can be reconciled, in order to decrease nationalism's challenge to democracy, particularly in multiethnic states. Can nationalism facilitate democracy, can it be a source of cohesion, solidarity and identity in the state? It would appear that every positive element nationalism has to offer to democracy is matched by its negative side, thus reducing the chances for compatibility.

Nevertheless, the contention here is that the reconciliation between nationalism and democracy is possible and depends on the compatibility of their objectives. The following case studies will provide the empirical evidence for this claim. Democracy presupposes a political unit and the implicit suggestion in the work of many democratic theorists (e.g. Mill,

Rustow, Linz and Stepan) is that democratisation is easier in a state with largely one culture, because there is less tension between nation-building and state-building policies. The clue to a successful transition to democracy then must lie in the establishment of a political community with corresponding identity and loyalty attached to that community. This does not presuppose the removal of cultural identities, which evidently is not so easy, but forging of an overarching identity that corresponds with the boundaries of the state and envelops all ethnic communities.

People's identity might draw on cultural roots, but it is also changeable and adaptable according to social and political conditions. It is precisely that human capacity to accept multiple identities, alongside with or over their ethnic identity, that makes democracy possible in multinational states.

The recent history of nationalism does not offer much faith in nationalism's capacity to promote such an identity, yet the beginnings of 'the nation' endowed with the status of a sovereign political body are to be sought in the revolutionary origins of nationalism. By the same token, the sheer magnitude of postcommunist changes was partially delivered by nationalist endeavour, hence there is no denying nationalism's capacity to facilitate democratic changes. Whether nationalism can sustain democracy longer term is doubtful. It depends on whether it is willing to promote the loyalty to the political rather than ethnic community, thus shift its inherent ethnic emphasis from 'one' nation to 'more' nations in order to contribute to democratic state-building. Such a shift cannot be just called into action, but depends on the socio-political conditions in the state, as the following illustrates.

## Theoretical Framework for the Case Studies

The discussion so far has concentrated on the prevalence of nationalism in postcommunist societies, and on the fundamental contradictions between nationalism and democracy as well as suggesting a possible compatibility. The purpose of this section is: first, to draw out the main arguments from the above theoretical discussion and thus introduce the theoretical framework within which the case studies will be conducted; second, to introduce the main lines of inquiry on which the following case studies are based.

The remainder of the book rests on the following propositions:

1.  Postcommunist world has witnessed the predominance of ethnic nationalism over a more civic dimension of nationhood. The reasons were discussed at length in the first chapter, but can be summed up by

saying that the absence of civic tradition, historically determined political inexperience, exacerbated further by the communist experience has made the advent of democracy even more tightly coupled with nationalism than it would have been otherwise. It is not certain that nationalism is by definition detrimental to democracy, but it is noted here with fair conviction that the ethnicisation of politics opens the stage to nationalist demagoguery and generally slows down the democratisation process. Whilst it is claimed that all nationalisms combine ethnic and civic elements, the prevalence of the former necessarily impairs the latter.

2. There is no denying the democratic potential of nationalism and the positive elements of national identity - all discussed above. Nationalism's greatest historical achievement is self-determination, yet self-determination conceals the tendency towards the appropriation of state power by the dominant majority and thus attempts to dominate the parts of the population that do not belong to 'the nation'.

3. Nationalism undermines state-building, a fact gaining in relevance in multinational states and since it is democratisation itself that facilitates the increase in nationalist mobilisation, democracy is better served by a weaker emphasis on national identity. This last point is even more pertinent in the newly independent states engaged simultaneously in nation- and state-building. Assuming that national identity is an important facet of peoples' existence and therefore relevant to democratic politics, the resolution of the tension between nationalism and democracy depends greatly on how anti-democratic elements of nationalism can be reduced to such an extent that the transition to democracy does not get overshadowed by the consolidation of the national rather than political community.

4. As with any major historical development, there is a considerable disagreement about the significance of nationalism in this process, generally vacillating between its positive and negative character, as the discussion above indicated. The proposition of this book, put to test in the forthcoming case studies, is that the role of nationalism in the democratisation process cannot be generalised and that under certain conditions nationalism can be conducive to democracy. Those 'certain conditions' however are in themselves a process which is contingent on many variables, ranging from historical determinants, the national development and the ethnic composition and consonance, through the recent past, to the formation of national elites in the transition, all of which are determining factors in the role nationalism will play in the democratisation process.

*Slovakia and Slovenia Compared*

It would seem unrealistic to assume that the relationship between democracy and nationalism is so one-sided that nationalism would be the sole driving force of the transition to democracy. The contention here is that democracy's capacity to contain nationalism within the limits of loyalty to the democratisation project has at least as much influence on the transition process as nationalism's capacity to endanger it. The case studies of Slovakia and Slovenia explore this dynamic, the key elements of which are: the communist legacy, the legitimacy of the new state and the democratisation process itself, and not in the least, the ensuing elite formation[48].

The findings of the case studies argue that Slovenia being able to use nationalism positively constitutes an example where nationalism played a relatively positive role in the democratisation process. Slovakia, particularly in the period on which this investigation focuses, between the independence and the last general elections (1993-1998) exemplifies rather the opposite case, whilst suggesting that the current configuration of the political elite and their commitment to democracy has reduced the relevance of nationalism in political life.

Before pointing out the main differences two qualifications are in order. First, I am not suggesting that Slovene nationalism is a 'good' nationalism, merely that its role in the transition process has been more positive than in Slovakia. Equally, it is not my intention to portray Slovakia as a home to 'bad' nationalism. My concern is rather with the conditions under which nationalism is more or less compatible with democracy – Slovakia is the 'less' case, for reasons that will become apparent.

The first point of comparison is the legitimacy of the new state and the transition process. Democratisation in Slovenia started long before independence, but due to the increasingly centralising policies of Serbia it could not continue further within the given constitutional arrangement. Thus independence became the culmination of that process, and moreover its guarantor - national emancipation in Slovenia did not start in the name of 'the nation', but in the name of democracy. In contrast, democratisation in Slovakia became subordinated to the 'national question' which, given the historical trajectory of Slovakia's national existence, assumed priority. The birth of independent Slovakia and the initiation of democracy were shrouded in disagreements; about the secession, about the conception of democracy and the role of the 'nation' in it, and about the identity and the purpose of the new state. The population, but mainly elites were divided mostly on political issues, but in order to camouflage the political disagreements, ethnic polarisation became instrumentalised into the main political cleavage. The actual conflict was between a populist-nationalist leadership, trying to halt the democratisation process and all elements of the political opposition who had entertained any reasonable doubts about Slovakia's independence and its democratic future.

In both Slovakia and Slovenia the economic and political inheritance were determined by communism. However, the recent history of Slovenia, was substantially different from that of Slovakia. Whilst the communist regime in Czechoslovakia was tightly controlled by Moscow and isolated the country from the Western world, Slovenes enjoyed open borders to the West and a guaranteed access to the Yugoslav market in which they assumed a leading position. In Slovenia communism did not leave behind a devastated country, but one which was economically relatively advanced, with a strong national consciousness and self-confidence of the politically and economically most developed republic within the Yugoslav federation. In contrast Slovakia was a weaker partner in the Czechoslovak federation and its national consciousness was based on negative comparisons with its larger and more developed and cultivated federal partner, and historically oppressive neighbouring Hungary.

In both cases the federal state failed to continue the democratisation process in the tempo which would be satisfactory to all its constituent units - whether for economic, cultural, historical or political reasons and usually due to the combination of all those factors. Whilst Slovenia was politically ahead of its federal partners, Slovakia was less prepared for the ever-increasing intensity of political and economic reforms advocated by the Czech side. Secession is often the last option by which to emphasise political differences in a common state and Slovenia decided that its future was best secured by independence. Slovakia on the other hand, was not given the opportunity to decide - the most important decision in the history of Slovakia happened without a referendum (the reasons and the consequences will be dealt with in detail in the following chapter). Neither Slovak independence, nor democracy could rely on a strong legitimacy that would give them a healthy start, and the years that followed confirmed one of the claims of this book that insecure democracy and insecure nationhood feed off each other and create a dynamic detrimental to further democratisation. The consequence for the transition was that the gaps in legitimacy were filled by nationalist elites trying to justify the fact after the event. Thus the political arena instead of being harmonised became increasingly radicalised on all issues involving the nation and democracy.

Thus, the basis of the comparison between the two transition processes lies in the legitimacy of democratisation and independent statehood which in Slovenia, unlike in Slovakia, formed a mutually compatible dynamic. There are moments in history when the interests of individuals coincide with national interests, therefore the difference nationalism has played in the democratisation processes in Slovenia and Slovakia can be summarised by the words of Ivan Bernik that in Slovenia 'nationalism was instrumental in creating a relatively broad consensus on vital national interests'[49]. In Slovakia on the other hand, the political developments became overshadowed by nationalism which was instrumental in widening political and ethnic cleavages, thus impeding the democratisation process.

## Conclusion

The point of the last two chapters was to argue the reasons why nationalism proved to be an integral part of postcommunist democratisation processes. The above introduction of the two case studies to follow demonstrates that the evaluation of the role nationalism plays in these processes, despite its evident capacity to distract the process, is nevertheless variable. This leads me to make the following assertions about nationalism and its role in the democratisation process:

1.   The overwhelming presence of nationalism in postcommunist transitions derives partly from the fact that the existing states lost legitimacy which signalled the reassessment and readjustment of identities, by majorities and minorities.
2.   The fundamental problem of newly independent democracies is the tension between the formation of a political community as the basic condition for democracy and the establishment of the state based on self-determination of the national community, which means the synchronisation of the two historically simultaneous, but ideologically different processes, nation-building and state-building. Nationalism and democracy are thus tied together, whilst they seek different and often contradictory objectives.
3.   Nationalism is an important element of the democratisation process; it affects the direction and the pace of transition, but does not wholly determine it. The level (intensity) of nationalism is an issue of mobilisation - there are no intrinsically nationalistic nations, only conditions under which nationalism finds more or less resonance with the public. Those conditions constitute in themselves a complex process contingent on the past and present socio-political developments.
4.   The democratisation process relies on the legitimacy of the state and the unity of political community. In short, the capacity of democracy to contain nationalism within the reasonable boundaries in order to move

the democratisation process forward is one of the pre-conditions for the continuation of that process.

## Notes

[1] J.Schwarzmantel *Socialism and the Idea of the Nation* Hemel Hempstead, Harvester Wheatsheaf 1991; L.Greenfeld *Nationalism Five Roads to Modernity* London, Cambridge Harvard University Press 1992; B.Fontana 'Democracy and the French Revolution' in J.Dunn *Democracy the Unfinished Journey* Oxford, Oxford University Press 1992.

[2] General texts are mainly: J.Dunn *Democracy the Unfinished Journey* Oxford, Oxford University Press 1992; D.Held *Prospects for Democracy* Cambridge, Polity Press 1993; G.Sartori *The Theory of Democracy Revisited* New Jersey, Chatham House 1987; D.Beetham and K.Boyle *Introducing Democracy:80 Questions and Answers* Cambridge, Polity Press 1995.

[3] P.Schmitter 'Dangers and Dilemmas of Democracy' *Journal of Democracy* 5:2 April 1994 pp.57- 74 p.58.

[4] A.Schedler 'What is Democratic Consolidation' *Journal of Democracy* 9:2 April 1998 pp.91-105 p.95. The author agrees that democratic consolidation is an 'intrinsically teleological concept', but defends it if three conditions are met: a) we have to avoid obscuring it; b) dissociate it from any belief in inevitable progress; c) acknowledge that there is a plurality of consolidations.

[5] S.Huntington cited in D.Beetham 'Conditions for Democratic Consolidation' *Review of African Political Economy* 60 1994 pp.157-172 p.158.

[6] G.Sartori 'How Far Can Free Government Travel?' *Journal of Democracy* 6:3 July 1995 pp.101-111 p.102.

[7] Compiled from M.Kaldor and I.Vejvoda 'Democratization in Central and East European Countries' *International Affairs* 73:1 January 1997 pp.59-82; See also R.Dahl *Dilemmas of Pluralist Democracy* New Haven, Yale University Press 1982 and D.Beetham in D.Held ed. *Prospects for Democracy.*

[8] E.Huber, D.Rueschemeyer and J.Stephens 'The Paradoxes of Contemporary Democracy' *Comparative Politics* 29:3 April 1997 pp. 323-341 p.323.

[9] D.Beetham 'Conditions for Democratic Consolidation' p. 159.

[10] D.Beetham 'Liberal Democracy and the Limits of Democratization' in D.Held ed. *Prospects for Democracy.*

[11] A.Ágh *The Politics of Central Europe* London, Sage 1998 p.9.

[12] A.Schedler 'What is Democratic Consolidation'. The author uses the term as a 'convenient shorthand for any kind of 'diminished subtype' of democracy. p.93.

[13] A.Ágh identifies four types of distorted democracies, particularly important to postcommunist states: a) formalist (e.g. Serbia, Russia); b) elitist (in the early 1990s Romania, Albania, Bulgaria); c) partyist, whereby parties are the only actors and try to exclude all other political and social actors from the policy-making; d) tyrannical majorities (e.g. Slovakia, Croatia) pp.11-15.

[14] P.Schmitter 'Dangers and Dilemmas of *Democracy*' *Journal of Democracy* 5:2 April 1994 p.65 and by the same author 'Transitology: The Science of the Art of Democratisation' in J.Tulchin B.Romero *The Consolidation of Democracy in Latin America* London, Boulder, Lynne Rienner 1995.

[15] L.Diamond and M.Pattner *Nationalism, Ethnic Conflict, and Democracy* London, Baltimore, The Johns Hopkins University 1994 p.xi.

[16] W.Connor 'Nation-Building or Nation -Destroying?' *World Politics* 24:3 April 1972 pp. 319-355 p.331.

[17] Cited in *Daedalus* 121 Spring 1992 p.140.

[18] M.Hechter *Containing Nationalism* Oxford, Oxford University Press 2000 p.7.

[19] M.Hroch 'From National Movement to the Fully-formed Nation' *New Left Review* 198 March/April 1993 pp.3-20 p.4.

[20] R.Schermerhorn 'Ethnicity and Minority Groups' in J.Hutchinson & A.Smith *Ethnicity* Oxford, Oxford University Press 1996 p.17.

[21] For a discussion about 'homeland' nationalism see O.Yiftachel 'Nationalism and Homeland' in forthcoming *Encyclopedia of Nationalism* (Academic Press) and 'Nation-building and the Social Division of Space: Ashkenazi Dominance in the Israeli 'Ethnocracy' *Nationalism and Ethnic Politics* 4:3 1998 pp.33-58.

[22] J.S.Mill 'Representative Government' in *On Liberty and Other Essays* Oxford, Oxford University Press 1991 p. 428.

[23] A.Stepan 'Multinational democracies' in J.Hall *The State of the Nation* Cambridge, Cambridge University Press 1998 p.226, refers to the former as nation-state building and to the latter as democracy building, which is how these processes are viewed here too.

[24] B.Parekh in *Rethinking Multiculturalism* London, Macmillan 2000 makes this distinction clearer by arguing that multicultural is a description of the fact, whilst 'multiculturalist a normative response to the fact' p.6-8.

[25] See also E.Harris 'Nacionalizmus a demokratizačný proces' *OS-Forum Občianskej Spoločnosti* 11 November 1999 (Kalligram Bratislava) pp.42-47 and 'Assessing the compatibility between nationalism and democracy in postcommunist societies' *Slovak Sociological Review* 31:6 Fall '99 (SAV, Bratislava) pp.587-602.

[26] P.Alter *Nationalism* London, Edward Arnold 1994, contrasts the 'voluntarist' (Risorgimento), liberal-democratic concept of nation with a 'deterministic'(integral) that can be undemocratic; R.Brubaker *Citizenship and Nationhood* Cambridge, Harvard University Press 1992, distinguishes between the 'French' (republican) understanding of nationhood as 'universalist' and 'secular' and the German idea of the nation as differentialist, thus in line with a often used distinction of 'western' and 'eastern' nationalisms as synonymous with 'civic' and 'ethnic' definition. See also D.Brown 'Are There Good and Bad Nationalisms?' *Nations and Nationalism* 5:2 April 1999 pp.281-302.

[27] L.Greenfeld *Nationalism: Five Roads to Modernity* Cambridge, Harward University Press 1992 p.11.

[28] See U.Özkirimli *Theories of Nationalism* London, Macmillan 2000.

[29] The best known representatives of the modernist and primordialist schools are E.Gellner and A.D. Smith respectively. See mainly: E.Gellner *Nations and Nationalism* Oxford, Cambridge MA, Blackwell 1983 and A.D.Smith *Nationalism and Modernism* London, Routledge 1998.

[30] U. Özkirimli p.83.

[31] T.Nairn *The Break-up of Britain* London, NLB 1981, chapter 9 'The modern Janus'.

[32] B.Anderson *Imagined Communities* London, Verso 1983.

[33] J.Breuilly *Nationalism and the State* Manchester, Manchester University Press 1993.

[34] E.Kedourie *Nationalism* Oxford, Blackwell 1993.

[35] For example M.Mann 'The Dark Side of Democracy: The Modern Tradition of Ethnic and Political Cleansing' *New Left Review* 235 May/June 1999 pp.18-45.

[36] B.O'Leary in J.Hall *State of the Nation* p.69.

[37] D.Miller *On Nationality* Oxford, Clarendon Press 1995 p.82.

[38] D.Miller (1995) p.89.

[39] D.Druckner 'Nationalism, Patriotism, and Group Loyalty' in *Mershon International Studies Review* 38 1994 pp.43-68.

[40] L.Greenfeld *Nationalism Five Roads to Modernity* p.7.

[41] For politics of identity see C.Taylor 'Nationalism and Modernity' in J.Hall *The State of the Nation.*

[42] D.Rustow 'Transitions to Democracy' in *Comparative Politics* 2:3 April 1970 pp.337-363. p.350.

[43] O.Yiftachel 'Nation-building or Ethnic Fragmentation?' *Space and Polity* 1:2 November 1997 pp.149-171 p.150.

[44] See C.Skalnik Leff *The Czech and Slovak Republics* Boulder, Oxford, Westview Press 1997.

[45] For the importance of shared national identity in democratic regimes see: M.Moore 'Normative justification of liberal nationalism: justice, democracy and national identity' *Nations and Nationalism* 7:1 2001 pp.1-20.

[46] C.Offe *Modernity and the State* Blackwell, Polity Press 1996 p.257.

[47] Cited in A.Ágh *The politics of Central Europe* p.78.

[48] The importance of the economy is omitted here, but not because I wish to ignore its importance. The role of economy in the postcommunist transitions is a separate issue, deserving a longer discussion than can be awarded to it here, whilst at the same time I do not feel that such a discussion would change the above propositions. Moreover, the issue of the economy as a contributory factor in seeking independence in both countries, even if for contrary reasons (Slovenia the most advanced republic within Yugoslavia, Slovakia the less developed partner within Czechoslovakia) will be dealt with in the case studies; in addition, I would argue that economy is not the most determining factor in nationalist mobilisation, but adds to the general unease about the political situation.

[49] I.Bernik and B.Malnar 'Ethism, Nationalism and State-Building:the Case of Slovenia' Paper presented at the Congress of the International Political Association, Seoul, August 1997 p.11.

# 3 Political and National Identity in Czechoslovakia

Political analysis of Slovakia's transition to democracy has generally become synonymous with questions about what has gone wrong and what type of regime has emerged in Slovakia, which till recently was mostly described as 'fragile' or 'semi' democratic[1]. The last general elections (September 1998), the fourth since the end of communism and second in independent Slovakia were still critical as to the direction of the transition. These elections raised questions of the observance of constitutional order and the rule of law, the treatment of minorities, the integration and the relations with the West, and the general commitment to democracy, all of which put Slovakia into a sharp contrast with other neighbouring countries. The contrast is even more striking in comparison to the considerably more successful transition of the Czech Republic, the ex-partner in Czechoslovakia, within which Slovakia began its transition to democracy. Slovakia's status as the only country among the Visegrád group[2], initially excluded from the first wave of entrants to NATO and applicants to the EU is therefore even more surprising[3].

The last parliamentary elections brought a political defeat to Mečiar's Movement for Democratic Slovakia (henceforth HzDS/ Hnutie za Demokratické Slovensko) which dominated the Slovak political scene since its foundation in 1991, and a victory for parties committed to democracy and closer ties with the West. Their victory appears to have reversed this process of exclusion and secure a new phase in Slovakia's transition to democracy.

Even if Mečiar's government, which was marked by nationalism, corruption and disregard for constitutional and legal propriety and the ambivalence towards Western institutions, is generally viewed as the obstacle to democracy in Slovakia, the following two chapters will argue that the 'derailment' of Slovakia's transition has deeper roots than Mečiar's administration. Slovakia constitutes a complex case of a postcommunist transition in the context of a politically and ethnically divided society, exacerbated by complexities of nation-building and minority issues; hence,

73

nationalism played an important role in the first decade of that transition process. The theme of this chapter is an historical analysis of the national question within Czechoslovakia in order to build a foundation on which the analysis of politics in independent Slovakia can rest. This is done because I believe that without at least a brief account of Slovak historical, political and national development, it is difficult to explain fully the peaceful disintegration of Czechoslovakia, the reasons for which directly influenced the political process in independent Slovakia. Slovak conception of democracy and the role the nation plays in it were significantly shaped by its national consciousness, whose main reference groups were the Czechs and Hungarians.

*Slovak question*  Slovakia came into existence in 1993 as a result of an understandable anxiety about the pace of economic transformation and what appeared to be an irreconcilable difference in cultural and historical understanding of the common Czechoslovak state. The split happened because the populations on both sides, in the midst of postcommunist struggles, saw it as an answer to the old 'Slovak question'[4]. This term has existed since the formation of Czechoslovakia in 1918 to describe the always uncomfortable position of Slovaks within that common state, a position that has too often been simplistically reduced to an inherent Slovak nationalism. However, the 'Slovak question' is broader. It concerns problems of national, political, economic, social and cultural relations toward the common state and the relationship between Slovaks and the larger, mightier, more cultivated neighbours, thus, all that here stands for national identity and (as I will argue) cannot be solved by independence. Slovakia might be an unfortunate, but by no means an anomalous case where insecurity about national identity, particularly in a new state, leads to a nationalist mobilisation, which in turn hinders the resolution of the most important issues that the state is facing - democracy, relations with the minorities and a good international reputation.

It will be argued that Czechoslovakia ended in the same way as it began: two nations with different aspirations and different expectations, on swept by the tide of a great systemic change and presided over by ambitious elites. The interwar state failed to narrow the gap between national aspirations and levels of development; these divisions were further exacerbated by communism and its demise. It seems appropriate to mention at the outset that despite regular appearances of dissatisfaction with the functioning of the common state from both sides (including their wartime separation 1939-1945), the ultimate collapse of Czechoslovakia was a surprise, not only to the international community, but to its own population as well. As late as April 1992, 77% of respondents in Slovakia agreed with the statement that despite all disagreements the ties between the two nations should not be broken, whilst roughly half of the population claimed to want to maintain the common state (CR 53%, SR 42%). Yet the constitutional confrontation continued, the Czech and Slovak voters aligned behind parties that were critical of the common state[5] and it must be concluded that even if the result was not desired by the majority of the population, it reflected the fact that the common state failed to create a firm sense of commitment to a continued coexistence.

The principal focus of this chapter is thus the importance of the establishment of a political nation as a foundation for a common multiethnic state. Without a sense of shared political destiny among all citizens there is no unity or solidarity. Under such conditions the common state is deprived of its full legitimacy and the democratisation project becomes unsustainable long term. Following this line of argument, the chapter proceeds in two parts. The first part charts the troubled history of Czechoslovakia from its democratic beginnings in 1918 through the temporary separation of Czechs and Slovaks during the Second World War to their coexistence during the communist period. It ends with the end of communism and the opportunity to re-establish democracy once more The second part deals with post-1989 politics of disintegration and its main protagonists. The conclusion argues that in Slovakia the democratisation in the post-1989 period was largely viewed as a resolution of the national question.

## Common State in Search of Common Identity: Czechoslovakia 1918-1989[6]

### Czech and Slovak Relations in an Historical Perspective

Czechoslovakia's creation in 1918 was a result of many factors, of which national struggle within the Austro-Hungarian empire was possibly the least influential. More than a culmination of national emancipation, Czechoslovakia was rather a result of the endorsement of the principle of national self-determination at the Versailles Peace Conference, a great diplomatic success of Czechoslovakia's founding president T.G. Masaryk and mostly a result of the policies of the Western Powers, who faced with crumbling empires and the Bolshevik Revolution sought a solution to stability in ECE. It is fair to say that the majority of the Slovak population was slightly confused by their new status of a Czechoslovak citizen and even by their new, for the first time officially recognised, Slovak nationality[7].

The Czech lands (Bohemia and Moravia) were incorporated in the Austrian half of the monarchy (after the defeat of the independent Czech kingdom at Bílá Hora 1620), whilst Slovaks from around the year 1000 were absorbed into Hungary. Despite sharing their existence in the Habsburg monarchy, the two nations historically defined their identities differently - Slovaks in terms of Hungarian absolute rule, the Czechs in relation to the Germans. The implications of this different historical experience will become apparent later; suffice to say that the two nations could not rely on any historical experience in which they shared a common political existence, unless one looked back to the 8th century and the Great Moravian empire.

The new states that emerged from the Versailles treaty remained multinational; large number of minorities, particularly the German (over 3.3 million in the new Czechoslovakia) and the Hungarian minority (1 million) became separated from their ethnic kin on the other side of the borders, the situation which in the Second World War would serve as an invitation for the Nazi intervention in the case of the German minority, and led to the annexation of parts of Slovakia by Hungary. Nevertheless, Czechoslovakia in 1918 set out to be a multinational democracy, a home to Czechs, Slovaks, Germans, Hungarians, Jews and Ruthenians. The new state was more ethnically diverse than any other Eastern European state with the exception of The Kingdom of Serbs, Croats and Slovenes (later Yugoslavia). Whatever the complaints, and it became apparent that in the first two decades of the new state's existence nearly everyone, except the Czechs, was dissatisfied with the unitary state, the fact remains that on the eve of the Second World War Czechoslovakia was the only functioning parliamentary democracy in the region.

Czechoslovakia from its inception faced the problems of conflicting approaches to national questions, particularly from the Slovak side, but it must be conceded that all good intentions to sustain this civic democracy were regularly obstructed by the events taking place elsewhere, and the state was never given enough time to solve its internal problems. In 1938 after the appeasement of Hitler by the Western powers at Munich the state was dismembered, in 1939 the independent Slovak State was established and the Czech lands occupied. The attempt to re-establish democratic Czechoslovakia after the war was quashed by the communist coup d'état in February 1948. In 1968 the Prague spring was crushed by Soviet intervention, only to be followed by more repression for another twenty years. The first real opportunity to establish democracy presented itself after the fall of communism, but as the pages to follow will show democratisation became a victim to the accumulation of historical, political and national grievances rather than a victory over them. The past and geography do not determine the future of states, but they do collude in the shaping of that future. Hence, the following chronological section turns to the Czecho-Slovak relations in which unification and disintegration met in equal measures from the very beginning of their coexistence.

*The First Czechoslovak Republic and the Interwar Period*

In the second half of the 19th century Slovaks began to see themselves as a separate ethnic group[8], a realisation that was substantiated by the codification of the Slovak language in 1843 by Ľudovít Štúr, who became and remains the personification of Slovak national consciousness. The revolutionary year 1848 shifted the emphasis from language to politics, and at the Slav Congress in Prague adherents of Štúr (Štúrovci) joined the Czechs in the first attempts for a political recognition of Slovaks, in a form of a demand for the federalisation of Austria, based on the historical-national principle. Since Slovakia could not provide a reasonable claim to historical entity the first idea of the Czecho-Slovak coexistence was abandoned.

The next steps in Slovak national revival aimed at the political and cultural recognition failed. The first rather ambitious[9] programme was wholly incompatible with the Hungarian revolutionary programme seeking to create a modern Hungarian nation and was rejected. This nevertheless led to the establishment of the Slovak National Council (SNR/ Slovenská Národná Rada). A misconceived anti-Hungarian uprising was led by Štúr, in the hope that Vienna would comply, but this too failed to secure any political gains. The next less ambitious attempt (Memorandum Národa Slovenského 1861 in Martin) was ignored by Budapest, and Slovak cultural and political life came to a near cessation.

The Czech and Slovak political and cultural life bifurcated completely after Austro-Hungarian compromise (1867), when the monarchy changed into two nearly sovereign states with different nationality policies[10]. The equality and the cultural autonomy of the nations under the Austrian constitution became a law, which meant that the cultural and to a certain degree the political life of the Czechs could continue (the same applied for the Slovenes). However the Slovaks became subjected to the modernisation policies of Hungary, degenerating into increasingly intensified Magyarisation. In the words of a Hungarian politician of that time:

We want a legal state, but we will build it after we have secured the national state. The interests of the Hungarian nation demand that the national state be built on extremely chauvinistic principle[11].

In practice that meant an attempt to annihilate the Slovak nation - eventually all Slovak secondary schools and cultural organisations were closed and prohibited.

The Slovak national movement of the 19th century displayed certain characteristics which influenced Slovak nationalism well into the twentieth century. First, Slovak nationalism emerged totally divorced from any attempt at state-building. It involved an ethnic population devoid of legal status or a tradition of such and is an example of purely ethnic nationalism. Second, the national consciousness, sentiment and ideology are usually created and promoted by elites, but the Slovak case is extreme in this respect. The mostly peasant population and the nation-building elites lived in different worlds and contact between them[12] was minimal. Third, Slovak nationalism of that time was fuelled by Romanticism not only in the ideology, but also in political action, meaning that the lack of political strategy was substituted by revolutionary zeal. Štúr wrote 'what has been expected in 20,30,40 years is already here, the time has caught us unprepared'[13]. As will be shown below, it would not be the first time that Slovak attempts to nation-building would take a similar radical route. Fourth, this period in Slovak history marked not only the future anti-Hungarian orientation of Slovak nationalism, but very importantly influenced the Czecho-Slovak relations by a different perception of their national history and by a considerable backwardness in political, cultural and consequently economic development of Slovakia when compared to the Czechs.

Thomáš Garrigue Masaryk, a half-Slovak and in close contact with some Slovak national revivalists, realised that the Czech lands, being geographically in close proximity to Germany and with a substantial German population, would not be able to sustain an independent existence. He realised that the needed corridor to other Slavs, the Russians and Poles, led through Slovakia. His conception was of a Czechoslovak nation, consisting of two ethnic nations, whereby in practice the Slovaks would keep their own language and would have a separate cultural life, but would be united with the Czechs in one political and national unit[14].

The idea found resonance in Slovakia and not only by a group round Masaryk[15], but initially also by the SNR (Slovak National Council), even though the Slovak side was always more inclined towards a purely political arrangement of the possible Czecho-Slovak unity. Around this time a strongly Catholic stream crystallised among the Slovak nation-building elites under the leadership of a Catholic priest Andrej Hlinka[16], which came to dominate Slovak nationalism for decades to come. Hlinka was in close contact with Czechs, but already then there was a widespread feeling in Slovak Catholic circles that the Czechs were 'godless', Hussites (after Jan

Hus, the medieval Protestant reformer) and 'pokrokáři' (progressive in a negative sense). Very soon Masaryk's 'hlasisti' were accused of being under Czech influence and the idea of 'Czechoslovakism' (the claim that the Czechs and Slovaks were actually one ethnic group) was rejected.

Masaryk's conception of the relationship between the two nations was moving increasingly towards one nation, in which the historical and cultural differences were of a temporary nature, therefore unimportant and would fade away with time. The rift between this notion and the Slovak apprehension about losing their authenticity was already detectable and would remain an integral part of the Czecho-Slovak relationship for the duration of its existence. Nevertheless, the uneasy beginnings shifted into another gear with the outbreak of the First World War, the chronology of events omitted here.

The First Czechoslovak Republic became a possibility, initially with an émigré Czech and Slovak intelligentsia and later at home. It is vital to reiterate the total lack of participation by the population of the future Czechoslovakia in the inception of their state, particularly on the Slovak side (a largely peasant population, the general absence of communication during the war and the totalitarian nature of the Hungarian state). The project rested on the support of various Slavic organisations, namely the Slovak League in the USA, which already before the war took a keen interest in Slovak affairs. The idea in the emigrant circles was for a loose federation (a constant feature of the Slovak national programme within Czechoslovakia and at the end of it in 1992), eventually formalised in Pittsburgh in May 1918 between the Slovak and Czech émigré organisations and Masaryk. The document was vague about the issue of the Slovaks 'own parliament' which for years fuelled disappointment often expressed by the Slovak side that Masaryk had never fulfilled the promise of Pittsburgh[17]. The importance of that document lies however somewhere else: in its text it refers to Czecho-Slovakia (the importance of that hyphen will become apparent below, for it is far from trivial to Slovak nationalism) and in its vagueness it laid the basis for the later interwar demands of 'autonomists', led by Hlinka's party and thus, became the antipode to the conception of the unitary state based on one political nation.

The First Czechoslovak Republic was declared 28 October 1918 in Prague, amidst more recrimination about the text of the declaration (Slovak delegation was not present) which supposedly did not contain the right text securing a degree of Slovak autonomy, by again referring to the 'Czechoslovak nation'. However, the 'Slovak question' was put on hold and the atmosphere of that time was one of mutual compromise[18], to the point of the Slovak side conceding that in the interest of international recognition and the liberation of Slovakia from Hungary, the centralised unitary state was the most desired solution, certainly in the beginning.

For Slovakia the early years of the First Republic meant a monumental growth, mainly in the field of education and culture. The official language was Czechoslovak (Constitution 1920), in practice both versions - Czech and Slovak were official in both parts of the country. The end of Slovak national repression was evident and amounted to 'Slovakisation of Slovakia'[19] with the help of Czechs. The near absence of Slovak elites was less problematic than the total lack of 'middle cadres'; thousands of Czech teachers, administrators, lawyers, policemen, doctors and technicians came to Slovakia to assist with schools, transport, the local government, hospitals and the general running of the new Slovakia, the fact which later (and even to this day) fuelled accusations of Czech domination.

The new state brought a considerable change in status for Hungarians and Germans who became unexpectedly a minority, after centuries of being the members of the dominant nations. The nationality policies in Czechoslovakia were based on the Austrian model which guaranteed the cultural autonomy for all minorities (i.e. schools, cultural organisation, the use of minority languages in official contact etc.). Ironically, the Hungarian minority in postcommunist Slovakia often referred to the First Republic as the example of progressive minority policies.

Although a democrat (even if of a paternalistic inclination), Masaryk had ambivalent feelings about federalism which reminded him of the efforts to salvage Austria-Hungary, the state he sought to destroy[20]. The unification of Czechs and Slovaks was an unification of two entities at divergent levels of development in all spheres of life, especially in the field of centrally controlled economy, which resulted in a large number of bankruptcies in Slovakia and a social tension which soon assumed a national interpretation. Despite the importance of the economy, the real issue, called the 'Slovak question' was always political and rooted in a different understanding of the common state and its conception of democracy. Seven decades later the state still marred by the same problem yielded to its weight. For Masaryk the 'Slovak question' was a mere facet of a much larger issue of humanity, in which national emancipation was a question of freedom and therefore would lose its relevance with more democracy. In crucial contrast to the Czech lands, Slovakia's preoccupation was not with the position of minorities, but with the position of Slovakia itself. Whether the vision of 'autonomists' of a loose federation with some overarching political roof, or a more 'centralist' vision similar to Masaryk (mainly social-democrats and initially agrarian parties), its basis was always Slovakia as a nation separate from the Czechs. This was contrary to the Czech notion (and often the world outside) that viewed the state as theirs and Slovakia as its region, separated by history. Hence, in Slovakia, the official doctrine of 'Czechoslovakism' instead of uniting the state, seemed to have strengthened the Slovak resolve for political and cultural autonomy advocated by increasingly influential Hlinka's party.

## *From the Second World War to Communist Czechoslovakia*

The Slovak national issue was exacerbated by diverging interests from various directions. Whilst the Slovaks in the Prague administration considered Hlinka's party an enemy, Hungary and Germany campaigned for Slovak autonomy, the motivation for which would become obvious only a few years later. Hence, all political demands from Slovakia came to be associated with irredentism and antagonism towards the central state. Another important facet of the conflict between Slovak demand for autonomism and the Prague government was that there could not be autonomy for Slovakia without considerable concessions to the German minority supported by Germany which by 1933 threatened the integrity of the state. The problem of the First Republic was that it equated an internally strong state with centralism and unitarism, even if intention was not to harm Slovakia, but rather the lack of mechanisms and the time for finding a 'better' solution.

The Slovak autonomy declared after the Munich agreement (September 1938) in which Czechoslovakia was partitioned and in which the Western powers acquiesced (and Czechoslovakia was not invited to share in this decisions) was seen as a betrayal in the Czech lands, subsequently occupied by the Nazis. This marks the beginning of the stereotypical depiction of Slovaks and their nationalism as opportunistic and ungrateful, seeking to triumph at any cost, mostly at the Czechs' expense. Czechoslovakia's precarious geographic position, the dependence on a favourable balance of power in Europe and the fragility of the state were manifest. The only alternative to the capitulation would have been armed resistance, which would have perhaps 'saved the soul of the nation', but 'would not have changed the outcome'[21].

Nazi rule was catastrophic for the Czech territory, called the Protectorate of Bohemia and Moravia with its authoritarian police, the complete subjugation of industry to German needs, transfers of the population and the mass deportations of Jews and the Romany. The fate of Slovakia was very different. Initially the declaration of autonomy was seen as a kind of achievement with admittedly a bitter taste, but generally the bitterness was not felt as acutely in Slovakia as in the Czech lands. Hlinka's party, after his death (1938) renamed as HSLS (Hlinka's Slovak People's Party) and led by the cleric Dr. Jozef Tiso, prohibited all other parties, but the naive hope that Slovakia could somehow hold affairs in its own hands prevailed. The combination of Slovaks' push for autonomy, intensified by Hlinka's party propaganda and Hitler's ultimatum resulted in the declaration of an independent Slovak State, declared by Tiso 14 March 1939[22].

Tiso's decision was probably not the cause of the Czech national disaster that followed, but Slovakia's independence was later interpreted by the Czechs as being 'knifed in the back'. The truth is that the very different situations in which the two nations found themselves left a significant gulf in their relationship. Slovakia's sovereignty was short-lived: four days later the Slovak government was forced to sign an agreement about the German 'protection' of Slovakia (Schutzvertrag). This signified a formal surrender of Slovak foreign policy, currency exchange and economy to the interests of the German Reich (Vienna 18 March 1939). When at the same time Hungary occupied Ruthenia and Slovakia turned to its 'protector', Germany refused and the result was a territorial loss and a further and a lasting complication in Slovak-Hungarian relations.

The Slovak State 1939-1945 declared itself as national and Christian. The former involved the elevation of the ethnic principle in all matters of citizenship and education, the latter stood for Catholicism. The Protestants became second-class citizens, atheism was officially denounced, religious education was compulsory, the sale of contraception products prohibited and coeducation at schools forbidden. Whilst open terror reigned in the Czech lands, Slovakia established its own form of national socialism, the economy grew (armaments) and generally some features of normality prevailed. This did not apply to the Jews who lost the right to property, were forbidden to frequent public places and eventually were deported to concentration camps where the majority vanished[23].

The nature of the clerico-fascist regime which suspended elections and relied on the paramilitary Hlinková Garda for the deportations of its own citizens remains to this day a controversial episode in Slovak history[24] and a blight on its nationalism[25]. Slovakia entered the war on the side of Germany, and Slovaks were expected to fight Poles and Russians for which they had very little reasons. War was deeply unpopular among Slovaks whilst it was becoming obvious that the existence of the Slovak state depended on a Nazi victory and by 1943 the Slovak regime was in crisis. The increased resistance by more democratic forces, combined with moderate nationalists, international resistance, partisans and Communists to the totalitarian regime culminated in the Slovak National Uprising (SNP/Slovenské Národné Povstanie August 1944)[26].

The abortive insurrection against German rule and the Slovak State was politically a significant event. Firstly, it was in favour of the restoration of

Czechoslovakia; secondly, a part of the nation revolted against its own state and thirdly, Slovakia despite its wartime regime was no longer viewed as an enemy by London, where Beneš's exiled government acquired recognition and planned the re-establishment of Czechoslovakia. The negotiations about the restoration of the common state, joined by the Moscow leadership of the Czechoslovak Communist Party (KSC/ Komunistická Strana Ceskoslovenska) led to a compromise (Košice 1945, KVP/ Košický Vládný Program), in which the constitutional position of Slovakia in the future Czechoslovakia was again postponed and not resolved[27].

After 1945 a form of democracy was restored, but proved short-lived. On the whole the Slovak Communists and Democrats advocated autonomy and agreed that Slovakia should be governed by its National Council in Bratislava, but in the 1946 elections the Communists lost in Slovakia (Democratic Party 62%,) and shifted towards the Prague centre relying on strong support among the Czech population[28]. The chain of events and power struggles that followed led to a Communist takeover in February 1948. Slovakia's status was not federal and not autonomous, but the status of Czechoslovakia was however confirmed: its geo-political position was within the Soviet sphere of influence. As in 1938, the government surrendered and Beneš personally signed the transfer of power.

The inauguration of the communist regime manifested what communists in all fairness never concealed, that to a Stalinist type of communism, the national question is merely a partner in the revolution and that once power is consolidated it must remain in the centre. Slovakia (and the Catholic Church) was closely observed for any rise of national demands, always labelled as the rise of separatism, which given the Slovak history was a convincing and successful strategy. A series of fabricated court cases and a crusade against the Slovak 'bourgeois' nationalists (ironically Gustáv Husák who was later to preside over the 'normalisation' after the Soviet invasion in 1968 was among the arrested) preceded the 1960 Constitution which changed the name of the country to the Czechoslovak Socialist Republic and reduced the already impotent Slovak rule in Bratislava practically to nothing.

## From 1968 to the End of Communism

The general dissatisfaction with the regime unleashed at the beginning of 1968 a reform process and inevitably renewed the national question. The fact that it was A.Dubček, a Slovak, who spearheaded the reform movement was not an accident. As a leader of the Slovak Communist Party he was used to protecting Slovak interests in Prague and it was his struggle with the strongly repressive regime of A. Novotný that won him the overall popularity and led to the state-wide leadership of the Party. The Party's Action Programme (April 1968) contained among other issues a pledge to resolve the Slovak question definitely, by federalising Czechoslovakia[29]. Federation would mean the establishment of parallel legislative and executive organs in two republics, and a governmental framework to limit the fact that Czechs could always outvote the smaller Slovakia (majorizácia). The committees were still working on the constitutional mechanisms when the Warsaw Pact armies occupied Czechoslovakia in August 1968. The Slovak achievement of nominal federal status (1 January 1969) was the only concession to democratic reforms of the 1968.

There are various reasons why the federation proved to be less than a solution to the national question. In fact it revived the friction and widened the gulf between the two nations, with hindsight irreparably. The law on federation came into being after the invasion, when the reform process was long buried and the era of 'normalisation' set in. Thus not only was the federation associated with the Soviet tanks, but it could not function in its intended form: it was a federation in which all competencies rested with the Party (called 'democratic centralism') not the federal government - a mere tool in the hands of the new neo-Stalinist regime. Already in 1970 a new constitutional law was adopted in order to curtail the federal institutions and Gustáv Husák, who enforced the federal idea originally, now in the process of consolidating his power did not tolerate any dispersal of it.

The most damaging facet of this federation for the national harmony was that it created a false consciousness on both sides. As far as Slovaks were concerned all decisions were still taken in Prague, even if the leadership was in Slovak hands (after Husák, the second in command was V. Biľak a great ally of Moscow). Two illusions stemmed from this situation. Czechs considered the state to be run by Slovaks and Slovaks resented the federal idea without having actually experienced it. Moreover, to the Czechs this was a repetition of the old Slovak betrayal - every time the country was in deep crisis (see the analogy with 1938), Slovakia tried to gain more independence. The relationship deteriorated and reached its lowest levels during the period 1968-1989.

The added dimension was the general feeling of powerlessness and the moral crisis in the society, exacerbated by the actions of a narrow political elite lacking wide support, thus proceeding to purge the party and the state of all reform-minded individuals and to suppress any form of open dissent[30]. These measures led to the decimation of the intellectual elite and a massive emigration to the West, but persecution was again less severe in Slovakia, where the resistance to 'normalisation' was limited and thus, economic benefits greater.

The 'normalisation' period carried great consequences for the future of Czechoslovakia and Slovakia itself. Slovaks, obviously more implicitly than explicitly decided for the preservation of their jobs, their families, the region and ultimately the nation. Whilst the Czech intelligentsia was reduced to hard manual labour, in Slovakia when people lost their positions, usually they remained within the same enterprise, the collaborators were tolerated, people retreated to their country cottages and nurtured their networks and generally adapted well. They accepted that democracy after all had proved to be a fiction and an unattainable goal. Ironically, it seems that Slovakia paid a higher price for the relative comfort of the 'normalisation' period; to some political analysts the continuing clientism in Slovak politics, inherited from that period and the corruption generally throughout the Slovak society was the main obstacle to the establishment of democracy in Slovakia[31]. At the end of the twenty years of this abnormal situation, Slovakia, despite the visible signs of environmental and moral decline and the growing technological and economical gap between it and the rest of Europe, showed little awareness of the unfeasibility of the continuation of this regime. The price was indeed high - the lack of conviction and commitment that democratisation requires left Slovakia behind its neighbours[32].

It would be wrong to conclude that there was no dissent in Slovakia, but it was small, mostly confined to intellectual, Catholic and environmentalist circles in Bratislava, whilst hundreds of people in the Czech lands were engaged in a coherent, robust and well recognized dissident movement initiated by Charta 77, in which only few Slovaks participated[33]. The Czechs and Slovaks entered the post-communist period having had very different experiences of the years immediately preceding it. The relationship suffered from a cultural, social and political difference that instead of being removed by their coexistence has been exacerbated by it. Particularly in the time of crisis this manifested itself by the pursuit of different goals and interests, which in Slovakia were regularly defined in ethno-national terms.

## Negotiating the Break-up: the Czech and Slovak Elite 1989-1993

Slovakia simply speaks in other ways, and we must finally take that calmly into account. We in the Czech lands should long since have followed Slovak publicists and Slovak culture more closely, and tried to understand other things than dissident speech because we otherwise do not hear that Slovakia is simply Slovakia and not the Czech lands, and we thus only vaguely apprehend what it all means! Interest in Slovakia is insubstantial and a tone of resignation about a common future resonates[34].

In the first days after the 'velvet revolution' (November 1989), the Czechs and Slovaks found themselves united in a struggle against totalitarianism, similar to 1968. The unity however did not last long and all problems hidden by the Husák regime were out in open with the national question leading the agenda in Slovakia. When the old question of federation appeared again the Czechs and the new post-communist government of Václav Havel were taken by surprise. The misunderstandings that plagued the Czecho-Slovak relations were well illustrated by 'the hyphen' conflict.

President Havel suggested (January 1990) that all symbols of the communist era should be replaced by new symbols in tune with the new developments, obviously including the omission of the word 'socialist' from the name of the country - from the 'Czechoslovak Socialist Republic' to the 'Czechoslovak Republic'. There was nothing ominous about that, except that no-one realised that in some Slovak circles there was always something wrong with the name of the country, namely that Slovaks felt 'invisible' and would chose the most innocent of occasions to press for more 'visibility'. The hyphen, the 'Czecho-Slovak Republic' was to make clear that there were actually two republics, thus indirectly invoking the Munich agreements when the hyphen first appeared in the name of the country.

The apparent triviality of the hyphen affair had deeper roots and should have signalled the difficulties the common state was to face. 'It is not about the hyphen, but about the name, a symbol of the nation that does not want to remain nameless, without identity', wrote a Slovak journalist at that time[35]. In the Czech lands this evoked indignation:

> if today we are offended by Slovak politics, then we are offended as humans and not as a nation! Rather than feeling something for that question, we are more tired of it... After Slovakia breaks away no one will prevent us from calling our state Czechoslovakia[36],

wrote the Czech writer L.Vaculík. At the end after what appeared endless bickering, the agreed name, the 'Czech and Slovak Federal Republic'(ČSFR) was the least important, more important was the fact that the national card was on the table and that the state, however named, lost its legitimacy, because its basic premise, the unity of Czechs and Slovaks, would eventually not withstand the pressure that the reassertion of the national question brought upon it.

*The Federal Question Post-1989*

The friction and historically accumulated latent conflicts between the two nations have conditioned future developments, but as important as those factors were, the final break-up was a result of the political system and the decisions of the leadership, all shaped in critical ways by the postcommunist situation.

The 1968 Constitution was still in operation after November 1989, when after the huge demonstrations in Prague (and smaller ones in Bratislava 16-18 November 1989) the communist leadership gave in and the new leadership led by V. Havel took up the leading position (V.Havel became the President 29 December 1989). The two-member federation and its two-chamber federal parliament had a complicated structure, in order to counteract the numerical preponderance of the Czech deputies (150 proportionally elected into the House of the People) and a provision which required that important laws be passed by both the majority in the House of the People and also by a majority in each of the national sections in the House of the Nations (75 in each of the Czech and Slovak section), thus in the final accounting 30 deputies from one section could block any constitutional law. Moreover, the right to veto was accorded to national sections and both republics had the right to secession - which gave the mandate to the deputies from the Slovak National Party (formed prior to the first free post-communist June 1990 elections) whose platform was the division of the state. The republics presided over healthcare, education and culture, all other areas (transport, post, state security, social security etc.) were shared between the republics and the federation, whilst foreign policy, defence, currency and federal legislation was under the federal government's authority. The Slovak political scene in post-1989 days was dominated by (Verejnosť Proti Násiliu/ Public Against Violence, founded in response to the demonstrations in Prague, November 1989, 29,3% in the 1990 elections in Slovakia), a civic movement and the Slovak counterpart to the Czech Civic Forum, led by Fedor Gál and a group of liberal intellectuals who were pro-federalist and closely connected to Prague from the days of Charta 77. Nevertheless even this most pro-federalist Slovak party in its first programme called for a 'consistent democratic federation', based on the principle of the 'factual equality' of the two nations[37].

Clearly, the national/federal question dominated the 'post-revolutionary' politics in Czechoslovakia and the problem became the various types of federation advocated by different points of view. The basic contrast was between the Slovak version of the 'dual federation', in which the constituent republics saw themselves as sovereign states, whilst the federation performed certain service functions for both of them (currency, defence and partially foreign policy), and the Czech 'tripartite model', whereby the federation was sovereign and the republics were subordinated to it in certain matters.

In the whole of this constitutional issue, money must not be forgotten - the money withdrawn by Slovakia from the federal budget bore no resemblance to its contribution throughout the 1980s and the Czechs thought they were paying for Slovakia and Slovaks believed that reforms were harming their national interest[38]. It could be argued that this destructive debate about 'who pays for whom', well illustrated by the Czech Prime Minister Václav Klaus's words 'money counts first', is a symptom of the loosening of solidarity ties when the parties concerned cease to think about themselves as one entity. On the other hand, Slovakia was already suffering from higher unemployment, not least due to the ill-considered decision to stop the country's armaments production based mainly in Slovakia. Slovaks thus felt that the foreign investors preferred the Czech lands, because Czechs monopolised foreign relations and Slovakia had no opportunity to press its own case.

The third suggestion made in order to resolve the constitutional conflict was Havel's 'authentic federation' - a compromise between the two previous models that divested considerable powers to the republics, including separate reserve banks and the eventual sovereignty of both republics in international law. This was to the satisfaction of the Czech side, for it allowed the economic transition to continue at a pace suitable to each republic's situation without the consequences of different outcomes being interpreted as national injustice. The model was legally so complex that it would have required 'clinically precise' policies, which considering the tense period of postcommunist transition were practically unachievable[39].

Here it may be appropriate to mention once more the role of dissidents and elites in postcommunist transitions. Political parties were very young and the affiliation of the public with them limited, whilst the shortness of time did not allow for lengthy pre-negotiations. Moreover, the dissidents now in governmental positions were as unused to negotiations and formal relations between various institutions as the communists were. Dissident activity had taken place clandestinely, had often been felt as an individual responsibility and decisions had usually been taken by a small group of trusted friends. The personification of politics is a postcommunist trait, shared by ex-dissidents and ex-communists alike and translates into politics mostly in two respects - politics are often conducted without the consideration for the wider consequences and in the context of general mistrust between politicians[40], based mostly on personal experiences of the past. The Slovak political scene in particular was splitting into various factions, including the VPN, whose split influenced the structure of politics in Slovakia for years to come and considering that Mečiar's HzDS sprung from that split, indirectly it influenced the break-up of the state.

## Slovakia in Transition to Independence

Vladimír Mečiar, already the Minister of Interior in the first post-communist pre-election government of 'national adjustment' (vláda zmierenia) and a member of the VPN, the leading party of the 1990 elections in Slovakia, became the Premier[41]. Mečiar was not an intellectual, he was a reformist ex-communist, but did not belong to the small dissident circle. He was not a separatist, but was nationally orientated and his ambitions for the nation matched his own. He became admired for the enormous energy and toughness he displayed and these characteristics made his popularity rise beyond any expectations. The public viewed him as a man who was personally changing the position of Slovakia within the federation, not by weakening it, but by 'strengthening the federation through the process of elimination of its old structures, centralism and bureaucracy'[42].

In the months between the summer 1990 and the spring of 1991, the endless meetings and negotiations between the republics, parties and federal government took place, with only one result - the radicalisation of the mood in both republics. The growing conflict between Mečiar and the leadership of the VPN became acute and the Slovak National Council recalled Mečiar from his post and replaced him with J.Čarnogurský, the leader of the KDH (Christian Democratic Movement), a well-respected Catholic dissident and the first politician to flirt with the idea of separation. However he very soon retreated from this position to offer a proposal that only the federation will be recognised by international law and the federal Constitution should precede the agreement between the republics. Mečiar's party HzDS was thus born as a splinter group from the VPN.

In summer 1991 the negotiations intensified around the major issue - the character of agreements between the federation and the National Councils, in other words about the fundamental question whether the federation or the republics were to carry more sovereignty. With hindsight it is obvious that any remaining good will had deserted all; the Czech side became dominated by the more right-wing politicians taking an uncompromising stance, invoking an aggressive reaction in Slovakia and thus confirming the growing Czech suspicion 'that it was impossible with Slovaks'[43]. Havel in desperation tried to put the pressure on the government by pushing for a referendum in order to find out public opinion, but parliament could not agree on the question and the referendum was not declared.

By February 1992 all negotiations about an agreement on the basis of which it would be possible to ratify the federal constitution failed. Everything was suspended in expectation of the general elections planned for June 1992. If one was to look for a sequence of errors leading to the dissolution of the state, this must be considered one of them. From the election there emerged two clear winners with parliamentary majorities in each republic, both with a hard and uncompromising stance towards each other and both clear on the constitutional issues. On the Czech side, the Civic Democratic Party (ODS/Občanská Demokratická Strana), led by Václav Klaus in support of a firmer 'functional federation' (no international recognition for republics and a clear sovereignty of the federal government). On the Slovak side Vladimír Mečiar's HzDS in support of a confederation, a loose association, a constitutionally dubious proposal, which stated in populist language appealed to Slovakia. The former unacceptable to Mečiar, the latter to Klaus, which left only a third option - the division of the state[44].

There was only one dilemma - how to make it legitimate without a referendum, which would be too risky for both leaders seemingly intent on dividing the state without having a mandate to do so, because it was not at all certain that the population wanted to break-up the state. On 17 July 1992 the Declaration of Sovereignty of the Slovak Nation was passed by the National Council. In August the HzDS and ODS agreed on the constitutionality of the break-up, involving three laws: on the end of the federation, on the division of property and on the successor rights of the republics. The Federal Assembly was still holding out and rejected the law on the end of the federation. The big question was how could deputies who swore fidelity to the state actually end it. Eventually, the government presented the Federal Assembly with a new law on the end of the federation, which was passed by the parliamentary parties to which National Councils adopted recommending resolutions. On 25 November 1992 the law on the break-up was approved on the second reading. On 1 January 1993 Czechoslovakia ceased to exist and Slovakia's first stage of democratisation was completed by its independence. The question of the legitimacy of Slovakia's statehood will be dealt with later for it had grave consequences for its nascent democracy, which lost some of its credibility in the whole process by being denied its fundamental feature - the consent of the citizens.

## Conclusion

The demise of the Czechoslovak federation highlights the complexity of processes that contribute to the conditions in which ethnicity can be mobilised to such an extent that it forms the most significant cleavage in society. The case of Czechoslovakia serves as a reflection on at least two points relevant to this book. First, it reflects negatively on the well-established idea that high economic interdependence, similar levels of technological and economic development and a high degree of social interaction[45] lead to political integration. The Czechs and Slovaks had more in common in that respect at the end of their coexistence than at the beginning, yet the differences in their political objectives increased rather than decreased. The point to stress is that the common state does not necessarily create a sense of common identity and that the establishment of a political nation under multiethnic conditions, requires ultimately constitutional arrangements that reflect the belief in a common purpose by all its ethnic and national groups[46]. Without a sense of common purpose there is no national unity and without national unity the major project of democratisation can hardly be sustained. Second, if it is true that the population was faced with a result it did not expect (and all opinion polls point towards this conclusion), the above case says something significant about the decisive role of political elites[47] in postcommunist transitions.

The following chapter, building on the above treatment of the Slovak pre-independence history, will concentrate solely on Slovakia. As the emphasis will be on the current political development and the role of nationalism in that process, I would like to stress a few points relevant in this context. Slovakia emerged from communist period relatively more developed economically than politically, by which I mean that the political development of Slovakia stagnated behind the level of industrialisation, urbanisation and education. In 1918 Slovakia had only one party, the Slovak National Party, its interwar period did not last long enough for other parties than the strongly nationalist Hlinka's Party to develop, only to be followed by the communist regime. Thus Slovak experience with pluralist politics is historically limited. The early postcommunist period and the first stage of transition to democracy marked also the beginning of political development in conditions of democracy. Slovak nationalism having historically encountered more resistance in asserting itself it intensified and the early stage of democratisation became to be viewed primarily as a resolution of the national question.

Hence, I would like to make a few concluding comments about the nature of Slovak nationalism. Slovak nationalism has indeed always viewed democracy as inseparable from the nation and its interests, with emphasis on ethnicity and history, whether it was Hlinka or Mečiar (by which I do not wish to draw any comparison between the two personalities, even if the comparison of their electoral support will be drawn below). Secondly, the central legacy of Slovak nationalism is fear of being engulfed by either Hungary, or more advanced Czech lands - Slovak national identity is defined against its neighbours and carries a sense of historical resentment. This gave Slovak nationalism often a dissatisfied and indignant character, easily seduced by demagoguery which is possibly its most negative trait in view of democratisation.

## Notes

[1]  S.Szomolányi *Slovensko: Problémy Konsolidácie Demokracie*   Bratislava, Slovenské Združenie pre Politické Vedy 1997 p.11. (henceforth S.Szomolányi 1997).

[2]  A security organisation, other countries: Poland, Hungary and the Czech Republic.

[3]  At the EU Vienna December 1998 summit Slovakia's entry in the first group of Eastern European associate countries was rejected and so was Slovakia's membership of the NATO (Madrid July 1997). However, in February 2000, Slovakia has become one of the 11 association countries and has since continued rather successfully with all accession negotiations. The Commission considers Slovakia to be now the most successful among the 'second wave' countries (Malta, Romania, Bulgaria, Latvia and Lithuania). All countries will be assessed individually, which means that, in theory, Slovakia could join the Czech Republic, Slovenia, Hungary and Poland in the first wave of the EU Eastern enlargement. 28 May 2001 Slovakia has hosted a summit of 11 association countries (10 ECE and Malta) in Bratislava (*SME* 28 May 2001).

[4]  R.Chmel P.Pithart and C.Kiss V.Bosáková *Slovenská Otázka v 20.storčí* Bratislava, Kalligram 1997.

[5]  Despite constitutional arrangements coming well behind unemployment, social insecurity and criminality as the issues of the greatest concern to Slovak voters. Z. Bútorová 'Premyslené "Áno" zániku CSFR' *Sociologický Časopis* XXIX:1 1993 pp.88-103 p.91.

[6]  The history of Czechoslovakia is based on the following literature: I.Kamenec *Tragédia Politika, Kňaza a Človeka* Bratislava, Archa 1998; D.Kováč *Slováci&Češi* Bratislava, AEP 1997; L.Lipták *Slovensko v 20. storočí* Bratislava, Kalligram 1998; E.Mannová ed. *Meštianstvo a Občianská Spolocnost na Slovensku* 1900-1989 Bratislava, AEP 1998; J.Musil *The End of Czechoslovakia* Budapest, Central European University Press 1995 (henceforth J.Musil p.); J.Rychlík *Češi a Slováci ve 20. století* Bratislava, AEP 1997; P.Pithart 'The Division of Czechoslovakia: the preliminary balance sheet for the end of a respectable country' *Canadian Slavonic Papers* 37:3-4 September/December 1995 pp.321-338; H. Gordon Skilling 'Czechs and Slovaks' *International Journal* LIII:1 Winter 1997-8 p.p.73-94; C.Skalnik Leff 'Czech and Slovak Nationalism in the Twentieth Century' in P.Sugar *Eastern European Nationalism in the Twentieth Century* Washington, University Press 1995 (henceforth C.Skalnik Leff 1995) and C.Skalnik Leff *The Czech and Slovak Republics* Boulder, Westview Press 1997 (henceforth C.Skalnik Leff 1997).

[7]  In 1919 census many Slovaks defined their nationality as 'Hungarian-Slovak', thus reflecting that Slovak national identity hardly existed divorced from the reference to Hungary. C.Skalnik Leff (1997) p.7.

[8] In the first half of 19th century the Czecho-Slovak relations were mostly limited to literature and language (Slovak Protestants to this day use the old biblical Czech) and that is where the first awareness of commonality between them stems from - linguistic similarity.

[9] 'Demands of the Slovak nation' (Žiadosti Slovenského Národa, Liptovský Mikuláš 10 May 1848): autonomy, national assembly, official use of the Slovak language, national symbols, army under the Slovak command, representation in the parliament.

[10] For nationalities policies in the Habsburg Empire see R.Kann *The Habsburg Empire* New York, Octagon Books 1973.

[11] Pester Lloyd (11 July 1906), cited in L.Lipták p.44.

[12] T.Pichler 'Past and Present in Slovak Politics' in L.Sørensen L.Eliason ed. *Forward to the Past?* Aarhus, Aarhus University Press 1997, suggests that the interaction between the two groups, thus the relationship between the leadership and the mobilisation of the people remains an underdeveloped field of academic research p.212.

[13] T.Pichler p.209.

[14] J.Rychlík p.37.

[15] Congregated round a journal 'Hlasy'[Voices], called 'hlasisti'.

[16] The founder of the Slovak People's Party (SĽS- Slovenská Ľudová Strana, the predecessor of the HSĽS / Hlinka's Slovak People's Party, also called 'ľudáci', after 'ľud'- nation/people. Strongly nationalist views in Slovakia are still described by this term or by the term 'hlinkovci', similar to the Slovak fascist paramilitary groups who also carried the name of Hlinka (Hlinková Garda).

[17] J.Rychlík p.47.

[18] D.Kováč p.66.

[19] J.Lipták p.101.

[20] V.Mastny 'The Historical Experience of federalism in East Central Europe' *East European Politics and Societies*14:1 Winter 2000 pp.64-97 p.74.

[21] H.Gordon Skilling p.77.

[22] According to the Czech historian J.Rychlík, independent Slovakia was in Hitler's interest and had Tiso not conceded Hitler would have found another Slovak leader p.171. For the biography of Tiso and detailed exploration of his motives and politics of the Slovak State see I.Kamenec *Tragédia Politika, Kňaza a Človeka* Bratislava, Archa 1998.

[23] The majority of 130 000 Slovak Jews (90 0000) remained in the Slovak State and 40 000 came under the jurisdiction of Hungary. Approximately 12 000 returned from the concentration camps. *Košice a Deportácie Židov v Roku 1944* Košice, SAV 1994.

[24] In an interview with V.Pálko (26 September 1997), the then vice-chairman of the KDH (Christian Democratic Movement), I asked about the connection between the wartime state, nationalism and the Church, because the rehabilitation of J.Tiso is very much at the heart of the Catholic Church and the Church is at the heart of the KDH. His views illustrated the ambivalence surrounding this period. According to Mr.Pálko: the state had discredited itself by the deportation of Jews, but not the Church; the president J.Tiso was executed for wartime crimes by communist propaganda in 1945; the national question is closely tied to the Catholic Church and that to the democratisation, which sadly has been hijacked by the ex-communists after 1989, thus taking the platform away from its rightful Christian values; the most important anchors in the Slovak national development were priests, Matica Slovenská (the national cultural organisation that openly defends the wartime state), Hlinka's Party in the 1920s and the Catholic dissidents. As for Hlinka, he has been unjustly treated by history, because of the paramilitary groups that had taken his name and conspired in the deportations, but added that Hlinka was lucky to have died in 1938, before his name could have been tarnished further. In another interview with

J.Sivák, an academic concentrating on the Slovak national philosophy and a distinguished member of the SNS (Slovak National Party, the only party openly defending the 1939-1945 state) I was told that the Slovak State was a just predecessor of the current Slovakia and that the type of regime is irrelevant to the recognition of the state whose existence was internationally recognised. It is important to note though that such views are generally considered extreme in Slovakia. However, the issue has so far not been dealt with properly and remains shrouded in embarrassment whilst causing unnecessary divisions among politicians and the population alike.

[25] Considerable attention is given to this period in Slovak history, particularly by some Western authors who try to explain postcommunist nationalism in the sinister light of the Slovak state and Hlinka's legacy. As much as I agree that there is a stream in Slovak politics that can be linked to this period, it is not advisable to seek the explanation of Slovakia's contemporary politics through this linkage. See for example S.Cohen *Politics Without a Past* Durham, Duke University Press 1999; N.Nedelsky 'The wartime Slovak state: a case study in the relationship between ethnic nationalism and authoritarian patterns of governance' *Nations and Nationalism* 7:2 April 2001 pp.215-234.

[26] L.Lipták p.241.

[27] D.Kováč p.85.

[28] The post-war success of the Communist party in the Czech lands was due not only to the longer tradition of labour movement, but also to the severity of the previous fascist regime Victory of Democratic party in Slovakia was partially due to the abolition of Hlinka's party.

[29] C.Skalnik Leff (1997) p.65.

[30] H.Gordon Skilling p.83.

[31] See chapters dealing with economy and privatisation in G. Mesežnikov and I.Ivantyšyn *Slovensko 1998-99* Bratislava, IVO 1999; further I.Mikloš 'Prepojenie politickej a ekonomickej moci' in S.Szomolányi (1997); In 1998 Corruption Perception Index for Slovakia was 47-8 (Hungary 33, the Czech Republic 37, Italy and Poland 40) 'Korupcia medzi kriminalitou a folklórom' *OS* August 1999/8 p.9-12.

[32] P.Pithart 'Towards a Shared Freedom' in J.Musil *The End of Czechoslovakia* p.212.

[33] In the Czech Republic over thousand people signed the Charta 77 of which few hundred were well known dissidents and activists, in Slovakia there were 10 cultural personalities known as dissidents and signatories of that document. S.Szomolányi in introduction to *Verejnost Proti Násiliu 1989-91* a collection of recorded testimonies and documents by the members of the VPN Bratislava, Nadácia M.Šimecku 1998, p.15 (henceforth *Verejnost Proti Násiliu*).

[34] Exile periodical *Listy* (9:1 January 1981), cited in P.Sugar *Eastern European Nationalism in the Twentieth century* Wasington, The American University Press 1995 p.107.

[35] Cited in S.Miháliková 'Narodné symboly Slovenskej štátnosti' *Politická Revue* 2 October 1996 pp.53-70 p.59.

[36] Cited in V.Žák 'The Velvet Divorce - Institutional Foundation' in J.Musil p.257. The following section concerning the institutional arrangements between 1989-1993 are based on this chapter.

[37] A few months later in a joint declaration with its Czech partner it called for a speedy resolution to the division of powers between the republics and the federation in the 'new understanding' as that of the 'two sovereign national state-forming republics'. See The VPN Programme Declaration, Bratislava 26.11.1989 p.311 and 'What we are and what we are not' Declaration VPN 28 May 1990 p.325.

[38] The opinion poll in Slovakia: 1991 57 % expected the Slovak economy to fall behind the Czech economy and by 1992 81% believed that the Czechs did not consider Slovaks equal partners. Z.Bútorová 'Premyslené "áno" zániku ČSFR' p.92.

[39] V.Žák p.249.

[40] S.Szomolányi in the introduction to *Verejnost Proti Násiliu* about the lack of knowledge how to transform a movement into a political party.

[41] In an incredible twist of irony his candidature was supported by the most liberal wing of the VPN, particularly personally by its leader Fedor Gál, who eventually had to emigrate from Slovakia after being physically threatened by the opponents of Mečiar for bringing him into politics and by his supporters for ousting him a year later.

[42] V. Mečiar cited in M.Leško p.37.

[43] V.Žák p.260.

[44] P. Pithart who was party to these negotiations, claims that Klaus asked Mečiar once more whether he really wanted Slovakia to be a sovereign state, to which he answered positively and was further not given the chance to explain how this could be done. Whether Mečiar really believed in this confederation, or simply remained faithful to his election promises is unimportant - the general assessment in the Czech lands was that the Slovaks asked for independence and they got it P.Pithart (1995) p.332.

[45] A sociological survey conducted in 1990 by the Komenius University in Bratislava revealed that in Slovakia 57% of the population had Czech friends and 31% had Czech relatives; in the Czech republic 23% and 45% respectively. *Kultúrny Život* 10 December 1991.

[46] A similar argument is at the heart of debates about multiculturalism. See B.Parekh *Rethinking Multiculturalism* London, Macmillan 2000.

[47] C.Skalnik Leff (1995) p.153.

# 4 Reclaiming the Nation: Politics of Independent Slovakia

The Commission concludes that Slovakia does not fulfil in a satisfying manner the political conditions set out by the European Council in Copenhagen, because of the instability of Slovakia's institutions, their lack of rootedness in political life and the shortcomings in the functioning of its democracy. This situation is so much more regrettable since Slovakia could satisfy the economic criteria[1].

This chapter seeks to address Slovakia's democratisation process, focusing mostly on the period 1993-1998. The underlying argument is that postcommunist development depends largely on the 'contemporary challenges faced by the state in question'[2]. In the case of Slovakia the roots of the postcommunist challenge are entwined not only with the legacy of communism and the period before that, but mainly with the identity - related issues, deriving from the simultaneity of nation- and state-building[3]. These ideologically often incompatible processes are further exacerbated by the historically complex relationship between the Slovak majority and the Hungarian minority[4].

The main criterion by which democratic progress in Slovakia can be measured is the level of tension between the two groups, a tension that cannot be explained by a cultural clash[5] only. Both ethnic groups share the same customs and mostly the same religion (Catholic), there is no significant economic division, nor any difference in their way of life, and generally the relations between people are good on the personal level. The Hungarian minority in Slovakia is a very close language community, and its political agenda is mostly concerned with the sufficient provision for the use of their language and the protection of their Hungarian identity[6]. The ethnic tension which marked the first years of the transition process was only partially due to what was by respective sides considered excessive demands. It stems more from the Slovak search for a conception of their new nationhood and the pursuit of national identity and unity, which due to historical developments have not been sufficiently resolved before.

The general thesis for this chapter is that insecure nationhood and insecure democracy feed off each other, therefore securing democracy means broadening of the nation-building agenda to include political identity as well as the narrow national one. As the second chapter argued, the reconciliation and constitutional recognition of ethnic diversity within a state, particularly a newly independent state, poses a considerable challenge (but also an opportunity) to the stability of democracy. Slovak transition to independence and democracy is also a testament to the well-known, but not enough emphasised fact that identity issues equal other ideological conflicts, i.e. economic distribution, but are less adaptable to compromise and can sustain a conflictual style of politics at the elite level[7]. Politics of independent Slovakia illustrate with a test-case clarity that a success of democratisation depends on the construction of a political community whose unity is rooted in commitment to the democratisation project rather than in ethnic identity.

The chapter is divided into three parts. The main part deals with the politics in independent Slovakia up to the last general election in 1998, the period dominated by Mečiar's leadership. It examines the political structure and seeks an answer to the political and ethnic cleavages in Slovak politics through the exploration of the Slovak political tradition. The second part focuses on the issues of nationalism and its most important manifestation, the minorities and the constitutional provisions for them. This is done through the examination of the Constitution and the State Language Law. The third part analyses the changes in Slovak politics after the last general elections in 1998. The assessment of the future prospects for Slovakia are positive, with some qualifications, of which the containment of nationalism within democratic system is the most important.

## What Kind of Democracy?

In theory, the second free elections in 1992 could have marked the beginning of the institutionalisation of a democratic regime in Czechoslovakia. As the previous chapter indicated, this period was marked by a prolonged constitutional crisis between political elites in two republics which resulted in the break up of the state. The subsequent formation of an independent Slovakia meant a considerable break in the continuity of the democratisation process which thus embarked on its 'second transition' under the conditions of simultaneous, and often competing processes of nation-building and state-building. In this period the 'instability of institutions' that has proved so damaging to Slovakia's initial application to join the EU, could be attributed mainly to the extreme polarisation of elites on nearly all issues concerning democracy and nationhood. Independence, instead of uniting the society behind a common project proved divisive; all political issues became interwoven with questions of loyalty to the state. The third victory of V. Mečiar's coalition in the 1994 early elections, meant the beginning of a particularly difficult period for the Slovak democratic development, in which 'politics of revenge'[8] that followed removed all opposition from key governmental, economic and media positions, despite the previously established rules which guaranteed the participation of the opposition in the government. This situation lasted until Mečiar's defeat in the 1998 elections, subject of the section below.

*Political Party System and Slovak Democracy*

The following attempts to outline developments in the formation of parties and the party structure in Slovakia in the period 1990-1998. The list of the parties and their abbreviations relevant to this period is in an alphabetical order:

DS      Demokratická strana / Democratic party.

DÚ      Demokratická Únia /Democratic union (breakaway factions from HzDS and SNS).

Együttéllés (hung.)  Spolužitie /Coexistence.

HZDS  Hnutie za demokratické Slovensko / Movement for Democratic Slovakia (splinter group of the VPN).

KDH    Kresťanskodemokratické hnutie / Christian Democratic Movement.

KSS     Komunistická strana Slovenska / Communist Party.

MK      Maďarská koalícia / Hungarian Coalition.

MKDH  Maďarské kresťansko demokratické hnutie / Hungarian Christian democratic movement.

MNI     Maďarská nezávislá iniciatíva / Hungarian Independent Initiative.

MOS    Maďarská občianska strana /Hungarian Civic party.

SDĽ     Strana demokratickej ľavice / Party of the Democratic Left.

SNS     Slovenská národná strana / Sloval National party.

SV       Spoločná voľba /Common Choice.

SZS     Strana zelených na Slovensku / Green Party.

VPN    Verejnosť proti násiliu / Public against violence (splinter group forms the HzDS).

ZRS     Združenie robotníkov Slovenska / Association of Workers of Slovakia.

## Table 4.1   Slovak Parliament: 1990-1994

| Party | 1990 seats in the parliament | 1992 | 1994 |
|---|---|---|---|
| VPN/MNI | 48.00* | | |
| KDH | 31.00* | 18.00 | 17.00 |
| SNS | 22.00 | 15.00* | 9.00* |
| SV (SDĽ+KSS) | 22.00 | 29.00 | 18.00 |
| MK (Coex.+MKDH+MOS) | 14.00 | 14.00 | 17.00 |
| DS | 7.00* | | |
| SZ | 6.00 | | |
| HZDS) (breakaway from VPN) | | 74.00* | 61.00* |
| DU (splinter from SNS and HzDS) | | | 15.00 |
| ZRS (breakaway from SDĽ) | | | 13.00* |

\* party of the governing coalition.
The National Council / Národná Rada Slovenskej Republiky / NR SR has 150 deputies.

*Source:* compiled by myself from various sources, mainly M. Bútora and P.Hunčík *Slovensko 1995* Bratislava, Sándor Marai 1996.

## Table 4.2   Slovak political parties and their ideological position[9]

| National particularism | | universalism |
|---|---|---|
| SNS/Coexistence/HzDS | KDH | /ZRS/MKDH/DU/SDL/MOS/DS/VPN |

| authoritarian tendency | liberalism |
|---|---|
| SNS/HzDS/ZRS/Coex. | SDL/SZS/KDH/MKDH/MOS/DU/DS/VPN |

| independence | federalism |
|---|---|
| SNS HzDS | KSS/SZS/SDL/DS/Coex/KDH/MKDH/MOS/DU/VPN |

| state intervention | | economic liberalism |
|---|---|---|
| KSS/ ZRS/ SZ/SDL | HzDS | VPN/DS/MKDH/Coex./KDH/SNS |

→from most conservative towards most accommodating

Looking at the tables above some facets of the Slovak postcommunist politics are immediately striking: the pivotal role of the HzDS and its leader Mečiar, the formation of the new parties as a result of the conflict in the existing parties, the discontinuity of the broad civic movement VPN, which initiated the democratisation process, the relevance of nationally-orientated parties, the strong ethnic division of the political parties along the

Slovak/Hungarian lines and the general incoherence of the coalition formations viewed through the adherence to economic policies.

*Conflict and the HzDS* During the 1990-1992 period, the party system could be divided into two major blocks, the pro-reform and ambiguous-towards-reform orientation. The first group consisted of VPN, KDH and DS (government coalition) and the Hungarian parties. The division along the ethnic line, in fact two party systems, the Slovak and the Hungarian was divisive as far as minority issues were concerned and obviously did not contribute to national unity (KDH and Coexistence ethnically more inspired than the rest), but both ethnic formations agreed on pro-transformation and pro-federal policies.

The second bloc (KSS, SDL, SNS, SZS and the new HzDS) either rejected or severely criticised the federal model and the pace of economic reforms, with SNS openly campaigning against the federation and the HzDS presenting themselves as the champion of the 'Slovak national interest', defined in legally dubious terms of a 'co-state' with the Czechs[10]. The VPN, despite it being a movement, whose appeal with a broad social base was ideologically fairly clearly defined, particularly in its lack of support for nationalist sentiments and socialist nostalgia. The movement however proved unable to address the prevailing mood in the country after initiating the change of regime and many of its members left in preference to the more specific political interests. After the protracted disputes within that movement, HzDS was formed by Vladimír Mečiar, the Prime Minister of the first post-communist government and the member of the VPN in spring 1991. As became obvious in the 1992 elections, the victorious HzDS attracted the majority of VPN's electoral support[11] and the second government of V.Mečiar was established.

In contrast with neighbouring countries (e.g. the Czech Republic, Hungary, Poland), where transformation continued on the intended path, despite the formation of more clearly profiled political parties, in Slovakia the reconfiguration of political forces and particularly the appearance of the HzDS meant a challenge to the direction of the transition. The HzDS retained the broad spectrum character of its parent movement VPN, but concentrated on the negative facets of economic transition with strong emphasis on national question, thus enabling to appeal to large sections of the population and form alliances with everyone, particularly with nationalists, previously unable to find a partner. Interestingly, despite this ideological ability, in practice the HzDS and Mečiar have found it difficult to collaborate in coalitions. This conflictual approach to opponents and allies alike created a further proliferation of parties and regularly increased the instability of the parliament. The primary causes of the international community's concerns about the state of Slovakia's democracy all resulted from the continued animosity between Mečiar, his supporters and the opposition.

In 1993 the issue of Czecho-Slovak relations became less compelling to the public, and HzDS and the nationalist SNS coalition found it difficult to maintain legitimacy. An internal conflict within the HzDS led to a defection of deputies and the failure to ree-stablish the coalition and further defections from both parties followed. Deprived of its parliamentary majority, the government fell to a vote of no confidence (March 1994), after a condemnatory speech of the then President M.Kováč, also in fact a defector from the HzDS. The new government led by the ex-foreign minister J.Moravčík (March 1994-October 1994) consisted of the new DÚ (formed by the defectors from the HzDS and SNS) aided by SDĽ and KDH. In the early elections (October 1994), Mečiar and his HzDS emerged victorious again (Mečiar's third government) and after the new parliament's legendary all-night sitting (3-4 November 1994), the new government was formed: HzDS, the newly formed worker's party ZRS and the right-wing SNS presided over the most controversial period in postcommunist Slovakia so far. It can be argued that Mečiar's political strategy for cementing and sustaining political power has been the preservation and exacerbation of conflicts deriving from ethnic and social divisions rather than a solution to them.

*'Fragile' Democracy*[12]   After 1994 elections the authoritarian tendencies of the HzDS, both inside and outside the party, led some observers to question the extent to which Slovakia could still be described as a democracy, whilst the regular defiance of the Constitutional Court was described by the opposition as 'the beginning of constitutional crisis'[13]. Following their victory in 1994, HzDS completely excluded opposition parties from any participation in bodies overseeing state functions, e.g. broadcasting, privatisation[14], the scrutiny of Slovak Intelligence Service, and it denied the opposition parties representation on parliamentary committees. HzDs began the new election period by an attempt to defy the Constitutional Court[15] (and continued to do so throughout 1994-1998), which became the 'only and key Slovak institution able to challenge the government'[16]; nevertheless the Constitution and its Court's rulings were often ignored and 'reduced to a mere recommendation', provoking a sharp criticism from the EU and OSCE[17].

Another issue that seriously damaged Slovakia's reputation was the deteriorating relationship between the President Kováč and Prime Minister V Mečiar. In an extraordinary example of the length to which 'revenge' in Slovak politics could go, the president's son was abducted in August 1995 in Bratislava and taken to the nearest police station across the border in Austria. Since the German Interpol wanted him for questioning in a matter of fraud they were investigating, he was held there for six months before the Austrian authorities decided not to extradite him because of the criminal manner in which he found himself in their custody and in which time the Slovak government made no attempts to have him returned. From the very beginning the Slovak Information Service was implicated in the case, which became more sinister by the removal of the police officers who investigated the case and death of a person involved in the case[18] (in an unexplained and uninvestigated explosion).

Possibly the most illustrative of Slovak democracy's descent from fragile to less than that is the thwarted referendum of 23-24 May in 1997. The case is legally too convoluted to explain fully here[19], but in short the events were as follows. The opposition parties in December 1996 put forward a proposal for a direct election of the President by referendum. The expectation was that after the end of Mr.Kováč's term in March 1998 and given the then configuration of the parliament it would be difficult to find a candidate who could secure a degree of balance against the ruling coalition in this important election year. Although the President did not enjoy a great executive power, he could (as M.Kováč regularly did) veto the laws considered unconstitutional. The veto could be overturned by a parliamentary majority upon its return to the parliament, but nevertheless it was a measure of democratic control very important to the opposition. Their fears proved justified[20].

The necessary signatures were collected and the President declared a referendum (the Constitution article 95). At the same time the government presented a new question for the referendum, relating to entry into NATO. At his monthly rally Mečiar presented his supporters with a set of questions about whether they wished for nuclear arms to be stationed on the Slovak territory and whether they agreed with Slovak army being deployed elsewhere - the audience reacted negatively. The thus initiated 'democratic discussion' seemed unnecessary since Slovakia had not yet been invited to join NATO and moreover NATO had no plans to station nuclear weapons on the territory of the new member states. The parliament nevertheless proceeded to request a referendum on NATO membership, an issue which de facto did not exist[21].

The President called for the referendum for both issues to be held on the same day, consisting of four questions, the first three relating to NATO, the fourth, its legality disputed by the government (and submitted to the Constitutional Court), relating to the direct election of the president. Wrangling about whether all four questions should be on the same ballot followed, with the government arguing against it. Eventually the Court produced a somewhat ambiguous verdict and rejected the government's application, for it claimed that referendum did not fall within the government's competence. The referendum ended in a complete fiasco, when the Interior Minister Krajčí, a HzDS member, took it upon himself to block the distribution of ballots with four questions printed claiming it was illegal to change the Constitution by referendum. In the ensuing chaos only 10% of the population voted and the referendum was declared invalid[22]. The point about the thwarted referendum and other cases mentioned here is that it manifested the fundamental problem in Slovak politics: the instability and the ruling coalition's desire to consolidate its control by any means.

## Political and Ethnic Cleavages in Party Formation: 1993-1998

There is a strong ethnic dimension to Slovakia's party system. The main purpose of the Hungarian parties' political activities is the protection of the Hungarian minority, which considering the presence of strongly nationalistic SNS in the Mečiar's government meant that MK supported the opposition, despite the difficult relationship with DÚ (unambiguously opposed to collective rights and regional self-government) and SDĽ. It would however be misleading to divide the political scene into nationalist government and democratic opposition, because nationalists were (and remain) in both camps. KDH does not shy away from 'national idea' and on questions of minority rights its position is unclear. It would be equally wrong to assume that the existence of Hungarian parties has been prompted by Slovak nationalism since they all were formed prior to the first postcommunist elections in 1990 and reflect a deep ethnic cleavage in Slovak society, the elimination of which would take more than a change of government. The MKDH's manifesto from the 1994 elections offers a kind of an explanation:

> the Hungarian population, attached to the homeland, has the right to express the linguistic and cultural attachment to the united Hungarian nation. The new state borders did not mean the creation of a new nation, but a branch was torn off, a branch from the same nation, which as a citizen is an inhabitant of Slovakia, but as a person is a Hungarian (p.20).

Nevertheless, the earlier radicalism has subsided and the MK, after having transformed itself into one party Slovak Hungarian Coalition for the 1998 elections, has joined the current government.

Another striking facet of the political scene 1993-1998 is what appears to be at first glance the ideological incoherence of the political parties. The governing coalition led by the HzDS on one hand and rather a standard collection of parties on the other, covering practically the whole political spectrum from left to right with the two extremes from both ends of the spectrum in the government. Economic policies do not offer an answer to the formation of these blocks. The HzDS came to power because it promised a gradual transition of the economy, slower privatisation and a more 'statist' approach to democratisation, which appealed to the population frightened by the rush to a market economy and confused by the sheer plurality of possibilities, offered by the end of communism. In that sense the HzDS is nearer to the SDĽ, with a nearly indistinguishable ideology as far as economics are concerned, than it is to its partner the ZRS with the explicitly workers orientated, state-centric, socialist policies. The ZRS, in the postcommunist ECE region an anachronistically left-wing party, was joined in this ruling coalition by the extreme right-wing SNS, subscribing to pro-market economic policies, more comparable to the rightist parties of the opposition, such as KDH. Clearly, the answer to the formation of coalitions is not in the economy, at least not in the official economic policies proclaimed by party manifestoes.

The answer to the configuration of political parties in Slovakia in the discussed period can be sought on two levels. Traditionalism still plays an important role in the party system[23], partly because all parties are new and thus seek to build on some historical tradition. SNS in particular expresses the affinity to the war-time Slovak State, SDĽ (and now irrelevant ZRS) make extensive use of communist stereotypical rhetoric with emphasis on egalitarian and anti-capitalist sentiments. Similarly, the HzDS builds on the communist period, with a black and white depiction of reality, formulated in populist language laden with enemies and praise for the 'ordinary man' and some residues of inter-war national conservatism, whilst KDH is inclined also towards the inter-war conservatism in the terms of religion and tradition (family, morality and confession).

More important level of the configuration of party system concerns the conception of democracy, often viewed as a zero-sum game in which winner takes all. In Szomolányi's view, the instability of Slovak democracy was rooted in the lack of consensual unity among elites about the parameters of democratic conduct, which meant that the 'struggle for the rules of the game'[24] continued; instead of a 'normal' competition for power between the government and the opposition, there was a struggle about the rules by which the political actors should regulate their competition. The role of political and economic elites, their power, thus the responsibility they bear for the direction of Slovak transition was one of the main points (the other being the role of nationalism) conveyed to me in interviews with academics and political analysts in Slovakia, conducted in the period August -October 1997[25]. The following is the much shortened summary of the answers to the question about the specificity of Slovakia's troubled transition: the extreme level of conflicts among elites (Zemko); the lack of a political elite which feels a sense of responsibility for the future of the state (Pichler); personal ambition under the condition of moral crisis in the postcommunist society (Pálko); clientelist networks and the incapacity of elites to unite the society which has no identification with the state (Weiss); the state unprepared for independence (Duleba); communist socialisation from which most elites have emerged (Podoba); confusing nationalism with the legitimacy of the state (Zajac). This indicates that the main problem seemed to be the combination of inexperienced and irresponsible elites and a passive population, both lacking in the identification with a state and the responsibility for it.

*Slovak Political Tradition: Socio-Cultural Analysis of Electoral Behaviour*[26] Whilst it may be true that the configuration of political parties has an independent and possibly final impact on the regime formation, the population itself does carry a certain responsibility for the decision how and by whom is the country governed. If political parties are representative of public interests and aspirations for the future, even allowing for manipulation by elites, then we must explore which interests and what kind of vision of society inspires that choice. That is usually referred to as political culture, the term which 'in keeping with the democratisation of post-communist societies is undergoing a spectacular revival'[27]. There is a danger in this 'political culture' interpretation, mostly that it is suggestive and that there is little data available from the communist and pre-communist period, therefore no continuity in comparing the surveys about values and orientations. Moreover, relying on surveys as a way of explaining the political system cannot do more than offer some cautious suggestions as to the possible outcomes.

None the less there is some relevance in exploring the political tradition as a way of exploring to what extent the past shapes the present and seeking an answer to how people perceive the world, what they consider important, how they formulate their desires, what they fear and whom, or what they trust[28]. In Slovakia, the political system is new and unstable and therefore the political culture relies mainly on historical developments some of which have been dealt with in the previous chapter and here will be explored through the comparative analysis of electoral behaviour.

What has been intimated thus far is a political tradition that includes a range of elements: anti-liberal tendencies; collectivism, manifested in strong national orientation; toleration of lawlessness by state authorities; high expectations from the state combined with egalitarianism and a general misunderstanding about how these tendencies affect long-term prospects. So, where do we look for the basis of these elements of political behaviour? The obvious answer is, firstly, in pre-socialist development; secondly, in the communist period and lastly in the end of communism itself.

**Table 4.3   Election results: Czechoslovakia 1920-1946**

| Party | 1920 percentage of vote | 1925 | 1929 | 1935 | 1946 |
|---|---|---|---|---|---|
| Czechoslovak Social Democrats | 39.4 | | | | |
| Slovak National and Agrarian Party | 18.7 | | | | |
| Czechoslovak People's Party in Slovakia | 18.1 | | | | |
| Hlinka's Slovak People's Party* | | 34.5 | 28.2 | | |
| Agrarian Party** | | 17.4 | 19.5 | 17.6 | |
| Czechoslovak Communist Party*** | | 13.9 | | | |
| National Christian Social Democrats | | | 15.9 | | |
| Bloc Hlinka's Party + Slovak National | | | | 30.1 | |
| National Christian Democrats | | | | 14.2 | |
| Democratic Party + | | | | | 62.0 |
| Communist Party | | | | | 30.0 |

*mostly in the ethnically Slovak regions; ** Eastern Slovakia and Protestant enclaves; *** regions with mixed Hungarian population; + in the Czech lands Communists won with a large majority – this however does not signal democracy, but the exclusion of Hlinka's Party from the political life, thus includes his supporters.

*Source:* V.Krivý *Slovensko a jeho regióny* Bratislava, Nadácia Média 1996.

The oldest polarisation of society was along the religious lines, between Catholics and Protestants. According to political analysts Catholicism (60% of the population) rests on irrational understanding of the world reflected in the hierarchical-authoritarian structure of the Church, as opposed to individualism and the rationality of Protestants[29]. The influence of the Catholic Church on political development was most visible in the interwar period, when Christian nationalism was the ideology of the leading Hlinka's Slovak People's Party. The rehabilitation of the wartime

Slovak State and J. Tiso remains an important issue with some segments of the Church, but on the whole it cannot be argued that in the present situation Catholicism has a strong influence on the politics of Slovakia[30].

More of a concern is the remaining division between Western orientation, and 'traditionalism'[31], whereby the latter stands for nationalism combined with anti-democratic tendencies. From 1925 the anti-liberal sympathies and the pressure for national identity and unity brought consistent victories to the traditionalist, even isolationist catholic party HSLS (Hlinka's Slovak People's Party). This movement was not only anti-liberal and anti-Czechs, but also subscribed to national-socialism and degenerated into a fascist state during the war.

The results of elections during the interwar period (see Table 4.3) show that with the exception of the 1920 elections, until the end of the war, the most successful parties in Slovakia were conservative, anti-democratic and directed against the unitary state. The anti-unitarian state parties do not have to be necessarily anti-democratic, but in the Slovak case they incorporated a strong nationalist element. The dominant feature of these elections was conservatism (the decreasing support for socialists, unlike in the Czech lands, can be explained by the anti-capitalist orientation of Catholic parties, as well as internationalist and Czechoslovakist orientation of socialists, thus their underestimation of national demands).

The first experience of Slovaks with parliamentary democracy confirms a preference for social equality, the role of the state and nationalism. However, Slovaks could not actually experience the consequences, nor advantages, of their political preferences, because Czechoslovakia was a centralized state that followed the policies of majority parties where Slovakia counted for a significantly smaller number of votes compared to the Czechs (including Moravians). Czechoslovakia, preoccupied with the idea of an unitary state, in the presence of many minorities (35% in total), treated all regional demands as a threat and eventually removed the already well established system of regional governments in Slovakia. Ironically, Slovakia now behaves in the same way towards the Hungarian minority, confirming the underlying argument of this book that nation-building, in multinational states has a tendency towards homogenisation at the risk of creating a situation where the lack of democratic institutions leads to citizens turning against the very basis of democracy. Moreover, the evident fact that the issues concerning nationhood and statehood influence transition to democracy is not a specificity of postcommunist transitions only; it is a specificity of all transitions which involve the reconfiguration of political and geographical space, and subsequently inspire the re-evaluation of the majority-minority relationship.

The degree and extent to which the population and elites are willing to undergo the changes affects the success of political reform. The above sections made it obvious that the willingness of the majority of Slovaks to undergo the all-encompassing changes necessary after 1989 was limited. Very soon after 1990 the economic reforms became unacceptable for Slovakia, even though it is absolutely essential to acknowledge the fact that the situation for Slovaks - due to the type of inherited industry (heavy and munitions) which became obsolete - was considerably worse at the starting point than for the Czechs. However, the lack of faith in the transformation began to play a role already before the economic reforms could take a significant hold to influence the political thinking, and therefore the negative reaction to economic transformation must be studied within the wider context of the socio-cultural sphere.

Let us look at the election results (only the main parties) up to 1994 again. The jump from 1946 to 1989 indicates the period of communist one-party state and makes analysis of electoral behaviour obsolete.

**Table 4.4  Election results: Slovakia 1990-1994**

| Party | 1990 | 1992 | 1994 |
|---|---|---|---|
| Public Against Violence | 29.3 | | |
| Christian Democratic Movement | 19.2 | 8.7 | 10.8 |
| Communist Party | 13.3 | | |
| Hungarian Parties | 8.7 | 7.4 | 10.18 |
| Movement for Democratic Slovakia | | 37.3 | 34.96 |
| Party of Democratic Left | | 14.7 | 10.41 |
| Association of Workers | | | 7.34 |
| Slovak National Party | 13.9 | 7.9 | 5.4 |

*Source:*  M.Bútora P.Hunčík *Slovensko1995* Bratislava, Sándor Márai, 1996; V.Krivý *Slovensko 1996* Bratislava, IVO, 1997

When comparing the election results from the interwar Slovakia and post-1989, a striking similarity appears in the pattern of electoral behaviour:

1.  1920 and 1990 elections show an enthusiasm and a reform zeal, by the elites and the population (1946 is comparable) following a major system breakdown;
2.  after the initial enthusiasm an anti-reformist, more authoritarian party wins and a substantial number of votes goes to either nationally (minorities too), or left orientated parties;

3. the party that initiates the change gives the direction of the new regime, but becomes obsolete as the carrier of transformation;
4. the regional similarities between the interwar Hlinka's national party and Mečiar's Movement for Democratic Slovakia, whereby both parties score the highest number of votes in ethnically pure rural areas[32] - a phenomenon worth noting, because it shows that nationalism can be effectively mobilised without the presence of minorities. On the contrary, the election results in ethnically mixed region of Eastern Slovakia (Hungarians, large Romany population, Rusyns and ethnic Germans) show a consistent resistance to nationalist parties, which would suggest that the co-existence with minorities in fact reduces the mistrust between majority and minority[33].

*Modernisation of Slovakia* The explanation for the above lies in the inquiry into the pre-1989 period and explains better the divergence in postcommunist development between the various countries. The starting point is the actual end of communism in Slovakia, which contrary to other countries, such as Hungary, Poland, Slovenia and the Czech lands was not preceded by a strong dissident movement. The opposition to the regime consisted of a small number of intellectuals, some Catholic activists and ex-communists, expelled from the party during the seventies 'normalization' period[34], but the majority of the population during the 1980s did not feel the need for social and political changes. This may be due to the industrialisation of Slovakia which began late, after the Second World War, and reached its peak in the 1980s - thus, the standard of living was rising markedly throughout the communist period, a point worth noting when comparing the Czech lands where the process took a downward spiral long before, because urban and industrial progress reached its peak before the war.

The 'velvet revolution' took place in Bratislava too and certainly demonstrated that Slovaks also had had enough of the old tired, discredited and corrupted regime, but somehow this did not translate into the understanding, or agreement on the depth of changes that lay ahead. The feeling of insecurity in Slovakia was rising and by 1991 76% felt insecure about their future[35], which shows that the majority of the population did not feel that the communist economy needed radical changes, but was persuaded by the general atmosphere of political development of that time. The opposition to the communist regime did not have a wide base among the population; soon after the euphoria wore off and daily life became full of insecurity and frustration, the population turned their sympathies back to politicians who spoke the language they understood and who promised the continuation of the life style they were used to.

Slovakia had undergone massive changes since the 1950s. The problems of modernisation are not specific to Slovakia, but the speed and the circumstances are. Industrialisation under communism was radical and marked by large industrial enterprises, mostly heavy industry, built in a rural, very traditional setting and was not accompanied by equal urbanisation; huge housing estates were built in rural areas thus traditional ties, networks and ways of life persisted. In 1960 only 30% of the population lived in the cities; now, it is just above 55% of the population, whilst 43% lives in localities of less than 5000 inhabitants, so that the country was not urbanised, rather cities became 'ruralised'[36].

Further specificity of Slovakia must be sought even further in the past, particularly in the assimilation policies of Hungary, discussed in the previous chapter. Nationalism in Slovakia is associated with rural tradition, conservatism of the church and large doses of resentment[37]. One must not underestimate the resentment as a part of national consciousness; it is rooted in comparison with more developed and cultivated national groups, often unflattering and therefore steeped in rejection, inwardness, hostility towards others and the idealisation of one's nation. The creativity of such nationalism is quickly exhausted and directs itself often to romantic deeds and illusions, something that is a remaining phenomenon in Slovak political thought.

From the elimination of the Slovak upper classes and from the absence of any political power derives not only a national ideology, but also a complete alienation of people from politics, always seen as something removed from them. The pre-industrial traditionalism, nationalism devoid of any state-building possibility and the persistently undemocratic regimes (with a too short period between the wars) meant that the population never developed a trust in institutions and in the rule of law, with a consequence that it is easily charmed by flattery and vague declarations about serving the nation and its ordinary people, instead of a serious future orientated political programme. Communism was a kind of organized social and political hypocrisy[38] in which people learned to live with trickery and develop strong patronage networks as a result of bureaucracy, scarcity at all levels of life and a general deformation of social structure and norms.

Thus, the political tradition of Slovakia derives its rigidity from a strange mix of rural traditionalism and the communist modernisation experiment. It is rooted in group solidarity, paternalism, devoid largely of individualism and democratic practices, thus it finds it difficult to adjust to the changes that transformation requires. This is not to say that Slovakia is incapable of completing this process, but given the cultural and institutional legacy of the extended history of political domination and the consequent political and economic backwardness in the combination with delayed nation-building, Slovakia needs a much longer time to do so. Slovak nationalism having all the hallmarks of ethno-cultural nationalism meant that the political thought centred round national identity and language - all ethnically determined. This tradition is of little use for building of a modern democratic state, particularly not one which comprises many minorities, yet it appears that the ethnic notion of the nation-state as a tool for the institutionalisation of national identity prevails in Slovakia, as the following section illustrates.

## The 'state-forming' nation and minorities in Slovakia

A comparison of Slovakia with its Central European neighbours and in the following chapter with Slovenia indicates that the country faces democratisation under less favourable conditions then they do. The absence of historical experience with statehood cannot be viewed as a determining negative condition, for the Czech Republic and Slovenia, both newly independent democracies, count among some of the most successful transitions in ECE countries. There is however a crucial difference. In the Czech Republic the oppressive communism shared with Slovakia pre-1989, was compensated significantly by industrial modernisation largely completed in the precommunist period and the less repressed past in the Austro-Hungarian Empire. These factors helped to create a stronger sense of nationhood and identification with the state following the creation of the First Republic. In Slovenia (also Hungary and Poland) a degree of liberalisation, however tentative, took place prior to 1989.

Whilst in other countries the independent statehood contributed to uniting the society, in Slovakia independence became a divisive issue. The combination of a higher degree of ethnic heterogeneity with greater ethnic polarisation of society and the circumstances under which the new state was established contributed significantly to the formation of national elite and the consequent deviation from the transition path followed by other comparative states. The processes of democratisation, nation-building and state-building overlapped and were compressed into a very short time with a result that democracy and nationhood both suffered from insecurity and the sense of failure. The founders of the newly independent Slovakia never really elaborated the concept of the future state, except for the notion of a state for Slovaks on which the legitimacy of elites was based.

The leading party of the ruling coalition after having brought independence, rather unwittingly and without the wide support of the population, proceeded to seek its legitimacy in the establishment of an independent state. This particularity of Slovakia, where nationalist mobilisation has significantly increased after independence, as it were justifying the fact after the event, is very damaging to finding a consensus among the political elites, because it suggests that only certain people deserve the right to act, or even argue on behalf of the nation. The division was not merely ethnic, between Slovak and non-Slovak, but was further compounded by 'good' (pro-separation) and 'bad' Slovaks (pro-federal), whereby the latter, following this logic, by not having contributed to the existence of the state had no right to govern it.

The building of democracy in Slovakia faces a major challenge, that of forging a workable consensus on the societal and elite level, a more coherent character of national identity which involves preferably the future of the country rather than its past. At this point there is no agreement, not even on the events that could provide an anchor for this new redefinition of identity; to some democrats it is the end of communism in 1989, to ex-communists and democrats on the Left the year 1969, which began with the federal Constitution of the then Czechoslovak Socialist Federal Republic; to some nationalists the 1939 Slovak state. Some of the more extreme nationalists go back to the Great Moravian Empire, yet to other kind of nationalists and some democrats the year 1993 is the only beginning of the truly independent democratic Slovakia[39]. The formation of the first Czechoslovak Republic in 1918 is missing, a surprising omission, considering that this is when Slovakia began its existence after being called the Upper Hungary for centuries.

The difficult question of how to reconcile cultural diversity with political unity is one of the major themes in world politics today and an issue of heightened urgency in Slovakia, where the minority issue is directly linked to the continuation of democratic transition. The main problem, apart from the speed in which all reforms have to take place in an era of heightened communication, creating a more easily aggravated political scene, is the simultaneity of nation and state-building. The nation preceded the state, gave rise to its statehood, but was rather badly prepared for that statehood and the responsibilities that the 'state-forming' nation carries towards the minorities living within its territory. Moreover, the largest and the most politically active minority in Slovakia considers itself Hungarian. In the Slovak historical experience Hungarians are synonymous with the suppression of Slovak language and all things national, thus associated with significantly delayed nation-building process (and territorial annexation[40]). What one observes are the actions of the nationalising state, its attempts to homogenise national culture and redress its historical position, perceived to be weak compared to its neighbours.

The process thus described centres round the main question as to what is the relation of the nation to the state. Slovakia extends the full citizenship rights to all her citizens regardless of their ethnic affiliation, so the ethnic/civic division does not explain the grievances of the Hungarian minority (for it must be stressed that the issue of minority in Slovakia is, at this point in time, confined to Hungarians). The tension is actually about the 'ethnicisation'[41] of the political community, by way of reaction to the disorientation about its civic identity, following the dissolution of the state that embodied and inspired that civic identity. Both groups are in the process of redefining their national identity; Hungarians who did not want an independent Slovakia and Slovaks who having established an autonomous state are seeking to justify it with all the consequences that the re-assertion of national identity brings.

If citizenship implies the membership of a political community, then in Slovakia one cannot speak of formal exclusion from citizenship as was the case with ethnic Russians in the Baltic states. It is rather an implicit and informal division between Slovaks, who perceive themselves to be the state-forming group and the owners of self-determining state, and 'the others', who are seen as less deserving of control in that state. In principle the demands of the Hungarian minority, which constitutes the majority in Southern Slovakia, are based on a similar idea of self-determination (i.e. control over their region) and that is precisely the point of tension - the control over the territory and the preservation of the 'immediate' identity[42] Citizenship in this case takes on a different meaning; the 'price' for the membership in the national community is expected to be paid, usually in the form of conforming to the dominant culture. That is where such issues as the Language Laws, disputes about signs, territorial reforms, the control over budgets for cultural activities, quarrels about what language school reports should be written in etc. come in, all in order to distinguish the real 'nation-builders', the ones who gave the name to the new state, from other citizens.

*Politics of Language*

Approximately 14%[43] of the Slovak population (5,6 million) declares themselves to be of other than Slovak nationality. The most numerous is the Hungarian minority with nearly 11% of the population (567 300), concentrated on southern borders with Hungary. The second most numerous minority is Romani, officially recognised since 1991 (76 000), but the estimated number is much higher and could be up to 250 000[44], followed by the Czech minority (59 300). Other smaller minorities are Rusyns, in the east of the country (approximately 30 500)[45], Germans, Poles and Bulgarians; the remaining Jewish population declare themselves as Slovaks. All minorities have cultural associations and institutions and regular press.

As far as political representation is concerned, only the Hungarian minority is represented in parliament (and since 1998 in the government) which reflects their position in political life as the 'measure' of the extent of Slovak democracy. In September 1995 Slovakia ratified the Council of Europe's 'Framework Convention for the Protection of National Minorities', including Recommendation 1201[46] which recommends the collective rights of minorities, but is not legally binding. In an attempt to settle the old disputes with Hungary, thus make the membership in the EU more realistic, a bilateral 'Treaty on Good Neighbourliness and Friendly Cooperation between the Slovak Republic and the Republic of Hungary', incorporating the Recommendation 1201 was signed (Paris, March 1995), but it took a year and further measures to ratify the Treaty (March 1996, the Hungarian government signed June 1995). It seems that in order to pacify the more nationalistic elements in the Slovak parliament a declaration had to be added which rejected the notion of collective rights, thus implying also the impossibility of establishing autonomous self-governing regions based on ethnic principles, and a law on The Slovak State Language (November 1995). Consequently, the tension between the Slovak government and the Hungarian minority became an integral part of the Slovak political scene, particularly in the 1994-1998 period. According to the Hungarian representatives, the language law, the territorial reforms (the change of districts in order to reduce the number of districts with the Hungarian majority) and the reduction in cultural subsidies made a mockery of the Treaty and showed 'that nationalism has become the official state policy'[47].

*The Constitution*[48] The Slovak Constitution was adopted 1. September 1992. The rights of national minorities and ethnic groups are dealt with in Chapter 4 of the Part 2 (Fundamental rights and freedoms), namely articles 33 and 34, which have been coordinated with the European Convention on the Protection of Human Rights and Fundamental Freedoms. The main points are:

art.33: membership in any national minority or ethnic group must not be to anyone's detriment.
art.34: citizens belonging to national minorities or ethnic groups are guaranteed the all-round development, particularly the right to develop with other members of the minority their culture, the right to spread and receive information in their mother tongue, to associate in associations based on their nationality, establish and maintain educational and cultural institutions. Details to be determined by law.

/2/ in addition to the right to learn the state language, citizens belonging to national minorities or ethnic groups are also guaranteed under the conditions to be determined by law: a) the right to be educated in their language; b) the right to use their language in official contact; c) the right to participate in solutions concerning national minorities and ethnic groups.

/3/ the exercise of rights by citizens of minorities... guaranteed by this constitution, must not lead to threats to sovereignty, nor territorial integrity of the Slovak Republic or discrimination of other citizens in the Republic.

This constitution was a great improvement on the Constitutional Charter adopted following the end of communism (January 1991) by the Federal Assembly of the Czech and Slovak Republics, which was meant to improve the Constitutional Act on Minorities from 1968, but in fact offered even fewer legal guarantees. All Hungarian MP's walked out of parliament, in protest, during the signing of the Constitution and it remains the subject of constant criticism by some Slovak representatives and international organizations[49].

There are two points in the above cited articles that immediately spring to attention. Firstly, the twice repeated clause 'to be determined by law', which makes the granting of these rights amendable by law. A simple majority in parliament can produce such a change and defeat the Constitution[50]. Secondly, article 34 /3/, which is concerned with the threat to sovereignty and territorial integrity. Many actions of minorities (and there is no doubt that this paragraph has been drafted with Hungarians in mind) could be construed as threatening, even a demand for more control over their own affairs, which is guaranteed under the above paragraph. It is an example of mistrust by the state towards the citizens who do not belong to the national majority.

Having said that, the escape clauses in the Constitution would probably not have led to such severe criticism, if they were not preceded by the preamble that set the tone of the document in such a blatantly pro-Slovak mode. Assuming that the purpose of the preamble is to situate the text in the larger context, then the debate and objections it inspires is deserved[51]. It reads:

We, the Slovak nation, in memory of the political and cultural heritage of our predecessors and centuries long experiences of struggles for national existence and stateness ...together with the members of national minorities and ethnic groups living in the territory of the Slovak Republic,...in the interest of lasting cooperation... thus we, the citizens of Slovak Republic...

More so then the actual operative articles, the preamble makes a clear distinction between the Slovak nation and other citizens. It puts minorities, even if involved in the aims and interests of the new state, explicitly into the second place and thus, implicitly leaves no doubt as to who the 'owners' of the state are and where their pre-eminence lies. In sum, the Slovak Constitution instead of providing a solid foundation upon which to erect a multinational structure had become a site for political and interethnic conflict.

*The Slovak State Language Law*[52] The law, which consists of 13 articles, took effect from 1 January 1996 and nullified the previous Law on the Official Language from 1990 (article 12). It created a legal vacuum, because the previous law granted the free use of minority languages, also towards the administrative authorities, in communities where the minority exceeds 20%, whereas this law made no such claim. The 20% threshold has has been brought back in the latest 'Law on the use of minority languages' in effect from 1 September 1999[53] This latest law whilst stressing that the state language is Slovak, 'acknowledges and values the importance of mother language to the members of minorities', and thus 'wishes' to aid the 'development of a democratic and tolerant society in conditions of European integration'[54]. The reason why I mention the Language Law, despite the many changes that have been brought to it since 1996 is that it hardly masks the intention of 'ethnicisation' of the state and the 'readjustment' of historical wrong; similarly as in the case of the Constitution, the Hungarian minority representatives were offended by its preamble and 'The Justification' It is important to keep in mind the fact that in the regions where the majority of the population consists of minorities, a normal situation is such that most officials, shopkeepers, doctors etc. speak the minority language and therefore the problem of the law lies in the possible implications it carries, rather than influencing the practicalities of daily lives.

The preamble starts off:

> The Slovak National Council, based on the fact that the Slovak language is the most important feature of the uniqueness of the Slovak nation, the most precious asset of its cultural heritage, the expression of the sovereignty of the Slovak Republic and generally the tool of communication for her citizens, which on the territory of the Slovak Republic, secures their freedom and equality in their dignity.

The justification[55] attached to the draft version submitted to parliament explains further that with the codification of the language, 'Slovak national unity was established' and that from the 18th century the Slovak language had to withstand the 'aggressive pressure of the Hungarian language'. It continues with a chronology of various laws adopted by the Hungarian court, from 1792 when Hungarian became a compulsory subject in every school, to 1907 Apponyi laws which Magyarised the last few public elementary schools. It ends with the 1920 Constitutional law of the Republic of Czechoslovakia that did not recognize two official languages but only one Czechoslovak language. One cannot but conclude that this justification is not about the building of a new state and its future, but about the revenge of the former 'victims' who are now in charge.

The second part adds the most questionable argument of this law, when it says that 'Slovaks comprise the only state-forming element of the Slovak republic', an argument that begs the question about the role of non-Slovaks in the new state. The Council of Europe's Framework Convention for the Protection of Minorities of which Slovakia is a signatory states that: 'any discrimination based on belonging to a national minority shall be prohibited' (article 4.1) and 'the parties undertake to recognise that every person has the right to use freely and without interference minority language, in private and in public, orally and in writing' (article 10).

By saying that Slovak nationhood is insecure, I also mean measures such as the above laws and the constitution which have as their main goal the confirmation of Slovakness as the pre-eminent identity in the state. These measures thus undermine the very concept of democratic citizenship in a multiethnic state. Without excusing the Slovak exaltation of their ethnicity, one must keep in mind that it is a novelty in their history, which has been marked by the feelings of resentment, mostly caused by their second class citizen status within the Austro-Hungarian empire and what they always considered a disadvantaged position within Czechoslovakia. The concept of ethnic equality and tolerance is not compelling enough to a politically inexperienced, culturally less acknowledged and 'sociologically insecure nation'[56].

As the development of national question in the previous chapter indicated, the Slovak apprenticeship into politics of ethnic identity has been more successful than with respect to civic identity. The result is a situation whereby the state is regarded as an expression of Slovak national identity, an achievement of their national consciousness. The consequence is that minorities, even if tolerated, are not given the incentive to feel more than a bare acceptance of the state, thus confirming their lack of affiliation, a suspicion they are already accused of - a vicious circle impeding the process of forging a new political community which should be the basis of the new state.

**Seeking a Consensus: The 1998 Elections and New Prospects for Democracy**

The general elections 25-26 September 1998 and the victory of political parties claiming unequivocal commitment to liberal democracy, economic transformation and closer ties with the West, instead of their predecessors' at best ambivalent attitude to those goals signalled a turning point in the direction of Slovakia's transition to democracy. As there is no historical or political inevitability for a transition to democracy to actually become one, these elections do not spell a definite consolidation of democracy in Slovakia, but they offer a reasonable chance for a change. As such the post-1998 period can be viewed as the beginning of the 'third transition' in Slovakia (1990-1993 as the first and 1994-1998 as the second attempt). The account of Slovak political and national development may end with analysis of this latest transition in this book, but the Slovak search for secure nationhood and democracy has some way to go yet.

*Coalition of Coalitions*

Jacques Rupnik, the French political analyst specialising in ECE politics, commented after the elections that 'the next problem is the unity of the winning coalition, because that is a coalition of coalitions, which in themselves consist of many different political streams'. He also asserted that the only way this coalition can survive the next 4 years is if the leaders can put aside personal and party interests in favour of common interest, because the fragile quality of this coalition is made even more fragile by the dire economic situation it inherited. He further expressed the view that even if it is difficult to describe the political profile of this new coalition, with its left orientation (SDĽ and SOP), he saw it as 'the weakening of a national-populist orientation, which hitherto dominated the Slovak politics'[57]. One would be well advised to reserve caution about such an optimistic assessment of the Slovak politics until the next general elections in 2002, as I will suggest below.

The most important new parties and coalitions in the 1998 elections were:

SDK   Slovak Democratic Coalition. Coalition of five parties transformed into one party: KDH (Christian Democrats); DS (Democratic Party); SDSS (Social-Democrats); SZS (Green Party); DU(Democratic Union).

SMK   Hungarian Coalition. Also an amalgam of three parties: MKDH. (Hungarian Christian Democrats); MOS (Hungarian Civic Party); Spolužitie (Coexistence).

SOP   Party of Civic Understanding/ Strana Občianského Porozumenia. A new party formed 6 months prior to the elections by the Mayor of Košice (now a President), a party of technocrats comprising of many ex-communists with a strong message (even if a lesser emphasis on the method) of political dialogue, European integration and a transparent completion of privatisation, social orientation in social policies and liberal in economy.

**Table 4.5   General election in Slovakia, 1998**

| Political party | Percentage of vote | Seats |
| --- | --- | --- |
| HzDS | 27.0 | 43 |
| SDK* | 26.3 | 42 |
| SDĽ* | 14.6 | 23 |
| SMK* | 9.1 | 15 |
| SNS | 9.0 | 14 |
| SOP* | 8.0 | 13 |
| KSS | 2.7 | - |
| ZRS | 1.3 | - |
| | | 150 |

**1994:**   HzDS 34.96%; SDĽ 10.41; SNS 5.4; ZRS 7.34; SMK 10.18
New coalition's parliamentary majority: 93 seats, 90(3/5) needed to achieve constitutional reform.
Turnout: 84.24%

*Source: SME* September 1998. Further *'Kto?Prečo?Ako?'* Slovenské Voľby '98 Bratislava, IVO 1999 and V. Krivý in *Slovensko 1998-99'* Bratislava, IVO 1999

*Political Structure Post-1998*

There are two important points worth noting about this election. First, the will to overthrow Mečiar's government was greater than disagreements between the coalition partners. Second, the HzDS despite the highest number of votes faced opponents who if not united among themselves were united in hostility towards Mečiar which blocked any possibility of the HzDS forming a government.

Political hostility, distrust and uncertainty characterised politics in Slovakia in the turbulent pre-election year, in which the presidential powers were in the absence of the President transferred to Mečiar and the President of the Parliament I.Gašparovič (also the vice-chairman of the HzDs)[58]. From about 1996 the opinion polls signalled that the strongest party of the government the HzDS was not getting more than 28% of votes, whilst the amalgamation of the opposition votes consistently reached over 50%, nearing what could be a majority in the parliament. Hence, the efforts to block the opposition through legislative methods followed. The first attempt to change the electoral system from the proportional to a combination system was introduced by the geo-administrative change of districts parallel to the HzDS dominance, based on an assumption that the fragmentation of the opposition under the new districts and the combination system would lead to their almost certain defeat. The smaller partners ZRS and SNS fearing the loss of influence, possibly existence, radically opposed the change of electoral system, but not the geo-administrative changes which went ahead anyway[59].

At that time three opposition parties, KDH, DÚ and the small DS formed a right-centre 'blue coalition' which declared the intention to form an electoral coalition and the will to cooperate with other democratic parties. In 1997, the all-party initiative (except the SDĽ) for a referendum (see above) led to a closer cooperation of all opposition parties including the Hungarian parties. In July 1997 the SDK was formed, whose strategy was to reduce the dominance of the HzDS and eliminate the possibility of the loss of votes for the smaller DS, SZS and SDSS. The first opinion polls proved the strategy well founded with the SDK reaching over 30%[60].

The next step by the government in order to prevent the formation of coalitions which would affect the position of the HzDS was to change the electoral law, so that each party within a coalition had to reach 5% threshold (May 1998, 5 months prior to the general election). The adoption of this law indeed ended the formation of coalitions which was precisely its intention, but ironically the law which was meant to eliminate the main opposition blocs, the SDK and SMK, resulted in its creator's demise. The Hungarian parties, used to cooperation and coordination even prior to the change of electoral law, chose to form one party, the SMK, in which the original member parties lost their identity and continuity at all levels, from the grass roots to the top. The two main ideological streams within the Hungarian movement, the Christian-democrats and liberals, determined one list of candidates according to the proportional preferences among their voters.

The SDK chose the strategy of one electoral party with one list of candidates, but the parties remained independent; they simply did not stand in elections. There are various reasons for this, mostly the disparate ideological orientation of the member parties, the consequent fear of loss of identity, thus membership in international party organisations and the personal ambitions of well established political figures from the large KDH and DÚ. The maintenance of the individual parties' identity has proved a great problem for the unity of the SDK thus posing the greatest danger to the new government's stability[61].

*A New Stage in Slovak Transition to Democracy?*

Broad coalitions across the left to right political spectrum have become a feature of Slovak politics. The question is whether it is a sign of a maturing political system, or a sign of yet another critical election, in conditions of an unstable undetermined democracy. It is possibly both; the elections were critical. Nevertheless the fear of irregular elections never materialised, the turnout was high, the outgoing government accepted the defeat and a strong desire for change was demonstrated by elites and population alike. The fundamental axis of political division in the period between 1993-1998 has evolved round the normative relationship to parliamentary democracy, constitutionalism, European integration, independence and the principles of rule of law. The division was deep and compounded by the ethnic division. The current government resembles something of a 'grand coalition', in which the ideological Left-Right division appears less important and the ethnic cleavage is considerably weakened by the Hungarian presence in the government[62].

*Hungarian issue* M.Duray, the founder of the Coexistence party and one of the most prominent Hungarian minority representatives, commented on the new situation by saying that 'the fact that SMK has entered government as an independent party constitutes a historical change for which we waited for eighty years'[63]. The presence of the Hungarian SMK in the ruling coalition is not merely symbolic and hopefully will not be limited to the minority issues. After years of confrontation, the presence of this politically highly mobilised minority in the executive (three ministerial posts in the new government, including the vice-chairman of the government for minority issues and the regional development) and in the legislature (vice-chairman of the Parliament and leaders of the parliamentary committees) must lead to a substantial change in Slovak-Hungarian relations.

It should signal a significant move towards the elimination of the 'Hungarian issue' in Slovak politics, thus the acceptance of a multicultural character of the state and the importance of minority participation in democratic politics. The most important implication is that this change could finally remove nationalism from political life; were that the case, it would show that nationalism is not inherent to Slovak or any other society. It would also demonstrate that the level of nationalist mobilisation depends on political developments in the state and on national elites, who can instrumentalise, but also reduce or even eliminate nationalism, according to their commitment to democracy. Ethnic identities despite their pervasiveness are not existential: the affiliation to the state and the strengthening of civic identity is a matter of politics and the minority-majority relationship reflects those politics.

*On a less optimistic note*  The reader must have noticed the caution with which I present the largely positive developments in Slovakia since 1998. As I am putting finishing touches to this book, the Hungarian Coalition is threatening to leave the government (decision postponed until September 2001), due to its dissatisfaction with the recently adopted laws on regional administration. Their departure would be a sad indictment on the Slovak-Hungarian relationship and a serious setback to new Slovak politics; it is to be hoped that both sides can come to a compromise in order to avoid such a disappointing[64] result. There are several further obstacles that the 'third transition' in Slovakia is facing. Firstly, the stability of the current coalition SDK-SMK-SDL-SOP which depended on the unity of its strongest member SDK has been severely disrupted, particularly due to the KDH's ambition to form an independent conservative party. SDKÚ formed by the Prime Minister M.Dzurinda is being weakened by the stubborn individualism and egoism of its potential coalition partners. The SOP which could never count on a stable electorate, its success being rooted mostly in the popularity of its founder R.Schuster, is unlikely to enter the next parliament. The continuing inter-party and inter-coalition fractiousness has resulted in a further proliferation (rather than profiling) of parties. The most important among the new 'alternatives' is ANO (Aliancia Nového Občana/ Alliance of a New Citizen) lead by the co-owner of the influential TV station Markíza Pavel Rusko and most concerningly, the splinter party of the SDĽ – SMER (Direction), founded by one of its most ambitious politicians Róbert Fico, who does not shy away from the exploitation of the Hungarian issue and provides a serious competition to the HzDS. Despite the notable successes of the post-1998 government, particularly in area of European integration, one must note the unchanging electoral popularity of nationalist SNS who together with the enduringly strong HzDS are forming a very destabilising element in the parliament.

The latest poll in electoral preferences illustrates my argument[65]. HzDS 24.9%; SMER 18; SMK (reflecting the stable Hungarian vote) 10,9; SDKÚ 10,1; SNS 9.2; KDH 6.0; ANO 5.9; SDĽ 5.0; SOP 1,6.

There are many possible scenarios, all of which share the same point of departure: the ruling coalition's raison d'être was the removal of Mečiar which in itself is a negative and limited position from which to sustain a lasting consensus about the future of multicultural democracy and its rules – only such a consensual force can eliminate political and ethnic cleavages in Slovak politics. If on the other hand, the conflicts have become a characterisation of Slovak political elite (and the judgment will have to be reserved until yet another 'crucial' general election which in itself is becoming a problematic feature of Slovak politics), then we can assume that nationalism will resurface as a mobilising factor for whichever party chooses it as its agenda[66].

## Conclusion

In the third chapter I have argued that nationalism is a part of transition, but does not necessarily assist the transition. Nationalism's compatibility with democracy depends on certain conditions which are contingent on historical, political and national development, the ethnic composition and the resultant elite formation. The journey through the troubled Slovak transition should have demonstrated the validity of this claim. The underlying argument was that the successful transition to democracy requires the construction of a political community whose unity is rooted in commitment to democratisation project rather than in ethnic identity.

The general motif running through the analysis of Slovak transition was the insecure democracy becoming overwhelmed by seeking the issues of national unity and identity, equally insecure, due to developments in the distant and very recent past. The priority given to nation-building was reinforced by political elites who after having secured independence rather unwittingly and without a convincing support of the whole population tried to legitimise their leadership and inflate the legitimacy of the state with excessive appeals to ethnic solidarity, thus excluding minorities and ignoring political opposition.

The function of the last post-1998 section was to raise an interesting question whether the change towards more democracy and civic integration means that nationalism has exhausted its influence on the political process in Slovakia. If so, is it because the change of elites means the greater commitment to democracy, or because nationalism has exhausted its appeal now that processes of state-building and nation-building are felt to be completed? It would appear that nationalism is an indispensable element of every democratisation process in a newly independent state; for how long will depend on how secure nation has become in its identity and in the purpose of its state - in sum, how long can nationalism inspire public imagination sufficiently, in order to serve as a legitimating tool in politics. Once the nation has been 'reclaimed' what other legitimate claim does nationalism have?

These questions about the role of nationalism in the democratisation process lead me to two propositions to be tested against the following case of Slovenia:

1. Nation-building and state-building are parallel processes in newly independent postcommunist democracies. However, the continuation of the democratisation process requires that at some point nation-building retreats in favour of state-building; and

2. Not disregarding political and historical developments concerning the national recognition and identity, the success of democratisation depends further on the level of consensus: between elites and the population and between ethnic groups, thus a less polarised society, whether ethnically or politically starts from a more advantageous position.

## Notes

[1] *Agenda 2000* The opinions of the European Commission on the Applications for Accession Strasbourg/Brussels 15, July 1997.

[2] G.Evans and S.Whitefield 'The Structuring of political Cleavages in Post-Communist Societies: the Case of the Czech Republic and Slovakia' *Political Studies* 46:1 March 1998 pp.115-139 p.134.

[3] For the similar argument see also P.Kopecký and C.Mudde 'Explaining Different Paths of Democratization: The Czech and Slovak Republics *The Journal of Communist Studies and Transition Politics* 16:3 September 2000 pp.63-84.

[4] The Hungarian minority is the largest among Slovakia's many minorities and is politically most organised. The relationship between the Slovak majority and the minority is compounded by a strong historical and emotional affiliation with the Hungarian state, situated along the Slovak Southern borders.

[5] This is contrary to the argument advanced by J.Batt in *New Slovakia* Discussion Paper London The Royal Institute of International Affairs 1996 p.vi 'the paper argues that the tension between Slovaks and Hungarians today can best be explained in terms of cultural clash'. Moreover, it appears that the most anti-Hungarian rhetoric and action comes from Central Slovakia, where there are practically no Hungarians. For this particular phenomenon whereby the strongest nationalist rhetoric comes from the least ethnically mixed region see V.Krivý *Slovensko a jeho regióny* Bratislava, Nadácia Média 1996.

[6] 94% communicate exclusively in Hungarian with their parents, 73% with their colleagues at the work place. See P.Frič F.Gál P.Hunčík C.Lord *Maďarská menšina na Slovensku* p.14.

[7] G.Evans and S.Whitefield p.135.

[8] K.Henderson 'Slovakia and the democratic criteria for EU accession' K.Henderson ed. *Back to Europe* London, UCL 1999 p.226.

[9] The table is put together by myself based on electoral programmes of all mentioned parties from 1994. Further *'Verejný Audit Volebných programov Politických Strán'* Bratislava, 21 September 1998 and G.Mesežnikov 'Štruktúra Systému Politických Strán' S.Szomolányi *Slovensko:Problémy Konsolidácie Demokracie* Nadácia Friedricha Eberta 1997.

[10] G.Mesežnikov in S.Szomolányi *Slovensko* p.27-47.

[11] K.Henderson p.226.

[12] S.Szomolányi *Slovensko* p.11.

[13] L.Fogáš MP(SDL) in *SME* 2 October 1997. In conversation with him (29 October 1997) Mr.Fogáš, who was one of the writers of the Constitution, told me that Slovakia ceased to be a formal democracy because there is no popular control and the lack of political will to regain it.

[14] To this end the voucher privatisation has been terminated in favour of 'direct sales' of the state property, regulated by FNM (National Property Fund), all top executives of which had direct links to the government, a body beyond the direct control of government. The sales were often to unknown companies, or could be traced to government (i.e. the largest steel works VSŽ to the Minister of Telecommunications A.Rezeš in the government till 1997). The list of proved and suspected corruption at the government level is long, as are the connections to organised economic crime. However, the question of clientelist structures in Slovakia is beyond the brief of this chapter, but for a few examples. The government has revoked the license of the largest investment corporation Sporofond, with some 40 000 investors in the second wave of privatisation despite the Supreme Court ruling. The case of Nafta Gbely, whose 49 % of shares has been sold to an unknown company at the estimated loss to the Slovak government 100 million USD), despite higher offers from other investors. For further information see I.Mikloš in M.Bútora and P.Hunčík ed. *Slovensko 1995* as before and M.Bútora *Slovensko 1996* Bratislava, IVO 1997.

[15] HzDS tried to remove the new DU from the parliament by disputing the signatures the party had to collect in order to stand in elections. In face of the Constitutional Court's rejection of this charge, the motivation must be seen as a revenge for the fall of Mečiar's government precipitated by their defection.

[16] C.Mudde and P.Kopecký 'Explaining Different Paths of Democratization' p.67.

[17] As expressed by A.D'Amato the Chairman of the American Commission OSCE in *Národná Obroda* 6 October 1997 in connection to the Gaudlieder case. Deputy F.Gaudlieder left the HzDS (November 1996) to sit as an independent in the parliament which is in agreement with the constitutional stipulation that MPs are guaranteed to exercise their own mandate. Nevertheless, the parliamentary majority stripped him of his mandate and refused to reinstate him even after the Constitutional ruling required them to do so.

[18] The current government has always accused Mečiar and his secret service chief Ivan Lexa of ordering the kidnapping to embarrass Mr.Kováč. *Domino Forum* 30 July 1998, *The Guardian* 21 April 2000. Lexa since has been arrested and charged, but released due to ill health, Mečiar has also been charged with abuse of power, but thus far neither has been tried.

[19] For the detailed study of the referendum see G.Mesežnikov M.Bútora *Slovenské Referendum '97* Bratislava, IVO 1997.

[20] President Kováč's term in office finished in March 1998. Due to the animosity between the government and the opposition no candidate was able to secure the majority of votes until May 1999 when the new government's law on the direct election of the President resolved the stalemate. In the direct election R.Schuster won, over V.Mečiar, who after losing in the general elections in September 1998 stood as presidential candidate, with a great success, it must be added.

[21] It was evident that with the other two coalition partners, the ZRS and SNS campaigning openly against NATO, it was unlikely that NATO would invite Slovakia to join the first group of Eastern enlargement at its Madrid July 1997 summit. On the other hand, the almost certain rejection of Slovakia could then be justified either way by referendum, either NATO refused a country eager to join, or the country did not want to join anyway.

[22] K.Henderson *Back to Europe* p.230.

23 G.Mesežnikov in *Slovensko...* p.37.
24 S.Szomolányi *Slovensko,* the subtitle *'Spor o "pravidlá hry" pokračuje'* translates as: the struggle for the rules of the game continues.
25 For the professional affiliation of interviewees see Appendix 2 in the bibliography.
26 The following analysis is based on V.Krivý, V.Feglová and D.Balko *Slovensko a Jeho Regióny* Bratislava Nadácia Média 1996 which is the most comprehensive and detailed study of the Slovak political behaviour since the end of the 19th century.
27 F.Plasser and A.Pribersky *Political Culture in East Central Europe* Aldershot, Avebury 1996 p.4.
28 'Democracy requires a distinctive set of political values and orientations from its citizens: moderation, tolerance, civility, efficacy, knowledge, participation' in L.Diamond ed. *Political Culure and Democracy in Developing Countries* Boulder, London, Lynne Rienner Publishers 1993 Introduction p.1.
29 V.Krivý, V.Feglová and D.Balko (1996) p.12.
30 The KDH counting on the catholic vote expected a clear overall majority in the 1990 elections, but came second with 19.2% of votes, after the purely civic movement Public Against Violence (29.3%).
31 For the role of 'traditionalism' and its translation into nationalist/populist politics see A.Ágh *The Politics of Central Europe* London, Sage 1998 p.63-69.
32 V.Krivý, V.Feglová and D.Balko (1996) p.28,48,53. The detailed election results according to districts in the 1925, 1992 and 1994 elections show a strong resemblance in voting patterns. Central Slovakia, the most ethnically Slovak region, voted overwhelmingly for Hlinka's national party and that is the region where post-1989 the populist stream HzDS/SNS was again the most successful. The Hungarian parties' stronghold remains the Hungarian South (interwar the same and Communist party).
33 Eastern Slovakia is a mixed region of Slovaks, large numbers of Rusyns and Ukrainians and Hungarians with a large Romani population and some remnants of Germans. Interwar: agrarian parties and Hungarian parties. In 1992: left parties (SDL/SDSS) and KDH and DS. In 1994: Left parties and KDH and DU. 1998: SDL and KDH and SOP (the new party of Civic Understanding). See V.Krivý, V.Feglova and D.Balko (1996) p.47-59, 103-107.
34 J.Podoba 'Ponovembrové Slovensko' in *Reflexie* IV Bratislava, Spoločnost pre trvalo udržatelný život Eurouni Press 1996 pp. 100 - 106 p.101.
35 V.Krivý, V.Feglová and D.Balko (1996) p.33.
36 See J.Pašiak 'Meštianstvo a občianská spoločnost v kontexte sídelného vývoja' in E.Mannová ed. Bratislava, AEP, 1998.
37 For discussion about 'ressentiment' as an unusually powerful stimulant of national sentiment and collective behaviour see L.Greenfeld *Nationalism Five Roads to Modernity* Cambridge, Harvard University Press 1992.
38 T.Pichler 'The Twisted Track of Culture and Modernization' in *Economics and Politics* V Symposium Bratislava, 1994.
39 During all interviews (19 in total) in Slovakia I asked 'when did Slovakia begin' and this was the range offered, with the majority divided between 1989 and 1993.
40 The annexation of Subcarpathian region in the Second World War marks the beginning of the Slovak experience with the Hungarian iredenta and the basis for the Slovak nationalist anti-Hungarian mobilisation. The mistrust is matched on the other side by the 1945-1948 Czechoslovak policies which declared Hungarians and Germans collectively guilty and led to tragic population moves and severe discrimination until the communist takeover in 1948.

[41] The term borrowed from S.Žižek 'Multiculturalism, or the Cultural Logic of Multinational Capitalism' in *New Left Review* 225 September 1997 pp.28-52 p. 42.

[42] See S.Žižek 'Multiculturalism, or the Cultural Logic of Multinational Capitalism' p. 42 for the distinction between the primary (primordial, immediate) identity and the secondary (nation-state, citizenship) and the tension the reassertion of the former causes in today's world.

[43] It is estimated that the actual figure could be between 18-20%, for not all members of minorities claim that status. Statistics from O.Dostál 'Menšiny' in M.Bútora P.Hunčík *Slovensko 1995 Súhrná Správa o Stave Spoločnosti* Bratislava, Nadácia Sándora Máraiho 1996 p.51-52.

[44] This is a figure according to the local governments in 1989. The size of Eastern Europe's Romani population is a heavily debated (and disputed) issue. Some statistics estimate the number of Romani in Slovakia to be around 10% of the population – 500 000. See Z.Barany 'Orphans of Transition: Gypsies in Eastern Europe' *Journal of Democracy* 9:3 July 1998 pp.143-156.The Romani are often a target of racist attacks from which they are not sufficiently protected by the police, the unemployment of the Romanies is 40-50%. For a detailed study of Slovakia's Romani see A.Jurová *Vývoj Rómskej Problematiky na Slovensku po roku 1945* Košice, Goldpress Publishers 1993.

[45] There is a division between Rusyns about whether they are a distinct ethnic group, or Ukrainians (17 200 the former, 13 300 the latter), but on the whole this is the most assimilated among the more numerous minorities. Their distinctiveness is more of a religious nature, as they belong to either the Greek Orthodox Church, or the Russian Orthodox Church.

[46] The text that most concerned the Slovak parties reads: 'minority shall have the right to have at their disposal appropriate local or autonomous authorities or to have a special status, matching the specific historical and territorial situation' in J.Batt *The New Slovakia* London, The Royal Institute of International Affairs 1996 p.32.

[47] Interview with L.Hóka the spokesman MK 17 September 1997.

[48] *Ústava Slovenskej Republiky* Bratislava NVK International 1992. All translation by myself.

[49] The post-1998 government has made considerable changes to the Constitution (February 2001, 85 articles), mostly in order to fulfill the criteria required by the candidate states for the admission to the EU; the use of minority languages is determined by a separate law (see below).

[50] Interview with L.Hóka the spokesman for the SMK.

[51] The change of this preamble remains an issue in the Slovak-Hungarian relationship; the post-1998 government which includes the Hungarian coalition has thus far been equally reluctant to do so.

[52] Zbierka Zákonov 270/ 1995 Národnej Rady Slovenskej Republiky z 15. November 1995 o štátnom jazyku Slovenskej republiky – all translations by myself.

[53] Zbierka Zákonov č.184/1999 which annuls and changes some articles from the State Language Law.

[54] This is a much shortened version of the preamble to the 'Law on the use of minority languages'. The acceptance of this law in the Parliament was accompanied by singing of nationalistic songs by some oppositional deputies whilst the Hungarian representatives would prefer a much more rigorous changes, leading to Hungarian becoming one of the official state languages.

[55] The excerpts from the 'Justification' are translated from the Minority Protection Association.

[56] G.Schöpflin 'Nationalism and Ethnic Minorities in Post-Communist Europe' in R.Caplan and J.Feffer *Europe's New Nationalism* New York, Oxford, Oxford University Press 1996 p.155.

[57] Interview with J.Rupnik in *SME* 28 September 1998.

[58] Among many incidents that seriously concerned the OSCE was the HzDS's petition to the Supreme Court to cancel the SDK's registration in order to exclude the main opposition from the elections (Constitutional Court confirmed their registration), the gross misuse of the state television in HzDS campaign, whilst the private television Markíza was also accused of the unbalanced broadcasts in favour of the opposition. See: 'Kronika udalostí v roku 1998' in *Slovensko 1998-99*. Also T.Waters 'Slovak parliamentary elections' Conflict Studies Research Centre by Ministry of Defence November 1998 pp.7-9.

[59] The changes of regions and districts reduced the number of the Hungarian representatives and the state funding awarded for cultural association - the territorial reforms were severely criticised by the Hungarian minority representatives (Interview with their spokesman L.Hóka 17 September 1999).

[60] The daily *Národná Obroda* 8 September 1997 HzDS 27.8% SDK 32.6%.

[61] KDH will stand as an independent party in the next elections, whilst the Prime Minister Dzurinda formed a new party, SDKÚ.

[62] G.Mesežnikov 'Voľby 1998 a vývoj systému politických strán' M.Bútora ed. *Kto?Prečo?Ako?* p.45.

[63] Post-election interviews in *Domino Forum* 7 5 November 1998.

[64] In July 2001, in compliance with the EU regulations, Slovak government created a new level of regional government. However, the law did not comply with SMK's wish that a region be created in which ethnic Hungarians would form a significant majority. The SMK demands the change of this new law. *Slovak Spectator* 7:29 July-August 2001.

[65] See also G.Mesežnikov and M.Kollár in an interview about the state of the country in *Kultúrny život* 22 May 2001. http://www.ivo.sk.

[66] For how conflicts are maintained by political parties P.Mair E.E.Schattsneider's *The Semisovereign People, Political Studies* 45:5 December 1997 pp.947-954.

# 5 National Communism in Yugoslavia: the case of Slovenia

*Slovene independence*[1]   Slovenia was a part of the Austro-Hungarian Empire for centuries, which, as far as Slovenes, Croats and the other Slav populations were concerned, never managed to solve the issue of equality of nations adequately. For that reason, when the empire collapsed after the First World war, the Southern Slav nations formed the State of Slovenes, Croats and Serbs, which after a very short existence merged with the Kingdom of Serbia (already including the Kingdom of Montenegro) and established the State of Serbs, Croats and Slovenes - under the centralising pressures of Serbia soon known as the Kingdom of Yugoslavia (1929).

After the Second World War the Communist party of Yugoslavia, having successfully combined national liberation struggles with the proletarian revolution managed to create a federal state[2]. In an attempt to finally resolve the 'national issue' in the federation, each of the constitutions that followed involved a greater degree of autonomy for the individual republics, until finally the Constitution of the Socialist Federal Republic of Yugoslavia (SFRY) of 1974 defined the federal units as states and acknowledged their right to self-determination. Following the process of constitutional amendments[3], which started in 1988 and reflected the fact that political and social developments in Slovenia had far outgrown the other republics, the Slovene people in The Plebiscite on the Independence and Sovereignty[4] adopted the Constitution of the Republic of Slovenia in December 1990.

*Slovenia: a special case among postcommunist transitions*   The following section on the disintegration of Yugoslavia in no way does justice to the complexity of its causes and the tragedy of its consequences, but will be touched upon in order to explain the position of Slovenia and why it viewed extrication from the federation as the only way to guarantee the continuation of the democratisation process that was ongoing from the early 1980s. It has been suggested earlier that the crucial point of comparison with Slovakia is precisely the reasons behind the secession - independence in both countries was a result of the transition to democracy, but for opposed reasons - in the case of Slovakia the extrication from the Czecho-Slovak federation was an unintended result. In both cases it appears that the federal state, as a whole, was unable to complete the transition in a tempo acceptable and suitable to all its constituent units, whether for political, cultural, historical or social reasons, but mostly due to the combination of all of these factors. Whilst Slovakia was not ready for the necessary steps, Slovenia was far ahead of the other[5] republics within the former Yugoslavia.

Equally, in both cases an essentially ethnic community became an inner condition for a political and legal community of a modern state and entered the world of global integration where there is little room for particularism, which in itself poses a number of dilemmas about democracy and its ability to reconcile political and cultural pluralism with the homogenizing tendencies of a new state. As will become apparent Slovenia seems to struggle with these dilemmas more successfully than Slovakia.

The process of transition by its very nature throws society into turmoil, the outcome of which will depend on that society's resources. If the differences in dynamics of transition and different conceptions of democratisation have affected the continuation of both federations (Czechoslovak and Yugoslav), then it is reasonable to assume that these factors will also have an effect on the continuation of democratisation in the successor states. As the postcommunist transitions have crystallised it appears that the only common link between them is that they were communist. That however means that a number of political and socio-economic dilemmas are shared by those countries and that the best way to identify causes of varying national outcomes is the systematic comparison between them; thus, that the 'general conclusions about the process of the transition can be made only in the framework of comparative analysis'[6].

The case of Slovenia in this book will be dealt with as a very special case[7] among postcommunist transitions. That is so for the following reasons:

1.  Former Yugoslavia was the most liberal among all socialist states (by liberal is meant the less harsh level of repression and the ideology of self-management, which permitted a limited degree of political pluralism, defined as a pluralism of self-managing interests). It was not a member of the Soviet camp and therefore enjoyed a very particular, even privileged status (supported by the West) in world politics.

2. Within that already different type of communism espoused by the Yugoslav leadership, Slovenia was further the most liberal among the republics. This was reflected in Slovenes feeling that they had almost achieved the 'third way' between capitalism and communism.

3. Because the independence of Slovenia and the ensuing disintegration of Yugoslavia was followed by the Bosnian war, mostly seen in the light of nationalist policies and ethnic conflicts (and regretfully less in the light of the disintegrating state of which those policies and conflicts were rather the result than the cause), Slovenian independence and the transition to democracy are too often reduced to the realm of politics of nationalism, whereby the central characteristic - democratisation - of that process is neglected in the analysis.

4. The specificity of this transition is that its roots go back as far as the 1960s and that this evolutionary process of transition was endorsed and eventually led by the self-reformed communist leadership who responded to the gradually increased pressures of the opposition organisations and civil movements.

It is my intention to argue that because the Slovenian transition was a gradual process stretching over a longer period of time, in which a degree of political reconciliation was achieved prior to independence, the issues of national identity, independent statehood and the polarisation of elites were sufficiently contained, thus less aggravating to the transition.

In order to justify this argument the following focuses on a number of interrelated factors, here considered to be the most influential in determining the path of Slovene transition: previous regime; the level of democratisation achieved prior to transition and the type of transition itself. The first part concentrates on the Yugoslav type of communism and its main feature, socialist self-management, and how this affected Slovenes and their perception of democracy. The second part explores the tension between the centralising state and the republics which eventually (and possibly inevitably) led to the disintegration of state authority - long before Slovenia and Croatia declared their independence.

The main theme of this chapter is the tension deriving from a combination of emphasis on the national/ethnic differences on one hand, and the centralist ideology of one-party rule, on the other. The conclusion proposes that even in the federation with a strongly autonomist legislation for the national units, the rising national awareness, exacerbated by radically different levels of ideological and economic development will lead to demands for political independence.

### Diversity Within Unity: the Yugoslav System

> To this awareness (about the right to self-determination), belongs the realisation that self-determination is not a self-determination of the Slovene peoples as a Nation, but self-determination of Slovenes as individuals[8].

> Slovenian independence is not a romantic story of a national movement reaching its goal, but rather a banal story of Slovenes not wanting to shoot Albanians in Kosovo, which is what staying within the federation meant[9].

*Slovene perspective* Interviews conducted in Slovakia in order to gain an initial grasp on the current situation could be characterised by the difference in opinions between those interviewed. The plurality of views on the transition, the current regime, the nationhood and the new statehood was overwhelming and indicative of the lack of consensus about the past and the direction the country was or should be taking, by opinion makers, academics and politicians alike. In contrast, the similar method employed in Slovenia showed surprisingly little disagreement about the appropriateness of the separation from Yugoslavia, the fast and unequivocal European integration policies of the current government, despite the pragmatic concerns for the country's economy and the newly acquired sovereignty, and what could only be described as a general sense of pride in institutional and economic achievements so far. The issue of independence, the pivotal point around which the Slovak political elites formed, but mainly polarised, proved the least divisive in Slovenia.

The interviews[10] confirmed the idiosyncrasy of the Slovenian case among Eastern and Central European countries. The salient points could be summed up as follows. First, an interesting combination of left-wing orientation by almost all interviewed, combined with a strong belief in liberalism and national identity and hardly any rejection of Tito's rule, a period seen as conducive to the growth of national awareness. Second, the positive role awarded to the ex-communist leadership (still in power) in the democratisation process and the formation of the national programme, with the exception of the representative of the Social Democratic Party of Slovenia, the main opposition party which bases its platform on the removal of these people from public life. Third, the concern about the role of the Catholic Church (too much influence or not enough). Fourth, the agreement on the main reason for the separation as that of Serbian centralist and authoritarian policies personified by Milošević and proved by the tanks of the Yugoslav army on the streets of Ljubljana. Finally, most of those interviewed claimed that Slovene nationalism is the 'right' kind of nationalism, that is, the strong sense of patriotism devoid of romanticism, future orientated and without an overtly ethnic element - a suspect conclusion[11] about Slovene, or any other nationalism for that matter, and most certainly not supported by this author who believes that the characterisation of nationalism is better served by a careful analysis of conditions in which it develops than by superficiality of labels.

The complacency was occasionally punctured by concerns about the possibility of the future ethnic conflicts between other ethnic groups living in Slovenia and their host nation, and about the maintenance of national identity and economic control for such a small country in the increasingly integrated European landscape. The concerns, however, were tempered by the recognition that there is no alternative to this process. A central point of discussion related to the question of whether independence was the logical culmination of the democratisation process and would have happened regardless of Serbian policies, or the only option left to safeguard that process given the circumstances. The majority of those interviewed, most of whom participated actively in bringing about the reforms of the late 1980s, agreed with the latter[12]. One person argued that the process was hijacked by nationalists and therefore not the culmination of democratisation[13]. Another, maintained that Slovene communists had always been nationalists (possibly comparable only to Poland), going back to the tradition of Social Democrats of the early century and that therefore, the reformers from 1988 onwards, knowing well what was becoming of Yugoslavia, formed an alliance with nationalists. Being aware that a small nation cannot exist without full international support, the declaration of independence had to be timed carefully, so as not to be seen as responsible for the break-down of the state[14].

What can be observed in these interviews is the extent to which the previous regime affected the nature of the present-day Slovenia, from the rise of national awareness, the Slovene social, political and economic existence, the formation of national programmes, the character of transition and the timing of independence itself.

## Yugoslav Communism

It has been implied a few times that politics in the former Yugoslavia differed considerably from the political system in Czechoslovakia. It therefore seems appropriate to question the use of the adjective 'postcommunist' in connection to the Slovak as well as Slovenian transitions. How communist was Slovenia, considering that Yugoslavia enjoyed 'most favoured Communist' state status, precisely because of the differences between the Warsaw Pact countries and Tito's regime, non-aligned to the Soviet bloc, wavering between West and East. The system of worker self-management, the lower degree of coercion of the population, the significant degree of liberalisation - in particular travel, some private ownership, the possibility of study abroad, the availability of Western goods and media broadcasts - was seen, if not as democratic, but nevertheless as a form of democracy, which always held the premise that it could evolve into more democracy. If the West saw it as an attempt to conform to Western liberal democratic values, the domestic population believed it to be their unique 'third way', with Slovenia leading the push towards more pluralism.

However, and here is the crux of the matter, Yugoslavia was not democratic. The fact is that Yugoslav communists never won a free election in any part of Yugoslavia, nor did the regularly proclaimed sovereignty of the republics ever stop the Communist party from using the threat of force whenever it deemed it necessary (Croatia 1971, Kosovo 1981 and Slovenia 1991)[15], and that it was the communist leadership of Serbia which resisted democratisation by the most brutal of methods - a war (1991). The Yugoslav political system, despite offering its population more rights than the systems of other Eastern and Central European countries, was nevertheless an authoritarian system, merely a different type of communist regime, possibly, as often argued by Yugoslavs[16] nearer to Marxism than Stalin's revision of it. A semblance of democracy does not stand for democracy which cannot fully develop in one-party rule. The variations in the degree of tolerance within a one-party state are rather a question of ideology adopted by the party bureaucracy itself in order to secure the party's hegemony than they are a question of adopting 'pluralist policies'[17]. Therefore, I continue to view the Slovenian transition to democracy as a postcommunist one, whereby the distinctiveness of communism in Slovenia (and the former Yugoslavia) will be explored only as a qualitative factor of that process.

*Tito's Yugoslavia*   The communists' accession to power under Josip Broz Tito after 1945 followed a period during the war which only served to exacerbate ethnic and political divisions within the country. The Croatian state (whose dominion included most of Bosnia) openly collaborated with the German occupier and carried out the 'final solution' policies of extermination and expulsion of not only the Jews and the Romanies (and the communists, including many Croats), but primarily Serbs. The latter rose in self-defence and joined either partisans or nationalistic Chetniks, who though originally aligned against Germany and the fascist Axis, increasingly collaborated with the occupiers against the ever-growing power of the partisan army led by Tito.

The war set Yugoslavs against each other in an unprecedented way and whilst they were massacring each other, in an attempt to eliminate enemies and their supporters, they were facing the Germans whose brutality stemmed from their general attitude towards Slavs, who similarly to the Jews were the intended target of the racial theory. More Yugoslavs were killed by each other than by foreign soldiers[18], each resistance movement including the partisans committed atrocities and engaged in civilian massacres. What was left of the old elites was disorientated, weakened and eventually destroyed by both the Nazis and the civil war (Communist-led Liberation Front vs. anticommunist military units) which raged simultaneously with the war against Germans.

After the Germans withdrew, the only power that seemed capable to restore Yugoslavia were the Communists, who in fact were the liberators (Soviet forces left after they helped partisans to free Belgrade), thus making the communist seizure of power a 'native' revolution. Even though the partisan army was a patriotic insurgency, the leadership had a clear political aim - the war of liberation became also a war for establishment of the Communist rule, a task made easier by the support of a significant part of the population radicalised throughout the upheavals of the war.

It should be noted that the organising bodies of the partisans and the Communist Party were established along national lines, meant as a step 'towards settling the national question and establishing the foundations of a fraternal community of equal and independent Yugoslav peoples'[19]. Of course the national issue was not settled[20], Yugoslavia became united, but again without a national consultation. The only thing that the establishment of ethnic-national institutions did was provide the lines along which the federation fractured half a century later. That was not the only contradiction that Tito's Yugoslavia contained. It was a federation with decentralised political and party organisations, but with central economic planning. Attempts to reconcile, practically and ideologically, the contradiction between a centralised bureaucratic Marxism and an ethnically diverse, unevenly developed, infant federation led to the evolution of socialist self-management, which ultimately became another contributory factor in the collapse of Yugoslavia.

Initially the Federal People's Republic of Yugoslavia (formed on 31 January 1946, re-named Socialist Federal Republic of Yugoslavia in April 1963) adopted a Stalinist model of central planning, rapid industrialisation and the total subordination to the hegemony of the Communist Party, despite some distinctions among individual republic's party organisations. In the late 1940's the commitment to collectivisation and long term planning in Yugoslavia preceded other communist-led countries, due to the revolutionary ardour and Tito's hold over his regime. The legacy of patriotism - the founding myth of the Communist Party's control - finally caused the break with the Soviet Union, after the latter's growing demands for subordination to Moscow. The expulsion of Yugoslavia from the Cominform (1948) not only magnified Tito's cult status, but forced the Party to seek different ways of legitimising its position, independently of the Soviet Union[21], which led to the greater involvement with the post-colonial world, and more dependence on the economic help from the West.

## Socialist Self-Management

The repressive measures of the late 1940s left the Party alienated whilst facing an economic crisis. In order to re-instate the legitimacy of the regime which was the only thing that all Yugoslavs had in common, the Party (in 1952 renamed the League of Communists, LCY) decided on a radical political and economic project. The legitimacy was based on the idea of 'double autonomy', that is of working people and nations, thus a self-managing society. In theory it involved 'de-etatisation' in the economic sphere by worker self-management and decentralisation in territorial terms through republic and communal self-management; in practice it amounted to the eventual break-down of the state authority. The irony is that the ideology designed especially to strengthen the federation was in the end the undoing of it.

The principle of breaking up the centralised structure stemmed from the 'withering away of the state' theory and was presented in its most positive meaning. Namely, 'the building up of another, different institutional system which would take over the performing of the functions necessary to the society, i.e. the functions which were formerly performed by the state', thus 'narrowing the conditions of a power being independent of society'[22]. The theme of direct participation and worker's control is well known in the socialist tradition and we can assume that Lenin's slogan 'all power to Soviets' was in its inception based on the same idea. The real power wielded by workers through the instruments of self-management would put Yugoslavia closer than other communist regimes to the 'dictatorship of proletariat', or what Lenin called a workers' state, an idea very appealing in the times of quarrel with Stalin and as a counterargument against criticism from orthodox Marxists.

The system of self-management was very complex and subject to many modifications during the four decades of its existence. Here I shall confine myself to the briefest of descriptions of its workings and failings, and to the influence self-management had on the perception of democracy in Slovenia. The economic reforms began in 1950 with the law that turned over the management of state firms and social services to worker's councils[23], initially more consultative than decision making bodies. Later, the enterprises planned their production, investment and wage administration; salaries were dependent on each worker's contribution and on the success of the enterprise as the whole. After 1961 workers decided how profits were to be divided within the salary fund and the accumulation fund, which after 1954 was owned by the enterprise. This resulted in the maximisation of wages out of profits, very high borrowing in order to finance accumulation and in the considerable decrease in the influence of the central state.

Decentralisation and 'de-etatisation' had contradictory results. The coordinating mechanisms between individual economic and political units either did not exist or were never established; they were filled by the Communist Party[24]. Because the economic reforms led to demands for further political democracy and decentralisation, the federal state allowed republics to gain more power and party rule became simply perpetuated on the lower territorial level, whilst self-management remained the instrument of the Party. The reduced power of the federal economic authority meant that the control over the allocation of investments was transferred to the republics, the individual enterprises and banks. If we now realise that Yugoslavia had become, in fact, a federation of eight competing economies[25], which together produced more than they earned, imported the raw materials for their industries without exploiting their own resources and borrowed heavily to the point when the central state had no control of the extent of it, we can understand what was meant by the 'Yugoslav disease'[26].

The result was the increased power of the establishment at local and republic level (the Party, banks and managers), low economic performance and conflicts between regions, so new reforms followed between 1971-1976. All economic reforms were matched by reforms in nationalities policies and led to the ever-increased autonomy of the republics. This final stage in the evolution of self-management (called 'contractual socialism') was double-layered. At the political level representative democracy was replaced by a complex system of delegational direct democracy and multi-chamber legislature at local, republic and federal levels. At the economic level it involved a further break down of enterprises into smaller units, each of which represented an integral part of work activity. The whole enterprise became thus a form of associated labour of two or more smaller units set up under the self-management agreement. The enterprises which shared production or other interests also could associate under those agreements into 'composite organisations of associated labour'. The idea behind this was to give the workers, down to the smallest unit, more control over decision-making and also, to replace the hardship caused by the market with more 'self-management agreement', so that all matters could be resolve through negotiation and agreement. Moreover, the public services were organised into self-managing 'communities of interest' whose main task was to provide a direct link between the suppliers and the users of the public services. The 'withered away' state reached, at least in theory, the highest point of autonomy of workers and citizens, realising the democratisation of economic decision making and the autonomy of nations and provinces.

However, the party thus divided into republic organisations controlled the selection process of delegates and became practically unconstrained in determining economic policy, due to the latest reforms becoming even more sheltered from the logic of the market. The state lost all control over monetary policy, which led to a rapid monetary expansion and uncontrolled inflation, exacerbated by the foreign debt (20 billion $ US in 1980, the time of slowing economies world-wide). The foreign borrowing which was much increased during the last two years of Tito's life[27], was used to quell ethnic unrest in disadvantaged regions in the time of political uncertainty. By 1989 inflation had risen to 3000% and the Yugoslav political and economic system was in severe crisis.

*Self-management in Slovene experience*[28]   In the Slovenian Public Opinion survey about the evaluation of the implementation of self-management (1978-1986) in response to the question 'is the situation better today, about the same, or worse than five years ago?', the 'better' answer decreased from 80.1% in 1978 to 18.8% in 1986, which would indicate that Slovenia had lost faith in the system of self-management. However, the idea of self-management remains well thought of among the majority of the Slovene population - in 1995 two-thirds of the public viewed it as a well conceived idea which was not put into practice effectively[29]. Despite the fact that Slovenes wholeheartedly supported the destruction of the system and reject its reinstitution, there is some logic in the positive evaluation, beside the fact that the founding theoretician and ideologue of the Yugoslav self-management system was Edvard Kardelj, a Slovene still considered an important figure in national mythology.

Historically there are various concepts of self-management, the Paris Commune, the Israeli kibbutz, the early workers councils in Soviet Russia and diverse forms of participation in industrial management in Western Europe spring to mind. The distinguishing characteristic of the Yugoslav system is that unlike others it was imposed from above, thus its ideological function of legitimising the rule of the Communist Party became paramount. When in the later years the Party was faced with the choice between liberalisation of the economy and political pluralisation which evolved out of the system, the Party chose to combat these tendencies by reconstituting self-management (1974) as primarily an ideological project in order to preserve the existing power relations. The authors, in particular Kardelj, emphasised corporatism in the form of 'interest communities'[30]; the 'pluralism of self-management interests', a concept which stood for controlled pluralism; a delegate system with some elements of direct democracy and the increased autonomy of the republics[31]. The rhetoric however did not correspond with practice and the concepts were not applied in reality, so that the highest levels of governing bodies were composed exclusively of the LCY members.

Slovenes took self-management seriously[32], but at the same time became critical of the situation in Yugoslavia and believed that the power of the state should be strengthened (in 1986 61.1% of respondents in Slovenia agreed that: 'a strong arm that knows what it wants would be of more use to our society than all the slogans about self-management'), which is surprising considering that Slovenes were the champions of de-centralisation and the freedom of individual[33].

It may therefore be legitimately concluded that Slovenes considered the system of self-management a failure as implemented by the LCY, not as an idea[34], and that the introduction of a multiparty system at the beginning of the 1990s (and ensuing independence) was the realisation of certain ideas, such as individual freedom, the participation of the majority of the population in decision-making and pluralism that Slovenes believed self-management contained. This explains why whilst rejecting the system that embodied self-management, the idea is still valued positively.

The importance of participation and the freedom of choice remain the defining characteristics of Slovene political thinking and were at the heart of the transition to democracy. Considering that a high level of public participation in decision-making process and a great degree of pluralism were achieved under the system of self-management, however limited, this meant that a certain level of democratisation, higher than in other postcommunist countries, was achieved prior to transition to pluralist democracy. More importantly, the Slovene public was also more aware of what participation and pluralism entailed, and equally aware of the limits that the Yugoslav federation imposed on the continuation of the democratisation process.

The reason lay in the system itself. The dichotomy between rhetoric and the reality, similar to other communist regimes, caused the accumulation of economic and political problems under whose weight the state was collapsing. The supporting pillars - Tito, the nations and their will to unite, and the ideology - which the federation was resting on, were either no longer there or lost their credibility. The increased threat of disintegration led to an increased pressure for centralisation, for which it was too late. The devolution of power to the republics, resentment towards

Belgrade and the already achieved democratisation, certainly in Slovenia and Croatia, combined with the divergent levels of economic and political development, could not be reversed. The nationality policy of the Yugoslav federation had an unintended effect (similar to the USSR) - nations turned to their own policies without regard for the federation.

## Failed Federalism

> The irony of history today is, that the measures whose political goal without question was to guard totalitarianism, unwittingly created legal and political conditions for Slovenia as an independent state[35].

Yugoslavia's most important, long-lasting and most influential characteristic is probably that it is a multinational community[36], in the words of an expert on the political system in Yugoslavia in 1979. This statement is somewhat poignant today, when a word 'long-lasting' brings into one's mind the tragic consequences of the disintegration of that multinational community.

Having a nationality policy meant that Yugoslavs considered the multiethnic composition of their state a potential problem and therefore the involvement of the Communist Party in that sphere was considered legitimate. The federal system with a wide degree of autonomy given to the republics had to be designed so that it could be justified by the ruling ideology and Yugoslavs claimed to have solved the 'national question' by defusing and containing nationalism through the political system based on mutual accommodation and cooperation. Had Yugoslavs succeeded, and the Kosovo riots of 1981 showed that even the most tentative assertions about the success of nationality policies were losing credibility, their model would have been worth emulating, for it suggested that Yugoslavia had created a political organisation able to contain nationalist mobilisation. Moreover, it would have suggested that only a certain type of socialism would provide the conditions for inter ethnic harmony. To Yugoslavs the 'working class was still national'[37], as opposed to the much-quoted dictum of Marx and Engels that 'the worker has no country'.

*Nationalities*

Nationality seen as an important factor in the consciousness of the working class comes very near to the Austro-Marxists' ideas, mainly Karl Renner and Otto Bauer[38]. Writing at the turn of the century in Vienna they sought to resolve the dilemma of socialists in the Empire - the continuation of the

Empire, rife with nationalist tensions, and the continuation of socialist politics, uninterrupted by those tensions. The solution was the distinction between nation as a 'spiritual and cultural community' (Renner) with the emphasis on language, and the state which would guarantee the cultural autonomy for peoples 'bound into community of character by a common destiny' (Bauer). To the Austro-Marxists national consciousness was primarily a matter of culture, which would thus be satisfied by cultural autonomy, whilst the potentially disintegrative administrative and political autonomy would be left to a supranational state. The bourgeoisie then could not hide behind the national antagonisms and manipulate working and peasant classes.

Particularly in Slovenia (and Croatia) the idea of intertwined nationalism and communism into one theme (national communists) goes back to the tradition of Social Democracy of the beginning of the century and the strong influence of Austro-Marxists on that movement[39]. In 1909 at the conference of the Slovene Social Democratic Party one of the most important guests was K.Renner, who expressed a vision that a united Yugoslav nation would 'easily become a powerful member in the chain of socialist nations'[40]. The Social-Democratic movement in Slovenia was inspired by Ivan Cankar (a leading figure in Slovene national history), who claimed that the struggle for 'social demands is nearly identical with national struggle' and that the 'Slovene nation is a nation of proletariat'. This claim was supported by the fact that the majority of the Slovene workforce (100 000 at that time) were Slovenes, whilst capital was foreign (90%)[41]. Cankar's ideas about the Slovene nation in connection to Yugoslavia are noteworthy in view of events that followed and show him to be a visionary. He saw Yugoslavia as a purely political decision and rejected all notions of a 'united Yugoslav nation consisting of three "tribes"', Slovenes, Serbs and Croats, popular at that time among many intellectuals. He noted:

> by blood we are brothers; by language we are cousins, by culture, which is the fruit of the separate upbringing, there, we are more foreign to one another, than one of our Upper Carniolan peasants to a Tyrolean[42].

Therefore, the state that such culturally diverse people would form would have to be a federal republic, if the people so wished, and would have to reflect the ethnic, social, economic and cultural differences. In 1913 Cankar was convinced that 'such a settlement of the Yugoslav question' would be 'a utopia', but nevertheless he maintained that 'utopias have a peculiar way of coming true'[43]. My concern here is more with utopias when they stop coming true, which they also have a way of doing.

*Federalism*

The early critique (1946) of centralism was directed at the economic policies, particularly on the part of the Slovene political elites. The policies intended to modernise and industrialise insisted on 'generous and active' [44] support by the more industrialised regions for those less developed areas. Slovenia as the most industrialised region had in this sense special obligations to the rest of Yugoslavia. The public debate on centralism and the national question, after being initially suppressed in the 1950s, soon showed that the pre-war prejudices and national concerns were not overcome. It was Edvard Kardelj[45], who was to remain on the forefront of the Party's ideology and constitutional policies until his death in 1979, who acknowledged the continuing relevance of the national issues, but saw them as the 'remnants of bourgeois nationalism', combined with the uneven development of the regions within Yugoslavia and the bureaucratic-centralist tendencies at the top. In his belief, the dilemma of Yugoslavia was to be tackled by socialist forces which would acknowledge the equal rights of all its peoples and thus provide foundations for 'patriotic consciousness'[46].

Post-war Yugoslavia was not just one idea, that of uniting Southern Slavs in one state, but became many ideas and it would be misleading to blame ideas alone, particularly with the luxury of hindsight, for the destruction of Yugoslavia; the execution of those ideas and the concrete policies they inspired is a more likely culprit. Whilst it is reasonable to criticise the Communist regime in 1945 for not having resolved the national polarisation left by the previous Kingdom of Yugoslavia, but merely bury it under slogans in the hope that they would come true, it is unreasonable in the extreme to blame the Communists for instigating ethnic antagonisms of the later years[47]. The newly formed state, traumatised by the war and isolated from the West by its regime and from the East by the split with Moscow, had to find its own way of remaining Communist, open to the West and modernising. Thus, a cooperative federation, 'a socialist, self-managing community of nations' would introduce 'essentially new category in interethnic relations'[48]. No amount of rhetoric could however stop the incessant wheel of transformation that the system had unwittingly built into its own mechanisms of functioning.

The focal arena of inter-republic cooperation (and controversies) was the Federal Assembly – Skupščina (Slovene, Skupština in Serbo-Croat), in particular the Chamber of Republics and Provinces, which was responsible for the federation. The role of this body was significantly enhanced with every constitution. Whilst in 1946 (called the Chamber of Nationalities), it had no decision-making power, in 1953, consistent with the ideology of the centralised state that would eventually disappear, it was replaced by the Federal Chamber and the Chamber of Producers. The 1963 Constitution, reflecting the struggles between the rising nationalist and the centralist forces, gave the Chamber (this time round called the Chamber of Delegates of the Republics and the Provinces) the basic responsibility for legislation. In 1967 Kosovo and Vojvodina became represented by their own delegations, rather than through the Serbian one. By 1971 the agreement of the federal units was necessary before Skupščina could pass any all-Yugoslav social or economic plans. According to the 1974 Constitution, the Chamber with the assent of republican and provincial assemblies passed laws, such as: social plan; monetary and foreign trade policy, including the fund for the rapid development of the underdeveloped regions; international agreements, that would require alterations in the regional legislations; agreement on federal funds. Autonomously it determined expenditures on national defence and state security, mediated in conflicts of jurisdiction between federal, republican and provincial organs and approved the extension of mandates of delegates in Skupščina.

The delegates were chosen by the republican and provincial assemblies and reserved their seats at those bodies whilst they were serving at the centre. In practice each delegation functioned as a 'bloc' and adhered to policies determined at the home base, i.e. the republic or the province. Whilst each delegation could propose new legislation, each piece of legislation required the unanimity of votes, which led to lengthy negotiations and the formation of alliances. In that sense the federation did rely on the cooperation between federal units, and the Chamber provided the arena for national concerns to be voiced and resolved.

The strong and unified position of federal units was replicated in the second house of the Yugoslav Assembly, the less effective Federal Chamber, which consisted of the representatives of self-managing and socio-political organisations, but carried out its decisions by majority voting, whilst each delegation wanted to veto any undesired decision. Finally, the system created a state presidency, which after Tito's death functioned as the executive (one delegate and vote per federal unit) and rotated annually in the 'president of presidency'; again the delegates were elected by their federal units to which they were responsible. In fact, not even the executive head of an already complicated apparatus presented the common vision for the common state. In 1990 Milošević, having reduced Vojvodina, Montenegro and Kosovo to mere satellites, held four out of eight votes in the presidency and could thus block any decision. This was not the reason why Yugoslavia ceased to function, but a symptom of what it had become.

## Political Disintegration of Yugoslavia

The interests of the federation were more often than not subordinated to the interests of the republics and the provinces, which indeed wielded considerable power and behaved according to their own national interests. There were many reasons for the 'national' character of each unit's leadership. The Party itself was organised along national, or ethnic lines. In 1969 the central committee of the Party was abolished and the unity of the Party relied almost exclusively on the personality of Tito. Moreover, each of the eight party organisations held their own congress, scheduled before the LCY congresses and indicating that the national organisations did more than merely approve the policies. In 1990 the LCS (the League of Communists of Slovenia) seceded from the LCY (immediately followed by the Croats), renamed itself the Party of Democratic Renewal and abrogated all obligations, including the financial ones to the LCY. By then the LCY was in an advanced state of decay, accelerated by the fusion of the Serbian Communists with the local 'Socialist Alliance' and the subsequent election of Slobodan Milošević as their leader.The real decision-making emanated from the regions rather than from the centre, whereby all conflicts deriving from the incredible diversity of the periphery were translated into 'nationally relevant conflicts of interests'[49], for the lack of any other category in which they could be expressed in an ideologically uniform communist system. Despite the external decentralisation the Party continued to function in a hierarchical and centralist manner, revealing the inconsistency between the national and political concept of Yugoslavia.

The social, economic and political problems led to national antagonisms which the Party was incapable of resolving. Meanwhile the huge foreign debt crippled the country and the Party called for each republic to help to pay regardless of how much of the debt each republic had incurred. This measure constituted a great burden for the successful export-orientated Slovenia, and became a source of loudly voiced discontent in those republics.

When discussing the collapse of Yugoslavia, it is paramount that the economic considerations are not overshadowed by ethnic and political considerations too overwhelmingly, for it would distort the fact that nationalism is usually an answer, a symptom of a development, which if not rooted in economy, certainly in tandem with it. The deep social and political crisis of the early 1980's was a result of Tito's death, the rise of oil prices and the tightening of the world's economy[50], to all of which Yugoslavia could no longer find an answer - the adaptation and reevaluation of Marxism had exhausted the whole repertoire and could not find a new direction. This time radical economic reform would have to be accompanied by political reform, of a much deeper character than a cosmetic reformulation of the long rehearsed phrases. It would have required a separation of political and economic powers, but politics did not allow for such changes.

Long before the political disintegration the country stopped functioning as an economically viable whole. Republics printed their own money, taxes were not collected, the republics engaged in autarkic economic policies to the detriment of the federation and built up their own systems. In the mid-eighties the party tried to restore its dwindling authority by calling for more centralisation in the educational, scientific and cultural fields which were very sensitive issues for Slovenia.

Belgrade and Ljubljana had less and less in common, each claiming defensive nationalism, the former preaching a strong Yugoslavia (or rather strong Serbia in a strong Yugoslavia), the latter rejecting its eternal role of an autonomous minority. The split between the centralist Serbian camp and the more autonomist Slovenia-led one, already manifested in the Kosovo riots in 1981, became deeper. Not for the first time in modern history the answer to the political and economic crisis became nationalism. This spelled an inevitable disintegration of the state in which all differences, whether they were the cultural, economic, structural, political or ideological, were linked to national/territorial frameworks, but in which nationalism and democracy were both denied.

Miha Kovač, the editor of the Socialist Youth Alliance oppositional journal *Mladina*[51](1988), explained that to understand the evolution of the political and cultural life in Slovenia, referred to as the 'Slovenian spring', one must go back to the 1970s. The emergence of a nationalist current within a broader context of a mass movement in Croatia was used as a pretext not just to crush nationalists themselves, but also to suppress the student movements and the liberal wing of the party who tried at that time to establish a market economy and liberalise political life, firstly in Croatia and later everywhere else. In Kovač's words:

> As the democratic upsurge ended, the nationalisms or local interests of Yugoslavia's six republics and two autonomous provinces became a kind of surrogate for all other political identities. You could be active within the existing political structure only on the basis of defending the interests of your republic or province. Thus, the system which had supposedly emerged through the defeat of Croat and other nationalisms turned out to be itself most conducive to nationalism. Nationalism is produced within the very structure of the Yugoslav system, its main root cause being the lack of institutionalised democracy[52].

The bureaucracy, the League of Communists, was exactly that, a League, not a monolithic apparatus of power, but a 'web made up of different national factions which - however resounding their clashes may appear - are never in a truly antagonistic relationship to one another'[53]. Retrospectively Kovač was wrong when he said that. As transpired later, the Slovene leadership embraced reforms and became very antagonistic to the Serbian leadership, but he was absolutely right claiming that 'without democratisation, there is no future for Yugoslavia'[54]. The consequence was that the regime's transformation could only proceed as a part of the national struggle for independence[55].

Independence or secession from a multinational federation is often the only way to make a clear political statement about the intended direction of political developments and how to differentiate one's republic from others. Slovakia distanced itself from the Czech Republic because its conception of the democratisation process was too different and Slovenia, equally so, by declaring its independence distanced itself from Serbian politics for ever. Kučan after he became the President in the first multi-party elections (1990) and talked of 'Slovenia's right to self-determination in a non-disruptive manner', stated also that 'in a way the election results are a demonstration of the criticism of Serbia'[56].

## Conclusion

The main reasons for the disintegration of Yugoslavia were rather paradoxical on at least three accounts. First, the measures taken to guarantee the cultural differences created a federation along national/ethnic lines with a strong autonomist legislation for the republics and provinces, which nevertheless saw the cultural autonomy as a substitute for a political one. The more classical theories of nationalism tell us that there is a certain trajectory of national awareness and that the rising awareness, particularly in combination with the divergent levels of development, which can be translated into national conflicts, will lead to demands for political independence[57].

Second, the strong emphasis on the differences was in constant tension with centralist ideology, which was never comfortable with the nationalities issue. The system considered nationalism an enemy, it linked the Party to the integrity of the state, so that to be anti-Party was equated with the nationalist movement. Such indiscriminate use of nationalist labels in combination with the growing power of federal elites induced many anti-Party activities to be labelled as nationalist movements. When the Party and the state it represented lost the affiliation of the greater part of the populations, in the multi-party elections in 1990, which preceded all Yugoslav elections, all opposition forces to the Party presented themselves as democratising national movements[58].

Finally, drastically different levels of development, ideologically on elite levels and economically at the federal level and within the federal units led to a situation which could not be brought to a final resolution within one-party rule. By the late 1980's certainly in Slovenia the 'peoples' democracy was no longer perceived as democracy as Tine Hribar stated in a seminal issue of *Nova Revija:*

> people's democracy, thus people's government is not authority of people as such, but the authority of the proletariat, in the forefront of which is the Party. Therefore, people's authority, as strictly people's democracy, actually does not mean anything else, but democracy in which the Party took the possession of authority[59].

## Notes

[1] Slovenia comprises some 20 000 km$^2$ and has a population of 2 million. For history see: J.Prunk *A Brief History of Slovenia* Ljubljana, Založba Grad 1996; J.Benderly and E.Kraft *Independent Slovenia* London, Macmillan Press 1997; L.Cohen *Broken Bonds* Oxford, Westview Press 1996.

[2] The Yugoslav federation and its political system were initially based on the Soviet model. The introduction of 'self-management' in the 1950's brought changes in the official rhetoric and ideology and set Yugoslavia on the separate path to the rest of the communist bloc.

[3] The process started in 1988 and was meant to harmonise the increasing democratisation in Slovenia with the Federal Constitution. Among hundred amendments that the Slovene parliament adopted the most important were: the introduction of the political pluralism (Amendment IX) and the reconfirmation of the right to self-determination of the Slovene nation (Amendment X) and intensive economic and social reforms. See M.Žagar 'The Constitution of the Republic of Slovenia' in D.Fink-Hafner and T.Cox ed. *Into Europe? Perspectives from Britain and Slovenia* Ljubljana, Scientific Library of Faculty of Social Sciences 1996, henceforth D.Fink-Hafner and T.Cox (1996).

[4] Held on 23 December 1990 whereby the overwhelming majority of voters (88.2%) voted for independence (electoral turnout 93.2%).

[5] In the case of Yugoslavia it is absolutely essential to recognise the immensely turbulent history of the region and the resulting complex mix of cultures, civilisations, religions, languages and peoples. The influence of these differences resulted in very divergent levels of economic, social, cultural and ultimately political developments in the different parts of the former Yugoslavia.

[6] M.Hafner-Fink 'Changing Social Structure in the Process of Transition from Socialism: the Case of Slovenia' paper prepared for the 68th Annual Pacific Sociological Association meeting San Diego, California, April 17-20,1997 p.2, henceforth M.Hafner 1997.

[7] R.Rizman 'Slovenia' in H.Neuhold, P.Havlik and A.Suppan *Political and Economic Transformation in East Central Europe* Boulder (USA), Summertown (UK), Westview Press 1995 p.57, henceforth *Political and Economic Transformation.*

[8] T.Hribar 'Slovenska državnost' in *Nova Revija* VI:57 a seminal issue of this very important journal around which the Slovenian intelligentsia concentrated throughout the late 1980's, dedicated to national program (Prispevki za Slovenski Nacionalni Program) Ljubljana 1987 p.29 All translations throughout are by myself.

[9] Interview 5 May 1998 Igor Lukšic.

[10] All interviews were conducted 21 April - 14 May1998 in Ljubljana, see Appendix 2 at the end of the book.

[11] Notable exception being prof. I.Bernik: 'All is circumstantial, Slovenes are the same as everyone else, if they were offered a state during the war as the Croats and Slovaks did, they would have behaved in the same way. The prime legitimacy in Slovenia is ethnic, as it is everywhere else. But, Slovenes had many advantages'. The 'circumstantiality' behind the Slovenian 'success' is part of the argument of this chapter.

[12] S. Gaber (one -time Minister of Education, the activist of the ex-Socialist Youth) 8 May 1998 'the independence was the culmination of democratisation, which started in 1981, but it is not true that independence was an integral part of that process at the beginning'.

[13] T.Kuzmanić, (Peace Institute), political activist of the 1980's 13 May 1998.

[14] L.Kreft (academic, the vice-Chairman of the National Assembly 1991-1994) 4 May 1998.

[15] S.Ramet *Nationalism and Federalism in Yugoslavia 1962-1991* Bloomington and Indianapolis, Indiana University Press 1992 p.38.

[16] See B.Denitch *The Legitimation of a Revolution: The Yugoslav Case* New Haven, London, Yale University Press 1976.

[17] For the discussion of the variations and characteristics of different types of non-democratic regimes see J.Linz A Stepan  *Problems of Democractic Transition and Consolidation.*

[18] S.Pavlowitch *The Improbable Survivor* London, C.Hurst & Company 1988 p.15.

[19] B.Ferfila P.Philips 'Nationalism, the State and Economic Restructuring: Slovenia and the Former Yugoslavia' in *Small States Compared: Politics of Norway and Slovenia* Bergen (Norway), Alma Mater 1994 p.31.

[20] For example Tito had promised Slovene partisans that they would be able to keep their own army with Slovene as the commanding language, but that promise was never fulfilled.

[21] M.Glenny *The Balkans 1804-1999* London, Granta Books 1999 p.572- 575.

[22] R.Ratkovic 'Socio-Political Communities in Yugoslavia - The Process of Self-Management Socialization of State Power' in *Socialism in Yugoslav Theory and Practice* Collection of Conferences Beograd, International University Centre for Social Sciences 1979 pp.113-119 p.116-118. Henceforth *Socialism in Yugoslav Theory and Practice.*

[23] The following section draws heavily from the B.Ferfila and P.Philips 'Nationalism, the State and Economic Restructuring' in *Small States Compared.*

[24] I was reminded by Prof. Rizman that due to the developments described here, it was not incidental that the first call for democratisation and political pluralism in the post-1948 communist world came from the member of Tito's 'triumvirate' M.Djilas *The New Class* London, Thames and Hudson 1958, who was later imprisoned for many years. The other member was the Slovene E.Kardelj, of whom more below.

[25] Republics: Slovenia, Croatia, Bosnia and Herzegovina, Serbia, Montenegro, Macedonia; autonomous provinces: Vojvodina and Kosovo.

[26] B.Ferfila and P.Philips (1994) p.33.

[27] Tito died 4 May 1980.

[28] All statistics from M.Hafner-Fink '(Trans)formation of the Idea of Self-Management: Slovenian Perspectives' Paper prepared for the 5th Conference of the International

Society for the Study of European Ideas 19-24 August 1996, Utrecht, Netherlands. Hence forth M.Hafner-Fink (1996).

[29] The longitudinal research project Slovenian Public Opinion has been ongoing since 1968 and covers a representative sample of adult residents of Slovenia. The project is conducted by the Centre for Public Opinion and Mass Media Research of the Faculty of Social Sciences in Ljubljana, led by Niko Toš.

[30] For the discussion of Slovene neo-corporatism and the utilisation of that concept in contemporary politics see the following chapter.

[31] M.Hafner-Fink (1996) p.4.

[32] In 1980 45% of the respondents asked about self-management responded that 'workers decide about everything themselves' and linked it to democracy. In the 1982 survey 68.5% agreed that 'self-management enables the exercise of human freedoms and creativity'. M.Hafner-Fink (1996).

[33] Survey June 1986-87 (Class, Structure of Contemporary Yugoslav Society, Toš 1989) about attitudes towards the state 73% agree that 'respect for individual freedom is more important than any state interest' (Serbia 57%, Croatia 66%, Macedonia 45.7%, Bosnia Herzegovina 64.4%, Montenegro 61%, Kosovo 63.2%, Vojvodina 63%).

[34] This would correspond with the general disenchantment with LCY. According to M.Hafner-Fink, in 1988 apparently only 4% of the respondents in the survey believed that the Communist Party has society at interest, whilst in 1990 this figure increased to 37% - the difference is significant, because whilst in 1988 the question referred to LCY, in 1990 it referred to LCS (League of Communists Slovenia).

[35] S.Žižek 'Tretja pot med univerzalismom in fundamentalizmom' in D.Rupel ed. *Slovenska Smer* Ljubljana Cankarjeva Založba 1996 p.95.

[36] D.Bilandzić 'History and Current Dimensions of Inter-Nationality Relations in Yugoslavia' in *Socialism in Yugoslav Theory and Practice* p.129.

[37] Stipe Šuvar, cited in S.Ramet *Nationalism and Federalism* p.42.

[38] See: P.Goode and T.Bottomore *Austro-Marxism* Oxford, Clarendon Press 1978; M.E.Blum *The Austro-Marxism 1890-1918* Lexington KY, University of Kentucky 1985 and J.Schwarzmantel *Socialism and the Idea of the Nation* New York, London, Harvester Wheatsheaf 1991.

[39] In conversation with Lev Kreft, 4 May 1998.

[40] M.Zver *100 Let Social-Demokracije* Ljubljana, Veda d.o.o. 1996 p.32.

[41] M.Zver *100 Let Social-Demokracije* p.33.

[42] M.Zver *100 Let Social-Demokracije* p.37.

[43] P.Vodopivec 'Seven Decades of Unconfronted Incongruities: The Slovenes and Yugoslavia' in J.Benderly E.Kraft *Independent Slovenia Origins, Movements, Prospects* London, MacMillan Press 1997 p.25. Henceforth P.Vodopivec.

[44] P.Vodopivec p.36.

[45] For a more detailed account of Kardelj's version of Marxism see extract from his book 'Democracy and Socialism' reprinted in D.McLellan *Marxism Essential Writings* Oxford, Oxford University Press 1988.

[46] P.Vodopivec in *Independent Slovenia* p.37.

[47] P.Vodopivec in *Independent Slovenia* p.26.

[48] Kardelj cited in S.Ramet *Nationalism and Federalism in Yugoslavia* p.63.

[49] The expression is borrowed from M.Hroch who used it as an explanation for the rise of nationalist movements in the 19th century Central Europe, where the absolutist oppression did not allow for more developed political discourse or argument, so that it became easier to articulate social problems in national categories. It is my belief that the analogy between the multinational Habsburg Empire and the multinational Yugoslavia

can be made on many levels and therefore the use of the expression is justified. See M.Hroch 'From National Movement to the Fully-formed Nation' in *New Left Review 198* March/April 1993 pp.3-20.

[50] J.Mencinger 'The Costs and Benefits of Secession' in D. Fink-Hafner and J. Robbins *Making a New Nation:The Formation of Slovenia* Aldershot, Dartmouth 1997.

[51] In the 1980's new ideological currents, searching for answers to ever more apparent political and economic crisis in Yugoslavia gathered round various new journals. The so-called structuralists (influenced by Michal Foucault) produced the journal 'Problemi'; the Marxist-orientated political economists' journal 'Časopis za kritiko znamosti'; the traditional intellectuals who saw themselves as defenders of the Slovene nation and its cultural heritage wrote for what became a very influential journal in voicing 'national' issues 'Nova Revija' and 'Mladina' which embraced the young socialists and the alternative cultural scene and disagreed with either dissident, or national orientations.

[52] M.Kovač 'The Slovene Spring' in *New Left Review* 171 September/October 1988 pp.115-128 p.115.

[53] M.Kovač p.119.

[54] M.Kovač p.127.

[55] D.Fink-Hafner 'The Disintegration of Yugoslavia' in *Canadaian Slavonic Papers* XXXVII:3-4 September/December 1995 pp.339-352 p.344.

[56] Cited in L.Cohen *Broken Bonds* Boulder, Oxford, Westview Press 1993 p.94.

[57] See M.Hroch 'National Self-determination from a Historic Perspective in *Canadian Slavonic Papers* 37:4 September/December 1995 pp.283-300, the same author in the above mentioned 'From National Movements to the Fully-Formed Nation' in *New Left Review* 198 and T.Nairn 'The Modern Janus' *New Left Review* 94 November/December 1975 pp.3-31.

[58] For the relevance of electoral sequences, that is, all-union elections prior to or after the regional elections as a way of dissolving or constructing all-union identity in the country facing stateness problem, see J.Linz and A.Stepan 'Political Identities and Electoral Sequences' in *Daedalus* 121:2 Spring 1992 pp.123-139. The authors explain, taking Spain, the Soviet Union and Yugoslavia as examples, that if all-union elections are held first (Spain), there are strong incentives for political activists to create all-union parties, and all-union agendas which can make or break the multinational polity. In the case of Yugoslavia I would say that the republican elections were only a contributory factor to the final stage of the disintegration that was in an advanced state anyway. The Czecho-Slovak split does not fit this model, because the all-state elections brought the victory to parties with a strong 'national' emphasis which then proceeded to press constitutional issues until the break-up, which was elite-led.

[59] T.Hribar as above in *Nova Revija* VI:57 p.21.

# 6 Independence and Democracy in Slovenia

We demand the right to self-determination, the right to democracy and independence which has already been granted to other European nations. We are able to constitute our own state, with all the attributes that belong to a democratic and open society. We legally confirmed this on June 25th with our Declaration of Independence. Alas, many lives have been sacrificed for independence in the past few days[1].

Only a sovereign nation* can give up a part of its sovereignty in a sovereign way and transfer to a transnational community[2].

Slovenia's independent status might have been born out of a nationalist endeavour, but true independence is more than autonomy of a particular nation. It is the independence to choose the institutional and social values of a new modern state opened to the advanced world. As for the role of nationalism in this process, the following case study of Slovenia suggests that the tension between nationalism and democracy can be managed more successfully than in Slovakia. There is little doubt that Slovenia, expected to join the first wave of the EU's expansion to the East, two consecutive governing coalitions comprising ideological adversaries able to adjust their different interests, and the high standard of the constitutionally guaranteed rights and protection of ethnic minorities, can be assessed as a successful transition to democracy. Moreover, there is little evidence to suggest that the present achievements could be eroded or that expectations of the regime's continuity are unrealistic[3].

Having discussed the concept and the character of the Yugoslav federation and the general conflicts and problems that led to its disintegration, I have tried to portray the starting position from which Slovenia embarked on the course of independence and democracy. The narrative of events prior to actual independence which follows in the first part of this chapter, will provide the basis for the main theme of this chapter: the evolving dynamic between transition, nationalism and democracy, with the purpose of drawing some general conclusions about that relationship.

The general thesis of this chapter is that the transition in Slovenia rested on a broad consensus about vital issues of national interest and commitment to democracy, thus that the processes of transition and independence were not subjected to pursuits of various alternatives. Proceeding on this assumption, the third part, after the analysis of the Slovenian political system, will address itself to the crucial link between legitimacy and nationalism in democratisation processes.

One of the safest methods to measure the progress of democratisation and judge the role of nationalism in that process is to look at the position of minorities. Thus, the chapter finishes with the constitutional protection of minorities, which in Slovenia, unlike in Slovakia can withstand the strictest of scrutiny. The conclusion, whilst assessing the role of the previous regime on transition and the role of nationalism in the democratisation process, will argue that in Slovenia both have been relatively positive.

Nationalism and democracy, certainly at the beginning of the democratisation process, formed a complementary dynamic and were largely conducive to each other's aspirations. The transition process, however tentative, having been ongoing for some time prior to the end of communism rested on a wide support of the population and nationalism reinforced it.

## Defending Democracy and the Nation: 1987-1991[4]

The previous chapter showed Slovenia as an increasingly disillusioned and uncomfortable partner in the Yugoslav federation, seeking its own way, parallel to the increasing economic and political malaise of the federation. From Slovenia's perspective, to continue the status quo was tantamount to 'national suicide'[5] for various reasons. The federation was destroying the Slovenian economy and showing less and less regard for Slovenian culture and constitutional arrangements; moreover, the Slovene leaders were repeatedly unsuccessful in influencing the federal government to bring about meaningful changes. As sketched above the federal government became a 'squabbling shop', where deals for each republic were brokered (this is if they bothered to tell the centre of the full extent of the deals they brokered elsewhere) and where decentralisation had gone so far that the implementation of any reforms, or, what by the late 1980s were mostly the recovery packages, became immobilised by the arithmetic of the alliances formed and enforced.

All the supposed achievements of self-management, presented as the most advanced economic system, became undermined by the 20 billion US$ external debt. Claims that workers had complete power over the distribution of surplus proved to be false as well - most enterprises no longer produced any surplus. If the founding myth of Yugoslavia and the Party was the 'external enemy', whether Moscow, or previously the expansionist West, Italy taking Trieste, Bulgaria concerning Macedonia etc., therefore justifying unity which implied the Serbian patronage over the small nations, the public opinion polls (1991) in Slovenia revealed that the perceived external threat came now from Serbia[6]

It must be stressed that the initiation of democratic changes in Slovenia was not expressed in nationalist language[7]. The need for change did not constitute a struggle against authoritarian power in the republic (the last decade was relatively prosperous and in political terms relatively tolerant), but was argued in the terms of 'democracy', 'human rights', 'Europe' and 'freedom'. Only when Belgrade threatened to stop Slovenia in its march toward fuller democracy did the demand for self-determination and integration into Europe become accompanied by more extreme nationalist claims. The road from defence of democracy to the defence of the nation was marked by a few important milestones, of which the first one must be considered the victory of the liberal wing of the League of Communists of Slovenia (LCS) over the party conservatives in expelling the latter from the leadership (spring 1987). A new leadership headed by Milan Kučan began to refashion the politics of Slovenia.

## Democratisation as National Project

Here it is impossible not to mention the development of social movements in Slovenia in the first half of the eighties, which actually initiated the democratisation process, divorced from the Party, but to which the Party eventually responded. Social movements in Slovenia started with punk[8] - a youth subculture, which managed to inspire the young intellectuals who lined up behind the movement and opposed the police violence proposed as the means of dealing with this social problem. The League of Socialist Youth also decided to follow its social base, rather than blindly follow the party line and the police. There is nothing unusual about that in a democratic system, but in a basically undemocratic one this amounts to a 'democratic breakthrough'[9]. The political parties that appeared in the late 1980 started off as social movements; pacifists, environmentalists, antimilitarists, feminists, gays and 'new spiritualists', together with punk, formed what was called in Slovenia the 'alternative scene'. Their high intellectual profile and an unusually developed sense for media contributed to the formation of a new political culture with a distinctive message. This was civil society, but opposed to the self-managerial version which, in the final analysis, was aimed at overcoming the distinction between state and society. The Slovene leadership for a while ignored the popularity of social movements[10], but eventually was unable to resist the developing process. It uniquely put itself at the forefront of this new democratic national project; the LCY in its criticism of developments in Slovenia used 'Slovene' and 'national' as identical to anti-Yugoslav. This was not without justification, one might add, but thus exonerating the socialist system from criticism and shifting the emphasis from reform to nationalism.

In 1986 the Serbian Academy of Arts and Sciences produced under the leadership of Dobrica Ćosić (who in 1992 became the president of the new much diminished Federal Republic of Yugoslavia, comprising only Serbia and Montenegro) a memorandum that complained about the unjust position of Serbs within the federation and contributed considerably to the nationalist defence of the Serbian nation. It touched every nerve, for its central claim was that the Serbs in Kosovo were dying at the hands of Albanians. It reminded Serbs that 'except for the time under the Independent State of Croatia, the Serbs have never been jeopardised as they are today' - and for what, asked the Memorandum - for 'being run by committees and apparatchiks?' Whilst Kosovo was demanding autonomy, Serbia after fighting for its independence over centuries 'was not allowed to have its own state'[11].

The powerful historical nationalism was invigorated with a new element, a possible repetition of the genocide. Of course, the Memorandum of a handful of intellectuals did not cause Serbian society to descend into the murderous nationalism they were later accused of, but it did allow for the type of language to emerge which later found resonance with politicians, particularly Milošević. One of nationalism's main concerns is to protect the nation and its language from danger; yet, it is worthy of attention to observe the language of danger that nationalism engenders. This is exemplified by Milošević in the speech he made to Serbs in Kosovo, who in fear of increasingly unhappy Albanians were emigrating in growing numbers, in April 1987:

> You should stay here, both for your ancestors and your descendants. Otherwise you would shame your ancestors and disappoint your descendants. But I do not suggest that you stay here suffering.... On the contrary! Yugoslavia does not exist without Kosovo! Yugoslavia and Serbia are not going to give up Kosovo[12]!

In view of such rhetoric, and similarly, 'if this so-called political pluralism is used as another term to supplant Yugoslavia and socialism, then we in

Serbia are against it' (Milošević 1989)[13], self-determination must become the only option.

To compensate for the lack of statehood, Slovenes have produced, for the size of the country, a formidable quantity of cultural institutions and literary publications, which throughout the 1980's became a forum for political opposition. A very important role in this was played by the journal *Nova Revija*, whose progress charted the political developments within Yugoslavia. After the publication of the 'Contributions for the Slovene National Programme' (February 1987), the leadership of the LCS, in defiance of Belgrade, refused to prosecute the authors; the Slovene prosecutor, after consultation with Kučan, rejected the federal prosecutor's request to start the legal proceedings against Nova Revija, and instead opened an 'all-Slovene' critical discussion of the journal and fired the two responsible editors[14].

The crucial controversy was of a military nature and of the greatest consequence for the mobilisation of the Slovene public. In May and June 1988, the police arrested Janez Janša and David Tasič, two young journalists of the increasingly popular countercultural journal *Mladina* (Youth) and their editor Franci Zavrl, whilst at the same time the military police arrested the army officer Ivan Borstner - the charge being the betrayal of military secrets with the intention of publishing them. Earlier in May, *Mladina* had published well-documented evidence that the Yugoslav People's Army (JNA) was preparing to arrest a large number of Slovenian liberals, thus trying to end the democratisation process. The public was outraged by the trial. Firstly, the civilians were tried by a military court in peacetime, kept isolated for a month and a half and denied civilian defenders. Moreover, the trial was conducted in the Serbo-Croat language in a court located in Slovenia, which was in contradiction with the Slovene Constitution (although it was a routine practice in the army). Kučan in a strong speech accused the military and reassured the Party and the Slovene public that he stood for national as well as class interests. He also disclosed that indeed the Military Council discussed the possibility of intervention in Slovenia[15]. The intervention was planned in case the police could not handle the civil unrest, which it was said was developing under the leadership of young journalists and academics. The legal Slovene leadership was also accused of if not inciting, then certainly tolerating this situation. The minutes of the meeting in Belgrade where Kučan criticised the possible implications of such a document (i.e. prosecution of dissidents) appeared in Ljubljana and the police arrested the four men who were presumed to be responsible for the dissemination of the minutes.

There were daily vigils outside the court and on 22 June, some 40 000 people took part in a demonstration in Ljubljana. The four men were found guilty and arrested. The support for the further democratisation was not dampened by the trial; on the contrary, the commitment to democracy deepened. In response to the trial a Committee for the Protection of Janez Janša[16] formed, but within days renamed itself the Committee for the Protection of Human Rights and proceeded with issuing bulletins and collected a protest petition signed by 100 000 people and thousands of small organisations. Slovene civil society, already considerably robust throughout the 1980's, was transforming itself to take the form of independent political parties. In the few months following the trial a number of parties were formed: Social Democratic Alliance, a Slovenian Democratic Union, a Christian Socialist Movement, a Green party and the Slovenian Farmers Union. Existing organisations such as the League of Socialist Youth of Slovenia (later renamed Liberal Party) and the Socialist Alliance of Working People, previously affiliated to the LCS, became new independent parties.

The society's pluralisation was driven initially by cultural and political motives, but the desired transformation of the regime, presumed in danger from the system identified with Serbia, changed the push for democracy into a national struggle. The Slovene Farmers' Union, the Slovene Democratic Union, the Social Democratic Union of Slovenia, the Greens of Slovenia, the Slovene Christian Democrats and Liberal Party formed a coalition called Demos (Democratična Opozicija/ Democratic Opposition of Slovenia) that won the first multi-party elections in April 1990. Its platform was a proper parliamentary system and an independent national state.

The Communist party wisely embraced the changes and in March 1989 published a Programme for Renewal, which abandoned one-party rule, jettisoned the communist doctrine of a 'single and eternal truth' and called for political pluralism. In January 1990 the Slovene delegation led by Milan Kučan, whose role in the transition of Slovenia cannot be overestimated, walked out of the Yugoslav Party Congress, renamed itself the Party of Democratic Renewal and became one of the parties in the first freely-elected Slovene government in May 1990. From there on the evolution of Slovenia into a democratic and independent state was as calm and committed to the rule of law as was its evolution from a communist state to a democratising one. Had it not been for the war that broke out after the Declaration of Independence, the whole process would have probably taken place unnoticed.

The interesting facet of this process remains that throughout the year 1990, Slovenia (and Croatia) still advocated a confederal solution and even in 1991, after the plebiscite which authorised independence (December 1990), the Slovene representatives took part in the Yugoslav consultations about the future coexistence of the republics. Whether this commitment to confederation stemmed from political shrewdness, intended to abate criticism from the international community so as not to be seen as the 'statebreakers', but as victims of the authoritarian state[17], as was intimated to me in some interviews, or indeed as a serious attempt to sway Yugoslavia to a different way, as I was regularly told, remains an unanswered question. I would argue that 1990 was the crucial year in Slovene national awareness, a point of no return to anything less than full sovereignty[18]. Slovenia in the spring of 1991 prepared for independence and started printing its own money (after it appeared that Serbia had 'borrowed' one billion US$ from the National Bank). According to D.Rupel on 21 June James Baker flew to Ljubljana to warn Kučan and himself against any one-sided moves. On 25 June, the Slovene parliament declared independence and on 26 June 1991 the Yugoslav People's Army attacked the border posts and Ljubljana airport. After the hectic diplomatic activity between the EU, the CSCE and the US, at the beginning of which the international community tried to reverse the Slovenian decision, Slovenia received international recognition and joined the UN 22 May 1992.

## Politics of Transition: Analysis of the Slovene Case

*Political Parties in Slovenia* (the first abbreviation stands for its latest name):

| | |
|---|---|
| LDS | Liberal Democratic Party (ex-Socialist Youth) / Liberalna demokracija Slovenije, a coalition of Socialist Alliance of Working People, Socialist Party, Democratic party and the ecological wing of the Greens. |
| SKD | Christian Democractic Party / Slovenski krščanski demokrati. |
| ZLSD-SDP | originally Party of Democratic Renewal (ex-Communists), just before the elections in 1992 renamed Associated List of Social Democrats / Združena lista socialnih demokratov (steps out of government coalition before the 1996 elections). |
| SLS-SKZ | originally Slovenian Farmer's Association, since second elections Slovenian People's Party / Slovenska ljudska stranka. |
| ZS | Green Party / Zelena stranka. In 1992 the party split and all deputies joined LDS. |
| SDS – SDZS | or SDSS Social Democratic Party of Slovenia/ Social demokratska stranka Slovenije (steps out of governing coalition in 1994). |
| SDZ | was Slovenian Democratic Union / Slovenska demokratična zveza (splinter group forms DS). |
| SNS | Slovenian National Party / Slovenska nacionalna stranka (1990). |

| DS | Democratic party / Demokratična stranka. In 1994 most of deputies joined LDS. |
| DeSUS | Democratic Party of Retired People/ Demokratična stranka upokojencev Slovenije. |
| NSi | New Slovenia / Nova Slovenija Krščanska ljudska stranka (established August 2000 and in coalition with SDS in October 2000 elections). |
| SMS | Party of Young People of Slovenia / Stranka mladih Slovenije. |

## *The Role of Political Culture in Democratisation*

The Slovene political tradition similarly to that of Slovakia has evolved without the tradition of independent statehood and with little tradition of independent political parties competing freely in an open system. Comparable to other ECE countries it had undergone industrialisation, urbanisation, mass education and other aspects of modernisation under socialism, which meant a considerable retardation in the modernisation of the political sphere. Whatever the differences between particular socialist systems, they all in various degrees of severity curtailed the freedom, whether of association, individual or the liberty of the political sphere. Even an apparent pluralist diversity of organisations and interest communities in the self-managing quasi-participatory democracy of the former Yugoslavia ultimately served the interest of the ruling party as the central mediating body between the citizens and the state.

This incongruity in the modernisation of the society between technological and educational advance and the political sphere has many consequences for the democratisation process. One of these is that politics is often viewed as something that 'the others' do and ordinary person's interests are not served by it adequately. This created a political culture lacking in participation and faith in political decision-making, precisely at the time when the advancement of the democratisation process requires a more 'democratic' attitude towards politics. The debate about the political culture in ECE at present is actually concerned with the (in)congruence between the democratisation of the political system and transformation of political culture, thus attempts to assess how the experiences of the past influence the present attitudes towards democracy, its stability and resilience in face of a crisis; in short, to what extent the public would resist populist appeals.

Slovakia did not show a great promise on that score[19] and it would appear that Slovenes' opinion of politics is equally poor. To the following four questions: 'politics is a struggle for power'; 'politics is a quest for common good'; 'politics is a battle for supremacy between special interests' and 'politics is a dirty business that honest people avoid' the positive answers were respectively 78.7%, 27.9, 69 and 60%[20]. There are two ways of evaluating such dissatisfaction with politics (a situation recognised in well-established Western democracies too). Either it is harmful, particularly in newly independent democracies which are in the process of constructing a new national and political identity, mostly because indifference and resignation can be at times 'woken up' by radicalism and populism, as was the case of Slovakia (in the West see political extremism in e.g. Austria, France, Italy). Or, a more optimistic view which sees the relatively low expectations the public has of the regime and its elites as an acceptance of the system with all its defects, thus expressing a pragmatic approach to politics. The high turnout at all elections (see tables 6.1 and 6.2 below) suggests that the public accepts its responsibility in the construction of the existing order, even if the only motivation is often to vote out the incumbent parties.

The Slovene political scene is not devoid of nationalist and extreme parties[21], mostly SNS[22], running on a strictly nationalist and xenophobic ticket. The SDS determines its position on the Left side of the political spectrum, but by focusing on the most severe criticism of the former regime (some of whose political leaders are still in power) and consistently pointing to 'scandals of transition'[23] and calling for the active role of the Church in the state education it approaches the voters from the Right. The political scene is polarised practically in half between the 'Left' and the 'Right' with the largest party the Liberal Democractic Party (LDS) Left of the centre, still less individualistically orientated than its Western counterparts. As the list of parties and their changing names and allegiances indicates, the Slovenian transition to democracy has not been particularly smooth. However, it has proceeded with less turbulence and less alienation from the West than in Slovakia; the populist leaders and overt nationalist mobilisation have so far not become characteristics of Slovene politics. After a short account of the evolution of the political system and coalition building[24], I shall suggest some answers as to what has gone right in the Slovene transition with a further elaboration on it below and in the concluding chapter of the book.

## *Historical Legacy*[25]

After losing their independent state in the Middle Ages[26] Slovenes became a part of the Austrian Empire. They did not have national autonomy, but had a written language codified in the 16th Century and a strong sense of ethnic and cultural identity, quite separate from their neighbours. In the second half of the 19th century, the small Slovene nation was divided into 6 administrative districts, of which the biggest (Carniolia) with the Slovene majority in the Assembly was something of a 'Slovene parliament'. The powers of the Assembly were limited and despite the representation in the all-Austrian parliament in Vienna (24 deputies), Slovenes in the Austro-Hungarian Empire failed to realise the main objective of their 1848 national programme – the unification of all Slovene territories under one representative body.

After the First World War, the vulnerable Slovenes having lost large parts of their territory to Italy joined the Kingdom of Serbs, Croats and Slovenes and found themselves in a centralised state where after 1929 the parliament was abolished and replaced by the authoritarian rule of the King. In the Second World War Slovenia was occupied and divided between Germany, Italy and Hungary. The Slovenian resistance under the leadership of the Communist Party joined the federal Yugoslavia dominated by Belgrade and all hopes (from 1943, after the capitulation of Italy there was a kind of Slovene parliament in operation) for a substantial autonomy (currency, army, political parties etc.) were dashed.

The philosophy and the workings of the system of self-management were described in the earlier section of this chapter, but important in this context is the functioning of the Assembly of the Republic of Slovenia (the Slovene Parliament). Slovenia's political system was a combination of one-party rule and an assembly style of self-management system, organised in a complex way from locally elected delegates from units of 'associated labour' (workers, the Chamber of Associated Labour), representatives of local communities (the Chamber of Communes) and representatives from five officially recognised socio-political organisations[27]. In spite of delegates being elected at the work place or local communities, the Assembly was not exactly a parliament for one main reason - the decisions at the top level remained directed by the interest of one single Communist party. Nevertheless, the experience of representation and community interests cannot be underestimated in the Slovene political system which has retained some of the socialist self-management character.

The new Constitution (December 1991)[28], declared Slovenia to be a 'social state' governed by the rule of law (Article 2) and 'the state of all its citizens based on the permanent and inalienable right of Slovenian people to self-determination' (Article 3). Large sections of the Constitution (Article 14-66) are dedicated to the protection of human rights and fundamental freedoms (Article 15, guarantees personal dignity and liberty, Article 19-21 secures the participation in political life, voting rights are defined by Article 42-44, the rights of children in Article 53-56). The unusual aspect of this Constitution are practically unchanged welfare rights of the previous regime (the right to social security and health care Article 50-51, the rights of children and obligations of parents Article 53-56), including the guaranteed freedom to work and the state's responsibility to create opportunities to work (Article 66).

The corporatist character of Slovenia, the tradition of which is not rooted only in the self-management system, but goes further back to the last century's cooperatives of farmers and artisans, strongly supported by the Church[29], is now encompassed in the political system. In the Slovene parliament, in addition to the main chamber, the National Assembly (Državni zbor, 90 popularly elected representatives of all people) which makes laws and decisions, there is a non-political second chamber, the National Council (Državni svet) composed of 40 deputies, of which 18 represent interest organisations, such as trade unions, nurses, physicians, employers, universities, agriculture, tradesmen etc., and 22 local communities. Despite its limited powers (it proposes laws, it can require a referendum and it can propose new laws for a further reconsideration before their adoption by the National Assembly), the National Council reflects strong ties between 'civil society' and the political system, inherited from the time of self-management and the beginnings of democratisation in the 1980s and has undeniably given the new democratic institutions a distinctive character, comparable more to Scandinavian countries or the Netherlands than to other post-communist democracies[30]. The consociational elements of the Constitution e.g. the permanent seats for minorities in the National Assembly are discussed below.

*Election Results and Coalitions Formation*

The transition to democracy in Slovenia, just as in all post-communist countries, must be considered in the context of general crisis of the communist regimes, but with special characteristics, apart from the national independence which it shares with other newly independent states. First, there was hardly any continuation of political parties from the interwar period (with possible exception of the SDS, claiming its origins in the Social Democratic Party from the beginning of the century), which is in great contrast to Slovakia. Second, one can point to the ruling Communist party elite's transformation whilst still in the position of power and its continued support for reforms. Third, since the collapse of Demos, the coalition of all new democratic parties which won the first free elections within Yugoslavia and could be compared to the Czech Civic Forum and Solidarnost, we can observe 'grand coalition' governments (parties of very different political ideas) in Slovene politics.

The first such coalition emerged from the 1992 elections: Associated List of Social Democrats (the former Communist Party, reformed into the

Party of Democratic Renewal), Liberal Democratic party, the conservative Christian Democrats and the smaller Social Democratic Party[31].

By the time of the 1996 elections, the political scene in Slovenia had lost its 'centre'. The Christian Democrats, previously interested in coalition with Liberal Democrats, but not receiving enough cooperation from them (the issue of religion being the crucial point of disagreement, with Liberal Democrats firmly behind separation of Church and the state) had joined the People's Party and Social Democrats forming the so-called 'Spring parties' and committing themselves to join only the coalition where these parties would be in the majority, assuming that that would be the election result, whilst all other significant parties were considered more 'left'(continuing the former system, according to 'Spring Parties').

The November 1996 elections split the electorate in half: 'Spring parties' got nearly 50% of vote (45 seats) and all others including the two permanent minority's seats also 45 seats. The Liberal Democrats retained their position as the strongest party (25 seats, 27%) and in the absence of the more leftist Associated List (who had lost many older voters to the Party of Retired People) they became the Left party in the governing coalition. The forming of the 1996 government took three months and became possible only after one of the 'Spring Parties', the Slovene Peoples' Party (SLS) agreed to form a coalition with the LDS[32]. The third party to join this 'pragmatic' coalition was the small DeSUS (Party of Retired People), a party without a particular ideology, more an interest group and a balancing party in the government, at that time not expected to last beyond this parliament.

Considering the divergent interests these parties represented, the coalition was an achievement and a sign of politically maturing and stable system. Indeed, the government was effective and presided over a very successful period in Slovenia's negotiation with the EU; the signing of Agreement on Cooperation in the Accession of Slovenia to the EU, involved the long resisted and controversial amendment of the Slovene Constitution (July 1997) allowing the foreigners to purchase the land. The coalition lasted until the SLS stepped out in April 2000 and joined with SKD to form a stronger right wing party; the government fell, but after two months of crisis the new government was formed and early elections avoided.

The last parliamentary election, in October 2001 was fought, again, between four major political forces: LDS, ZLSD, SLS+SKD, SDS. The older establishment of the 'Spring Parties', lead by Janša, pushed unsuccessfully for majoritarian system which led to a split in the SLS+SKD and the formation of a new right wing party NSi, who in turn formed a kind of coalition with SDS (Coalition of Slovenia)[33].

## Table 6.1    Election results: Slovenia 1990-1996

| Party | 1990 | 1992 | 1996 | 1996 (seats) |
|---|---|---|---|---|
| LDS | 14.5% | 23.5* | 27.1* | 25* |
| SKD | 13.0* | 14.5* | 9.6 | 10 |
| ZLSD (SDP) | 17.3 | 13.6* | 9.0 | 9 |
| SLS (LS-SKZ) | 12.6* | 8.7 | 19.4* | 19* |
| ZS | 8.8* | 3.7 | | |
| SDS (SDZS, SDSS)+ | 7.1* | 3.3* | 16.1 | 16 |
| SDZ | 9.5* | | | |
| SNS | | 10.0 | 3.2 | 4 |
| DS | | 5.0 | | |
| DeSUS | | | 4.3* | 5* |
| | | | | 88 |
| Hungarian minority representative | | | | 1 |
| Italian minority representative | | | | 1 |
| Total | | | | 90 |
| Turnout | 83% | 86% | 74% | |

\* coalition formation
   threshold: 2.5%.
+ SDS steps out of coalition in 1994.

*Sources:*  D.Zajc 'Parliament of Slovenia - Democratic Pluralism and Forming of
   Coalitions' *Conflict and Consensus* D.Fink-Hafner 'Development of a Party
   System 'D.Fink-Hafner J.Robbins *Making a New Nation: The Formation of
   Slovenia* Aldershot, Dartmouth 1997.

Notes relevant to the election results:
1990: within Yugoslavia, 3-cameral parliament 240 deputies. The ruling coalition DEMOS -
47 seats (coalition Christian Democrats, Farmer's Union, Greens, Democratic Alliance,
Social Democrats and Craftsmen's party, also called 'spring' parties) fell apart in 1991(the
other two main parties the ex-communist 'Renewal' Party -14 seats and the Liberals-11), the
early elections were called for 1992.
1992: changes to two-cameral parliament National Assembly 90 and National Council 40
Only 4 parties (LDS, SKD, ZLSD, SLS) have got large shares of votes in all three elections.

The government[34]
Proportional Representation system is composed of the Prime Minister, proposed by the
President after the consultation with leaders of the parliamentary committees and may be
deposed by a vote of no confidence by the ministers, vice-versa, the Prime Minister can
propose a confidence vote in the government. The President is a representative function with
limited powers, elected directly in general elections for a term of 5 years (2 terms
maximum), but nominates the Prime Minister and dissolves the National Assembly and calls
new elections in case there is no candidate for Prime Minister with enough votes. The
judiciary as the third section of the government is entirely separate from the executive and

legislative sections of the government - judges do not hold any other governmental or party position, whilst the Constitutional Court, besides the judgement upon the validity of legislation mediates in disputes between all state bodies.

The Prime Minister is Janez Drnovšek (LDS).

President: Milan Kučan 55.5 % in 1997 (non-partisan, suspended membership in the Party of Democratic Renewal, ex- leader of LCS, President of the presidency in 1990, President of Slovenia 1992, 1997).

**Table 6.2   General election in Slovenia, 2000**

| Party | Percentage of votes | Seats in parliament |
|---|---|---|
| LDS* | 36.21 | 34 |
| SDS | 15.80 | 14 |
| ZLSD* | 12.07 | 11 |
| SLS+SKD* | 9.53 | 9 |
| NSi | 8.76 | 8 |
| DeSUS* | 5.16 | 4 |
| SNS | 4.38 | 4 |
| SMS | 4.33 | 4 |
| | | 88 |
| | | + 2 ethnic minorities |

\* coalition
New threshold 4%
Turnout 70.37%
SLS+SKD established April 2000
NSi, breakaway from SLS+SKD
SMS new party in the Parliament

*Source:*   Personal correspondence with A.Krašovec
www.uvi.si/eng/new/background

*More consensus?*   The above has shown the evolution of the Slovene political system from the initiation of democracy and independence to the present. The question to ask is why the Slovene transition, despite its obvious problems and similarities with Slovakia, has been more successful. The proposition here is that the main reasons are the politically more mature electorate and national elites due to a more participatory system prior to the transition, more consensus on the issues of independence, and the less divisive ethnically determined composition of the society.

The interrelation between democratisation and nation-building and state-building has been discussed in the earlier chapters, but in this context it must be repeated that in Slovenia the former has been ongoing longer than the latter, which gave the democratisation process a less 'revolutionary' character. Despite the former communists' victory in the

1990 elections, the self-reforming leadership was forced into opposition to the communist regime due to the impossibility of reforming further within the Yugoslav federation. This meant that the redefinition of the Slovene position within Yugoslavia became inevitable. Once the independence option became accepted by all major political actors, nationalism ceased to be a divisive political issue among political elites (and their supporters), and the political agenda could shift to internal problems, the economy, the establishment of democratic institutions, European integration[35] etc.

Moreover and very importantly, the ethnic composition of Slovene society and the history of ethnic relations within it did not lead to the formation of ethnically based parties. The minority groups in Slovenia did not oppose the secession of Slovenia from the federation and had little reason to expect any change in their position for either historical or political reasons. All in all, the democratisation process did not become absorbed in the issues of the nation and this enabled the differentiation of the political parties to proceed along a path more compatible with the democratisation process and the promotion of international relations instead of preoccupation with inter-nationalities relations within the state itself.

It has been argued throughout that the role nationalism plays in the democratisation process is contingent on other processes: the pace of democratisation which influences the formation of national elites, the degree of consensus concerning independent statehood (in the newly independent democracies), on the historically predetermined level of political development (political culture), which contributes in a greater or lesser degree to the legitimacy of the transition, and on the ethnic structure of the society which affects majority-minority relations. Concluding this section, I would argue that all of those elements were more compatible with the democratisation process in Slovenia than they were in Slovakia.

## Legitimacy of the transition

The introduction to this chapter stated that the specificity of the Slovenian transition lies in the fact that it was a gradual process, which was endorsed and eventually led by the self-reformed communist leadership which responded to the gradually increasing pressures of the opposition organisations and civil movements. The preceding account of the initiation of democracy in Slovenia illustrated significant differences from the Slovak case. However 'homegrown' the transition in Slovenia was, it is unlikely that it would have happened, at that time, without the fall of the Berlin Wall, which removed the last ideological barrier between the East and the West. It demolished whatever was left of the faith in the communist system (certainly for the time being), and made the desire to join 'Europe', in this sense more of a political than geographical meaning, attainable for the first time since 1945. The possibility of attainment makes the formalisation of demands easier and the goals clearer.

All postcommunist transitions, whether they preceded the attainment of independence (as in Slovenia), were contemporaneous with independence (ex-Soviet republics), resulted in independence (Slovakia), or in unification (East Germany) share the same aspect, that is the unravelling of state power and the reassertion of the national question in response to a totally new set of circumstances. Such an historically unprecedented situation, in some cases more revolutionary than in others, warrants a review of all set ideas about the conduct of nations in determining the course of their future. Therefore any discussion about developing democracy in the newly formed states cannot sidestep nationalism and its evident role in the transition process.

Transitions in postcommunist states - whether the Slovenian one with a head start on the others, or in the established states, such as Hungary and Poland - became national projects. Where the project involved the establishment of independent 'statehood', thus at the same time the reconfiguration of borders, nationalism naturally became a more prominent force. The relations between individuals, the nation, the ethnic groups and the state had to be reconceptualised and that is the 'space' within which nationalism operates. Whether the result is compatible with democracy or not, whether it took NATO bombing to stop the Serbian nationalist onslaught on Kosovo, or whether nationalist sentiments have declined in Slovakia depends on how those relations are construed. In any case the reconstruction of states and redistribution of power in the postcommunist transitions have been accompanied by nationalism. Why this was not the case with other transitions from other authoritarian regimes is quite another story, which would involve a systematic comparison between them.

The argument presented in the case of Slovenia in comparison to Slovakia is twofold. Firstly, the transition in Slovenia, starting with liberalisation[36] of the communist system from below, progressively moving towards the issues of human rights, participation, accountability and pluralism, eventually embraced and initiated by the leadership itself. It thus rested on greater legitimacy, by having had enough time to reconcile societal and elite differences about the form and the pace of transition. Secondly, secession became the guarantor of the continuity and the pace of democratisation, thus giving nationalism a more positive role in that process and removing its relevance once independence was achieved. In Slovakia, where minimal liberalisation took place prior to the change of the regime, the population was largely unprepared for the transition and its consequences, which allowed a section of the political elite to make the decision about independence, thus filling the gaps in legitimacy with nationalism long after independence.

What we are exploring is the question of how nationalism relates to the transition to democracy and under which circumstances is nationalism less or more compatible with the democratisation process. The key to the answer seems to be the legitimacy of the unfolding democratisation process. Legitimacy as used here corresponds with commitment, consent, recognition, appropriateness and the authority to act on behalf of others, whereby it is a sum of all those elements. Thus, legitimacy requires the recognition that a state and its governing regime are appropriate internally (and externally) and that the overwhelming majority of the population consents to the authority of the government. Most former communist regimes have failed to achieve this, including Yugoslavia, despite the experiment with self-management as an alternative to political democracy - at this point in history, almost uncontested as the most legitimate political system. If we consider the difficulties and insecurities that the transition to democracy brings, it is obvious that legitimacy is a driving force of the transition and that the progress of transition in new democracies depends on its attainment. The correlation is symmetrical - the more legitimate the democratic change is, the more likely it is to succeed.

The preceding sections showed that Slovenia found itself at the point where democratic reforms could not continue within the existing constitutional arrangements and thus national self-determination became the only way forward. The communist leadership in order to stay in power had to share it with other parties and uniquely, it did not just step down, it transformed itself. Instead of being in the forefront of the Party it was now in the forefront of the nation[37]- much the same as with the Serbian leadership, and in response to the nationalist platform Serbia assumed. The motivation however was very different: Serbia was seeking hegemony, not democracy. Accusing Slovenia (and Croatia) of unconstitutional secessionist tendencies, it increased the motives of those countries to dissociate themselves from a structure which no longer served them well; moreover, the dissociation became the declaration of the difference and the intention for the future.

Nationalism, ethnicity (and religion for that matter) can only be exploited when there is a rift in society on those issues. At the present time, when politics have stabilised and political parties have to create a sharper profile of identification against domestic rather than external opposition, some parties, namely SDS, SNS, SLS+SKD, campaign more on the issue of national identity, religion and ethnicity than they did at the time when independence encompassed all of those issues against external pressures. It appears that in Slovenia nationalism in the beginning of the transition added to the legitimacy of democratic change, instead of exploiting the new enlarged political arena by seeking alternatives to that process.

Nationalism can adjust the pace and the direction of transition - in Slovakia its role was more negative, it slowed the process down and brought more radicalism into politics. Then again in Slovakia neither democratisation, nor national independence enjoyed the legitimacy they did in Slovenia. The already complicated relationship between nationalism, democratisation and legitimacy was exacerbated by the polarisation of society, which ran precisely along those lines - the affiliation with the federal partner that pursued a different form of transition and the presence of the large minority opposed to Slovak national independence.

*Does Nationalism Exclude the Possibility of Democracy?*

The mobilising potential of nationalism is rooted in the simplicity and immediacy of the appeal it makes to 'the nation'; this ability is easily utilised for any political purpose and largely explains the negative view of nationalism. None the less, nearly all authors on Slovenia agree that nationalism had a positive function there, that 'it was instrumental in creating a relatively broad consensus on vital national interests'[38] and that:

> it is obvious that the basic sources of the awakened Slovenian nationalism should be sought in the tendencies to set up a political nation and to build a nation-state, as the two necessary frameworks for more rapid comprehensive modernisation processes[39].

In the opening of the first chapter, which dealt with the rise of nationalism in the postcommunist Eastern/Central Europe generally, I mentioned an essay by Ghia Nodia, which states that 'democracy never exists without nationalism' and argued that the evident link between democracy and nationalism should not be confused with their compatibility. On the other hand the issue of compatibility in the 'up and running' democratic system is a different question from how compatible nationalism is at the inception of democracy. Newly emerging democracy combined with a new statehood cannot be compared to a more mature democracy, or a new system in a long-established state.

Nationalism in Slovenia at the time of the self-determination era must be viewed as a strong force moving the changes forward with the population acting as its agent. Obviously there would have been some manipulation by elites and by the media (and not to forget the actual political events that took place), but to a much lesser extent than we have seen in Slovakia. If anything, the legitimacy of the political elite derived partially from the response to what was happening among the people, which is the reason why some activists of that time claim that the leading reformers allied with nationalists. But what if 'nationalists' were democrats too? The point is that, and here I sympathise with Nodia's argument, nationalism does not exclude the possibility of democracy. When nationalism is blamed for the break-up of Yugoslavia, it is because it led to a war, which is not the same as Slovenia becoming independent, without border disputes and without ethnic mobilisation against minorities within its territory, or elsewhere.

The criticism of nationalism is rooted in its intolerance of an individual cause and the preference for the 'collective', from which there is only a small step to 'the tyranny of the majority' and political values confused with cultural, racial and other characteristics devoid of universal norms of liberal democracy (which is of course what we are talking about). Slovenia demonstrated that at a certain time in the nation's development the individual cause can be identical with that of community. It is not intrinsic to nationalism which seeks its own state to demand the exclusion of other national groups, it is however one of nationalism's traits to suggest exclusion, if it will benefit its political cause.

Due to the regular appearance of the latter kind and the challenge it poses to democracy, the debate about the theoretical compatibility of the two concepts has been dominated by the negative influence of nationalism on anything to do with democracy. This is rather long-lead to the idea which dominates this book: that nationalism is a part of the democratic process with better or worse consequences for the process itself, and even that depends on too many variables and is imbued with a strong normative element. Whether the Slovene nationalism at the time of transition was good, or less good, thus 'ethnic', is not that relevant; the point is that an ethnic community, with a number of cooperating minorities, became a political nation[40]. We are still looking at a predominantly ethnic nation, but en ethnic nation that made an unreserved commitment to liberal democracy. If the character of its nationalism thus shifted the emphasis from ethnicity to democracy, it did so in accordance with the goals and aspirations of its nation.

Ethnicity is not by definition undemocratic or conflictual, it is the uncertainty about how it forms the relationship with the state that can lead to undemocratic or conflictual ethnic policies. Hence, in view of postcommunist developments, the assessment of the relationship between nationalism and democracy is worthy of renewed reflection which does not exclude compatibility.

Postcommunism is synonymous with one prefix – 're' – revival, restoration, reidentification etc. Thus, forging the new out of what there was, neglected or interrupted and therefore national(ist) can mean many things; it could be democratic, more socialist, less authoritarian, more liberal, even fascist. What it can hardly be is a transition without being national, which makes nationalism a difficult, but necessary partner of postcommunist transitions to democracy. Nationalism, in a way similar to legitimacy, drives the transition, it can add to its legitimacy, just as much as it can minimise it, it can speed it up or slow it down, therefore, its role is regulatory. However, the final direction democratisation takes depends much more on the level of commitment to democracy than on the level of nationalism.

## Ethnic policy of Slovenia

The issues of nationality, citizenship and the protection of ethnic minorities are some of the central themes in the process of transition of Central and Eastern European countries. Not only because it is often for the first time that these have to be formulated in fully independent conditions under democratic principles, but also because they determine the level of democratic credentials and the country's international reputation. Ethnic policies have two dimensions: external and internal, and both condition their formulation[41]. In its internal dimension the ethnic policy adopted is an index of the democratic development of modern society; it is important to add that the number of ethnic groups or the size of ethnic minorities should not be a determining factor. Of course it is easier to offer a high level of protection to small minority(ies), but in the long run, tolerance is a question of education and perception of its importance for democracy. Intolerance permitted against one group can soon change its targets - as such it is always detrimental to social and political stability and pluralism, without which there is little democracy.

The external dimension has two aspects. First, the less positive one, which is the use of ethnic policy towards a certain minority (or immigrant community) in bilateral negotiations with neighbouring countries. The principle of reciprocity holds a political value and functions as political leverage, even if the moral value of such political bargaining is questionable. Secondly, despite the ethnic policy being considered an internal affair of each state, in the increasingly global world the international community can demand the implementation of certain standards in the exchange for admission to international organisations and monetary programmes.

Slovenia had traditionally a good record on the protection of minorities, already within Yugoslavia and was often cited as the best example of the Yugoslav system, in which the protection of minorities did not count among its many problems. The 1991 Constitution followed this positive tradition and tried to translate it into a new social situation. Slovenia is a full member of the Council of Europe, it signed the European Charter on Human Rights, it has signed and ratified the European Convention on Human Rights including all Additional Protocols. The Slovenian Parliament adopted the European Charter for Regional or Minority Languages and as an internal measure the Law on Self-governing Ethnic Communities. In addition, Slovenia is a member of IMF, World Bank, GATT, NATO's Partnership for Peace and finally, it has been accepted as a future member of the EU in the first round of its enlargement into the East (June 1998). So, how is all that international recognition reflected in the ethnic policy of Slovenia, or the question could be posed the other way round. What kind of ethnic policy leads to such international approval?

Whichever way, it can be argued with certainty that ethnic policies influence international recognition directly, which in turn reinforces the commitment to democratisation internally, thus that there is an explicit link between ethnic policy and the transition to democracy.

*Citizenship*

The first consideration in the Slovene case is the status of the immigrant population from other Yugoslav republics, which constituted 10% of the population. According to Article 39 of the Law on Citizenship (Uradni List RS No.1/1991) everybody who had citizenship of SFRY (every Yugoslav citizen had double citizenship, federal and republic, so that everybody who acquired a republic citizenship automatically had also federal Yugoslav citizenship) became a citizen of the Republic of Slovenia. Article 40 of the same Law provided a special procedure for the granting of citizenship to every citizen of former Yugoslavia, who actually resided in the territory of Slovenia on the day of Plebiscite (23 December 1990), and who applied for Slovene citizenship within six months after the adoption of this law (25 June 1991). Some 170 000 people became Slovene citizens under this article 40. Their application could be refused if they had actively participated in the aggression against Slovenia (as a member of JNA in the 'Ten Days War'). After the 6 months period everyone could apply for citizenship by naturalisation on the basis of general conditions (Article 10), which are not particularly easy or difficult, but similar to other laws on citizenship in other states[42]. The result of the referendum showed that immigrants voted for the independence of their new country of residence, which increased the vote by an extra 10% (88,2%, turnout 93%). The commitment to Slovene independence by the immigrant population does not have to be sought in ideology, most of them voted for a better life, which was what brought them to Slovenia in the first place.

## *Ethnic Minorities*[43]

A minority is (according to the Additional Protocol to the European Convention on Human Rights and Fundamental Freedoms, concerning National Minorities and their Members): 'a group of persons in a state who a) reside on the territory of that state and are citizens thereof, b) maintain long standing, firm and lasting ties with that state, c) display distinctive ethnic, cultural, religious and linguistic characteristics, d) are sufficiently representative, although smaller in number than the rest of the population of that state or of a region of that state, e) are motivated by a concern to preserve their culture, their traditions, their religion or their language'[44]. Minority rights should therefore assure the existence and development of ethnic minorities, their distinct language, culture and identity, establishment and functioning of their own organisations, and their participation in the process of decision-making within the political system.

Following a very common practice, the Constitution of Slovenia guarantees special rights and protection only to those autochthonous ethnic communities[45] who have traditionally lived in a specific territory, which are the Hungarian and Italian minority. Concerning the role of the state in the protection of ethnic communities, the Constitution (rather uniquely in the region) adopted the 'positive concept of protection of ethnic minorities and their members', which in practice means an active role of the state, an obligation to act and to assure the realisation of individual and collective rights. The words 'collective rights' are significant - it is the recognition of the duality of the rights of ethnic minorities, whereby collective rights belong to ethnic minorities as distinct communities and as individual rights to every member of a certain ethnic community. Concerning their nature, some of the rights are realised mostly as collective rights, while others are realized mostly as individual[46]. The state's role in the protection of minorities is covered by Article 5 in the Constitution, which also defines Slovenia's active role in attending to the welfare of Slovene minorities in neighbouring countries and in promoting their contacts with the homeland. In addition: 'Slovenians not holding Slovenian citizenship shall enjoy special rights and privileges in Slovenia', the extent of which shall be determined by statute.

The official language of Slovenia is Slovenian (Article 11). In those areas where Italian and Hungarian ethnic communities reside, the official language is also Italian or Hungarian. The main provisions regarding protection and rights of ethnic communities are located in Part II of the Constitution under 'Human Rights and Fundamental Freedoms'. Besides the general provision of 'equality before the law' (Article 14), there is the guarantee of equal human rights, irrespective of national origin, race, language, religion, political or other beliefs, financial status etc. 'Each person shall be entitled to freely identify with his national grouping, to foster and give expression to his culture and to use his own language' (Article 61). Each person has the right to use their own language and script in official proceedings (Article 62) and the Constitution prohibits (Article 63) 'all incitement to ethnic, racial, religious or other discrimination' and the inflaming of intolerance.

In addition to the basic human rights, belonging to each citizen, the Constitution guarantees special rights to the Hungarian and Italian minorities. The most important of those (Article 64 and further elaborated in various laws) are: a) the right to the use of their native language - in the mixed areas Slovene, Hungarian and Italian are equal and all public services are bilingual; b) the free use of national symbols; c) the right to establish autonomous institutions; d) the right to foster the development of their own culture and the right to be informed in their own language; e) the right to education and schooling in their own language and to become familiar with the history and culture of their mother country; f) the right to cooperation with the nation of their homeland and very importantly, and finally g) the right to direct representation in the National Assembly (Article 80 - two seats permanently reserved for the Hungarian and Italian deputies, elected by their local authorities in the Slovene Parliament).

It should be emphasised that all these right are: a) irrespective of the number of minority members, b) that the state is obliged to support financially and morally the implementation of these rights; c) that the Constitution provides a minority veto (Article 64) in the process of decision-making within the political system, that is, any legislation which exclusively affects the Hungarian and Italian communities, 'may not be enacted without the consent' of their representatives. As far as education of members of the above minorities is concerned, it is based on two different models: the Italian minority attends monolingual schools, while the Hungarian minority attends bilingual schools with Slovene pupils. The curricula of these schools differ from other schools in that they teach both the minority and Slovene language and pay special attention to familiarising the pupils with the culture and history of their native country in order to maintain their ethnic identity. The common goal of these measures is to establish bilingualism, also by the majority population, so that the generations that grow up in these mixed areas do not have communication problems. This provides for a better understanding and more active coexistence.

Slovenia recognises also Romani/Gypsies as an autochthonous ethnic community (Article 65), approximately 2300 people, although they have no 'mother' state to exercise the special connection with, or to be protected by. Despite being given the status and special rights by the Constitution (an improvement on other Constitutions in the region), these rights 'shall be such as are determined by statute' - they are still not in operation. The representation of the Romani community is made more difficult by the specific situation in which they live; their communities are usually very small and dispersed, there is little sense of a common identity, made worse by the traditional lack of education. The problem of education is exacerbated by the lack of teachers who speak their language and by the fact that the children are usually socialised in a different way, which is not always compatible with the one in schools.

It would appear that in treatment of minorities it is important to recognise dual culture and affiliation and accept plural loyalties[47]. The evidence from Slovenia shows that civic and ethnic identity are not always in conflict and that narrower smaller ethnic community (in this region usually based on language) and the larger civic attachment can satisfy basic human needs. Understanding this is of particular importance in East Central Europe, where many people live in the sphere of influence of two cultures. Rejection of dual loyalties by a state forces minorities into a narrow choice between assimilation and antagonism. Both choices are incompatible with democracy: the formal unacceptable, and the latter undermining.

## Conclusion

I have concluded the chapter on Slovakia with a set of propositions to be tested against the case of Slovenia. These concerned: the simultaneity of nation- and state-building; historical and political developments concerning national recognition, identity and political tradition; and the polarisation of society.

The evidence which has emerged in the course of this chapter points to the following conclusions. First, Slovenia's national consciousness at the time of independence was much more developed than in Slovakia. The reasons are numerous; firstly as a consequence of the different development within the Austro-Hungarian empire and secondly, as a consequence of different national policies within Yugoslavia and the special position of Slovenia within that already different communist system. As a result the Slovene nation-building process was ongoing and maturing throughout the communist period, culminating in independence, which gave the state-building a more prominent role in the democratisation process.

Second, political participation and a degree of democratic awareness existed in Slovenia prior to the collapse of Yugoslavia and the initiation of democracy. The more lenient type of communism allowed for reforms from above and the pressures from below to be coordinated over a longer period of time, thus more consensus was reached on all issues concerning the nation and democracy. More radical elements in the Slovene political scene could be neutralised before they could aggravate the transition.

Third, the transition from communism, which was a kind of partial (or deformed) modernisation to a modern state, participating fully in the economic and political integration in Europe, became a national project, the completion of which was only possible by secession from Yugoslavia. In the Slovene case nationalism and democracy were not only conducive to each other's aspirations, they became dependent on each other, which gave democracy high legitimacy and nationalism reinforced it.

The thrust of the argument has been that in Slovenia, nationalism and democracy formed a complementary dynamic at the beginning of the transition process, which has increased the level of consensus among elites and the population, thus consequently, reduced the level of potential conflicts, translatable into nationalist issues. Whilst recognising the political efforts in Slovenia, the situation was aided by historically predetermined positive conditions; among those were a greater ethnic harmony, a strongly developed sense of national identity, a politically more aware population and lastly, but very importantly the unequivocal commitment to democratisation above all other issues. This however does not mean that Slovenia is not susceptible to an increase in nationalist mobilisation in future, or certain stagnation in the democratisation process, both still fluid as much as in Slovakia.

## Notes

[1] Slovene Writer's Association in an Appeal for International Recognition of the Independent State of Slovenia, written under siege (Yugoslav Army occupied Ljubljana 26 June 1991) 2 July 1991, in *Nova Revija* Special Edition 'The Case of Slovenia' Ljubljana, July 1991.

[2] Asterisk refers to the distinction in the Slovene language between words 'nacija' - nation having its own state (political nation), and 'narod' which implies cultural nation (for the cultural/political nation distinction see P.Alter *Nationalism*). Since English does not have two different words for these two different notions, the text indicates the former, 'nacija', with 'nation*'. V.Hribar 'The Slovenes and European Transnationality' in the same special edition of *Nova Revija*.

[3] Despite the expected continuity of democracy in Slovenia, it is not a consolidated democracy; this in reference to 'the term democratic consolidation should refer to expectations of regime continuity' A.Schedler 'What is Democratic Consolidation' in *Journal of Democracy* 9:2 April 1998 pp. 91-105.p.103.

[4] This period in the Slovene history is often described as the 'Slovene spring'. Many different phrases appear in the publications, all describing the trajectory of the transformation in Slovenia. For example: 'from ethnos to demos', F.Medved 'A path towards the cartography of Slovene national identity' in *Razprave in Gradivo* 29-30 pp.177-210; 'from the Party to a Party', T.Mastnak 'From Social Movements to National Sovereignty' in J.Benderly E.Kraft *Independent Slovenia* London, Macmillan 1994 p.103.

[5] J.Seroka 'The political future of Yugoslavia: Nationalism and the critical years, 1989-91' in *Canadian Review of Studies in Nationalism* XIX 1:2 1992 pp.151-160 p.156.

[6] Z.Mlinar 'Autonomy and (Dis)integration in Post-socialist Transformations' in J.Subrt and N.Toš *Crossroads of Transition* Praha, Philosophy Faculty of Charles University 1995 pp.33-37. The following data expressing the mood in pre-independent Slovenia from I.Bernik, B.Malnar and N.Toš 'Slovenian Political Culture: Paradoxes of Democratization' in D.Fink-Hafner and J.Robbins *Making a New Nation:The Formation of Slovenia* Aldershot, Dartmouth 1997 To the question of whether Yugoslav republics should have greater autonomy in the future, 59.1% of the responses were positive (1987), whilst 52.9% believed that Slovenia's development opportunities would increase outside Yugoslavia. 58.5% (1988) saw the industrialized Western countries as the most important region to cooperate with regarding future economic, cultural and political developments.

[7] R.Rizman 'Slovenia: A special Case' in H.Neuhold, P.Havlik and A.Suppan ed. *Political and Economic Transformation in East Central Europe* Boulder, Westview Press 1995 p.58.

[8] Punk-rock was initially tolerated as just another rock style. As its message became more aggressive, the state authorities began to focus on its often sinister Nazi message. This mainly due to the band 'Leibach' (German for Ljubljana) whose totalitarian message (a combination of Stalinism and Nazism) provoked authorities. 'Leibach' soon became a part of an artistic avant-garde, admired and financed by the League of Socialist Youth, as their way of protest against the party's political activities. Once the political campaign against the rock culture ended, both official youth organisations and punk groups lost interest in each other. Nevertheless, punk contributed to the liberalisation of Slovenia, despite the controversy. For detailed discussion see G.Tomc 'Politics of Punk' in J.Benderly and E.Kraft *Independent Slovenia*.

[9] T.Mastnak 'From Social Movements to National Sovereignty' in J.Benderly and E.Kraft *Independent Slovenia* p.94. For a more theoretical discussion of 'civil society' generally and in Slovenia particularly see A.Bibič and G.Graziano *Civil Society, Political Society, Democracy* Ljubljana, Slovenian Political Science Association 1994.

[10] The crude simplification of this important facet of developments in Slovenia of that time is due to the fact that the subject is too encompassing, whilst I do not believe that the deeper exploration of civil society in Slovenia would change the basic arguments in this book.

[11] Memorandum of the Serbian Academy of Arts and Sciences cited in T.Judah 'The Serbs: The Sweet and Rotten Smell of History' in *Daedalus* 126:3 Summer 1997 pp.23-45 pp.38-9. Further reading: M.Glenny *The Balkans*.

[12] T.Judah p.40.

[13] L.Cohen *Broken Bonds* Boulder, Westview Press 1993 p.79.

[14] One of them being D.Rupel, the author of the article this section draws on and who later became the foreign minister of the first post-communist government. D.Rupel 'Slovenia's

Shift from Balkans to Central Europe' in *Independent Slovenia*. The other sources for this chronology of events are: P.Vodopivec and T.Mastnak in the same publication. R.Rizman in *Political and Economic Transformation in East Central Europe* as above; S.Ramet 'Democratization in Slovenia - the second stage' in K.Dawisha and B.Parrot *Politics, Power and the Struggle for Democracy in South-East Europe* Cambridge, Cambridge University Press 1997; S.Ramet 'Slovenia's Road to Democracy' in S.Ramet and L.Adamovich *Beyond Yugoslavia* Boulder, Oxford, Westview Press 1995.

[15] D.Rupel p.189.

[16] The hero of the trial remains a controversial political figure in Slovenia, and the leader of the opposition party, the populist Social Democracy Slovenia of which more later.

[17] Here note the difference with Slovakia, always perceived as the responsible party for the break-up of Czechoslovakia. For that reason Slovene politicians preferred to use the term 'razdružite' (dissociation) from Yugoslavia rather than 'secession'.

[18] Prior to the landslide Referendum on Independence in December 1990, the Slovenian Assembly had amended and annulled some 100 federal laws in economy, politics and defence. For the process of drafting of the Slovene Constitution see M. Žagar 'The Constitution of the Republic of Slovenia' in *Into Europe?*

[19] In Slovakia in 1995 55% of respondents answered 'no' to the question 'do you understand what is going on in our politics?' and 61% believed that current political parties in Slovakia are not a sufficient guarantee for democratic politics. Focus 'Current Problems of Slovakia' Bratislava, Centre for Social and Market Analysis 1995.

[20] A.Bibič 'Slovenian Public Opinion on Politics' in F.Plasser and A.Pribersky *Political Culture in East Central Europe* p.62.

[21] For 'Radical Right Politics in Slovenia' see R.Rizman in the unpublished essay with the same title, Ljubljana 1996.

[22] With anti-foreigners, pro-workers slogans, e.g. 'We will not give our forests to foreigners and the Church' (Manifesto, 1996 elections.) Slovene National Party is, unusually in the region, opposed to the Catholic Church, the position of national and Catholic party is in Slovenia taken by the Social Democratic Party.

[23] Meaning the privatisation, the presence of ex-communists in the government, the possible return of foreigners through the repatriation of the land etc. Interview with Milan Zver, a prominent member of the party 11 May 1998.

[24] Based on D.Zajc 'Parliament of Slovenia - Democratic Pluralism and Forming of Coalitions' and S.Kropivnik 'Voting Behaviour in Slovenia' and I.Lukšič 'Social Partnership in Slovenia' S.Kropivnik, I.Lukšic and D.Zajc ed. *Conflict and Consensus* Third Regional Conference of the Central European Political Science Association Bled (Slovenia) November 1996, published by Slovenian Political Science Association Ljubljana 1997. Further interviews with F.Adam, A.Krašovec, I.Lukšic and D.Zajc May 1998 Ljubljana.

[25] J.Prunk *A Brief History of Slovenia* Ljubljana, Založba Grad 1996.

[26] Ancient state of Karantanija, the story of which is now often recalled for its ritual in which the free people transmitted their sovereignty to the ruler (by the French historian Jean Bodin described as 'without comparison in the world [1576]) and which, it is said, inspired Thomas Jefferson in the drafting of the American Declaration of Independence as the contract between the 'people' and the sovereign.

[27] The Socio-Political Chamber, the War Veterans, Trade Unions, the League of Communists, the Socialist Alliance of Working People and the Socialist Youth.

[28] *Constitution of the Republic of Slovenia* (Ustava 1991), Časopisni Zavod Uradni List Republikc Slovenije Ljubljana 1993.

[29] There is a long tradition of Slovene political thought rooted in the protection of the community, traditionally associated with the Catholic Church (in the absence of aristocracy and political citizenry, the Church came to represent the society, mostly peasantry), such as the movement 'Krekovstvo', the peasant cooperatives 19th century and the idea of popular self-government of Andrej Gosar (1930's). The concept of corporatism was further developed within socialist ideology by E.Kardelj, see the previous chapter. The notion is that of society as one living body, in which each organ is equally important to the health of the whole. For corporatism as the main feature of the Slovene political culture see I.Lukšič 'Political Culture in Slovenia' in F.Plasser and A.Priberski *Political Culture in East Central Europe.*

[30] Another facet of the Slovene political system worth noting is that political parties (developed mostly out of interest organisations and deemed to defend functional interests - retired people, farmers, etc) are provided for by public funds.

[31] Social Democratic Party stepped down after its leader, the controversial Janez Janša, the hero of the above mentioned trial and the Minister of Defence was dismissed, which marked the beginning of the anti-establishment campaign by this party.

[32] D. Zajc 'The role of national parliament in the process of accession to European Union – the case of Slovenia'. Paper presented at XVIII IPSA conference Quebec 1-5 August 2000.

[33] SDS despite securing the second place in 2001 elections remains a severe critic of the government. Its chairman Janša, referring to the change of threshold to 4% and the remaining PR system, opposed by his party commented: the elections were legal and the outcome legitimate, but morally contentious. www.uvi.si/eng/new.

[34] Based on interviews with A.Krašovec, political analyst Faculty of Social Sciences Ljubljana. Further,: A.Krašovec 'Parlamentarni deli strank vs.centralni deli strank' *Teorija in Praksa* let.34 June 1997 pp.919-933 and *Moč vPolitičnih Strankach* Ljubljana, Faculteta za družbene vede 2000.

[35] I.Bernik 'Slovenian political culture' in D. Fink-Hafner J.Robbins *Making a New Nation: Formation of Slovenia.*

[36] There is a difference between democratisation and liberalisation. The latter can occur in essentially non-democratic system and involves, as in the case here, the greater freedom for the formations of associations, the lesser censorship of the media and more open criticism of the regime, the better treatment of prisoners, the more tolerant approach to opposition, artistic freedoms, more open borders etc. The former is much more a political concept which simply put means that the ruling ideology and therefore the control of government can be contested in elections. Democratic transition clearly refers to democratisation, not merely liberalisation.

[37] In 1990 74.6% believed that the Slovenian Communist Party was more in accordance with the interest of the people than a few years ago (41.7% in 1989; 26.4% in 1988). I.Bernik and B.Malnar 'Ethism, Nationalism and State-Building: the Case of Slovenia' Paper prepared for presentation at the Congress of the International Political Association, Seoul, August 1997. Henceforth I.Bernik and B.Malnar (1997).

[38] I.Bernik and B.Malnar (1997) p.11.

[39] P.Klinar 'Ethnic Conflicts in Postsocialist Societies in Europe' in S.Devetak ed. *Kleine Nationen und Ethnische Minderheiten im Umbruch Europas* Munchen, Slavica Verlag Dr.Anton Kovac 1993 p.284.

[40] Slovenia is often said to be practically ethnically homogenous, which is far from the truth. As all states of the former Austro-Hungarian Empire it comprises of many minorities, however small. Officially recognised are two - Hungarian and Italian in total 0.59% of the population. However, during the Yugoslav period many immigrants from other republics

settled in Slovenia, mostly for economic reasons. At least further 10% of the population is of that origin. Then they are some other very small communities (Romany, Germans, Austrians, Albanians etc.) and people of 'undetermined' ethnic origins. According to the 1991 data 87.84% of the population is ethnically Slovene (Ethnic Minorities in Slovenia Institute for Ethnic Studies Ljubljana 1994).

[41] M.Žagar 'Nationality, protection of ethnic minorities and transition to democracy: the case of Slovenia' in *Teorija in Praksa* 32:3-4 March-April 1995 pp.243-254 p.250.

[42] There are 4 ways to acquire Slovene citizenship: 1 - ius sanguinis (birth and blood, at least one of the parents to be Slovene); 2 - ius soli (born in Slovenia); 3 - international agreement; 4 - naturalisation (18 years of age, 10 years of residence, 5 permanent, permanent employment, no longer than 1 year of imprisonment, should be able to communicate in Slovene, dual citizenship to be avoided etc. All in all citizenship laws of all countries are restrictive. The greatest problems are encountered by refugees, at this time still some 17 000 whose status is covered by The Law on Temporary Protection, which hinges on always the dubious concept of evaluation of the circumstances in the country of origin and the possibility of return - particularly problematic after the Bosnian war.

[43] The following draws on *Constitution of the Republic of Slovenia* Ljubljana, Časopisni Zavod Uradni List Republike Slovenije 1993; *Ethnic Minorities in Slovenia* Ljubljana Institute for Ethnic Studies Information Bureau Government of the Republic of Slovenia 1994; *The Law on Temporary Protection* Ljubljana, Peace Institute 1998; M.Žagar 'Nationality, Protection of Ethnic Minorities and Transition to Democracy: The case of Slovenia I and II in *Teorija in Praksa* 32:1-2 January 1995 pp.88-95 and 32:3-4 March 1995 pp.243-254; R. Jóó 'Slovenes in Hungary and Hungarians in Slovenia: Ethnic and State Identity' in *Ethnic and Racial Studies* 14:1 January 1991 pp.100-106. Forthwith known only by the name of the author.

[44] M.Žagar p. 244.

[45] The Constitution uses strictly term 'ethnic community', not 'ethnic minority' in order to avoid the possible negative connotations of the term minority.

[46] For example: the right to be educated in minority language belongs to individual and collective rights simultaneously; the establishment of an appropriate educational system is a collective right of a certain minority, whilst giving the possibility to attend a bi-lingual school in the language of minority is an individual right of every member of a certain minority.

[47] R. Jóó p.106.

# 7 National Identities in Post-Cold War Europe

Much of the traditional discussion about the relationship between nationalism and democracy deals with the nation and the state, with the borders of the state constituting the limits within which this relationship is played out. This chapter enlarges the field and turns its attention to the international environment, beyond the Cold War generally and to new democracies in particular. It explores how international relations and integration shape nationalism and democratisation in the newly independent states of Eastern/Central Europe.

The previous chapters have pointed to some conclusions about democratisation and nationalism, which could be summarised as follows: communist states of the region have always differed, but their levels of divergence have increased with democratisation; the success, stagnation or failure of the democratisation process depend largely on domestic conditions which in postcommunist states can generally be characterised by a limited experience of democratic politics combined with relatively high intensity of nationalist sentiments; if formal democracy (fair and free elections) is not backed up by more substantive institutional and constitutional mechanisms which are able to curb majority nationalism and offer substantial provisions for minorities, the democratisation process is likely to be arrested by the rise of nationalist sentiments among all ethnic groups within the state.

It appears that the relationship between democracy and nationalism in the newly independent postcommunist states is locked in a paradox of inevitability. Both processes are simultaneous, promoting each other and posing a challenge to one another. The most challenging task of democratisation is to withstand the pressures from nationalism, which democratisation itself called into prominence. National self-determination, minority rights and identity are the key elements of the contest, whilst democratisation policies seek the creation of an all-inclusive, culturally tolerant and politically united community. This task can be achieved only if nation-building policies include tolerance and pluralism among their aims.

The argument of this chapter is that the current international environment is a close partner in this relationship, and it is suggested, for better rather than for worse.

The pages to follow address the nation and the state in a world where both are increasingly enmeshed in either overlapping or mutually exclusive coexistence required by various internationally accepted norms, accords and arrangements, willingly or because non-participation is not a feasible option. Moreover, it is argued that sovereignty is no longer the ultimate accolade for a nation, for national recognition by the international community involves more than independence. It requires the ability to relinquish part of sovereignty to transnational organisations, and this means a significant redefinition of what was a classical aim of nationalism. The key elements of nation-building, the national identity and the subsequent role of the state are thus expected to expand their meaning and include supranationality, difference and the expanded horizon of the state on board. The following discussion starts with the end of the Cold War and outlines agendas, dilemmas and the chances of states in a global world and the resulting character of nationalism. The final part explores the main theme of the book, the relationship between nationalism, democratisation and international environment through the case studies of Slovak and Slovene foreign policy-making since independence. The conclusion will emphasise the difficulty of the transition to democracy in a newly independent state that faces a multitude of tasks, often contradictory, but always under a close scrutiny of the international community. Finally, it is suggested that international relations and integration, for all their possible reverse effects, including a nationalistic backlash, shape the relationship between democracy and nationalism in favour of the former.

## New World Order

The much-debated issue in international relations remains the extent to which external factors influence domestic developments, which is not the same debate as the one about how low on the list of the electorate's priorities lie the issues of foreign policy. However, no politician in a democratic state can risk ignoring public opinion in matters of the state's standing and functioning within the international system. The system itself reverberates with the echo of major systemic changes that are often brought about by a change in domestic policy of one important unit. The 'Prague Spring' of 1968 failed to loosen the hold of the Soviet Union over Eastern and Central Europe, but the violence with which the status quo had to be reinstated showed a glimmer of the weakness of such an artificial division of the world. The 'limited sovereignty' of the Brezhnev doctrine which sent the tanks into the former Czechoslovakia did not change the world, but the denunciation of the doctrine by Gorbachev did. There could be little doubt that 'the Gorbachev effect'[1] linked the changes in the Soviet Union to the developments in Eastern Europe, though 'the effect' was more what the USSR did not do than what it did in connection to the surrounding countries. The end of the Cold War was therefore not an agreement about a new world order, but a withdrawal of one major player from the Cold War order, thus a tacit admission of radical changes.

The radicalism of this situation, however, is paradoxical. Firstly, there is the notion that the end of the Cold War means an unstable and insecure world. The absence of one major threat is replaced by a multitude of threats, from various less controllable sources. This is rather strange considering that the 'safety' of the Cold War was rooted in an ideological division of the world, backed up by an arms race of frightening proportions at a very high human cost, and that 'the only one threat' was a nuclear one. There are further assertions about the 'safety' of the Cold War[2], such as that there were fewer armed conflicts and certainly less of that murderous nationalism, which have by now become a standard assessment of the previous era and are a witness to the selectiveness of human memory and the creation of myths.

This is not the place to list the wars and conflicts of the 1945-1989 period, but mentioning Korea, Vietnam, Afghanistan, the Middle East, possibly indicates where this argument, were it be elaborated upon, would lead - to the conclusion that the wars of the Cold War were fought by proxy in the periphery. The dismantling of the Soviet Union has cost fewer lives than the dismantling of other European empires following the Second World War and possibly even fewer than the withdrawal of the British from India, whilst the expectations of the ethnic conflicts in the ex-Soviet Union have far exceeded the reality. Whilst on the subject related to nationalism and self-determination of the peoples, Bosnia and Kosovo loom large, but they are not a symbol of our time, they are a lesson the international community has not learned, blinded by that other myth that under the Cold War conditions nationalism died.

Had it died it could not have been revived as quickly and as vigorously as it was; the point is that the conflicts were labelled differently and that we have come to associate nationalism strictly with fragmentation and instability, instead of equally closely related self-determination and democratisation. The fragmentation of the empires at the end of the First World War was a celebration of the self-determination doctrine, yet much of its implementation was regretted later, for the principle itself, as lofty as it is, was never meant to guarantee peace. The end of the colonial era was as much in the name of national liberation and self-determination as is the revived nationalism in the postcommunist world. There is an important extra dimension to this wave of nationalism - it carries strong tendencies towards integration (EU, NATO). Many nationalist leaders have claimed (whether with conviction or for mobilising purposes), that only 'a sovereign nation can give up a part of its sovereignty in a sovereign way, and transfer it to a transnational community'[3], and in similar vein, 'that the establishment of the state means that all its citizens can directly participate in European and world integration'[4]. The other type of ethnic reassertion, also prevalent in the post-Cold War context, seeks the way back to traditional societies. This form of ethnic politics is more a result of fast technological, cultural and political advance in the modern world, when some societies, unable to adapt to the rapid pace of modernisation, political or technological, feel disenfranchised and turn inwards (e.g. some Islamic countries).

Secondly, the new order was actually an acceptance of the existing order, by the previously resisting side of the ideological barrier. The radical change applied, so it seems, only to the East, whilst the West remained at worst unchanged and at best challenged. The change for the West is that capitalism as a system no longer needs any justification[5]. It has proved more resilient and economically sustainable than the other (communist) system, and its compatibility with liberal democracy means that there is a certain exhaustion of political alternatives[6]. The fact that some 30 % [7]of the world's work force is unemployed, that a large part of the world is politically marginalised, that there is a detectable sentiment of uncertainty and impending environmental crisis is a part of the sophisticated, but largely ineffective (as solutions to these problems go) debate about postmodernity as the only critical debate of the new world order.

*The New Agenda*

The new agenda for the countries of the region, thus plunged into the new world order, suddenly and without guidance, became very complex. While the West struggles with the redefinition of the role of the state in the era of global economy, political integration and a militarily insecure world system, and with the construction of national identities which would reflect the fast changes and movements of people and goods, then the new democracies face a double struggle. The insecurities about the role of the state, a general condition shared globally, is in the new states compounded by the fact that the state, discredited by the previous regime, has now an important role to play in the transition to the new system of political democracy.

The new states are facing a multitude of challenges where each challenge is exacerbated by the other. The agenda is often contradictory:

1. nationalising and homogenising and anchoring one's national identity through old myths revamped for the new conditions, whilst implementing the universal rights and protection of minorities;
2. catching up with the 'history', that is forming a nation and joining the world as an equal and independent state, at the same time as the historical project of modernity - whose main achievement was the nation-state - has apparently 'ended' and the relevance of the nation-state is being questioned, thus being given little time to make that national 'history';
3. seeking recognition by the international community under closer scrutiny than any old states were ever subjected to, and conforming to the rules of international law inspired by countries with a much longer tradition of doing so; and
4. finding a niche for national economies in the extremely competitive and technologically advanced global market which may require a reluctant acceptance of the fact that democracy, certainly in the early stages, leads to a greater inequality than in previous regime.

These are mammoth tasks and I would like to contend at the outset that pessimistic assessments of the postcommunist transitions, however valid in some cases, at certain times, should take this into consideration. Postcommunism defines an agenda but the order in which the items on this agenda are dealt with varies with each country. The assessment of the progress should therefore be more appreciative of the progress achieved in each individual country, rather than critical of the time scale in which this ambitious agenda is fulfilled.

The challenge for a new state is thus how to harmonise its own view of itself and its desired international image with an identity accorded to it by the international community; the answer to the question how this discrepancy between the two shapes nationalism and democracy is the subject of this chapter. It is argued here that more encouragement on the part of the international community produces better results and that exclusion is a self-fulfilling prophecy. The transition has pushed the new states towards the West, but such orientation only confirmed their peripheral position, which is hardly conducive to self-esteem. National recognition was a way out of the dysfunctional system, and hence, the most important rationale behind the establishment of the new states was the emancipation based on national identity. However, the harmonisation of the 'national' and internationally imposed conditions has in nearly all cases proved difficult - the external influences and expectations and internal expectations do not always meet. The international community expects political stability as a precondition for integration, yet the instability of societies in transition is exacerbated further by the fact that the agenda of international relations is not designed to meet the most urgent needs of societies in transition - on the contrary the transitional societies are having to adapt by bringing more transformation into already changing societies.

## Universal Principles and Idiosyncratic Conflicts

A central feature of the modern global era is the tension between centripetal tendencies of the global market and regional integration on the one hand and, on the other, centrifugal forces of many different identities and cultures forced into coexistence by these globalising and integrative processes and reinforced by the universal acceptance of democracy and human rights. The 'age of rights'[8], cultural diversity and globalisation might at times not accommodate one another, but connections that form between them make clear that there is a limit to state-centricism in international politics. This fact alone requires a redefinition and conceptual re-examination of the role of state, nationalism and democracy - the following sections are merely a modest suggestion towards possible avenues of exploration.

### Globalisation

The first thing to mention about globalisation is that it carries an aura of inevitability with it[9]. A state can perhaps decide on the degree to which it wishes to be globalised, but not whether it is being globalised - it is a process so all encompassing that everything is swept away by it. Not joining in means impoverishment and isolation, whilst joining in is an exercise in unpredictability. So, globalisation is the main characteristic of this new world order, feared and revered at the same time. There are broadly three views on globalisation.

First is the new globalist orthodoxy: we are talking about a true global world ('that is the creation of genuinely global markets in which locational and institutional - and therefore national - constraints no longer matter')[10], thus, states are becoming powerless, empty vessels carrying symbolic flags, as it were. The second, in contrast, views globalisation merely as the internationalisation of economies, made much more visible by the higher degree of communication. States are seen as the instigators of the whole process, taking control whenever necessary as the only authority in charge of the national economy and therefore well capable of adapting to the global world[11]. In this case not much has changed, history has seen a high degree of economic interdependence before, even if the scale is enlarged. This view sees the modern nation-state embedded in a very dynamic economic and inter-state system, its essential characteristic being adaptation, so that the relevance of the nation-state will increase rather than decline.

According to the third option, globalisation means a redefinition of sovereignty and the role of the nation-state, which is neither declining, nor is wholly empowered, but is engaged in a balancing act between remaining indispensable as the ultimate source of legitimacy, but at the same time somewhat impotent to take complete charge of certain developments, which exceed the boundaries of territory and sovereignty. Apart from the two issues of the economy and environment, possibly the two most internationalised ones, these developments are often connected to the phenomenon of identity and to society. The agenda of governmental debates and intergovernmental collaboration and conflicts is weighty with issues such as regional autonomy, cultural autonomy, federalism, the forms of political representation, human rights, religious freedom, immigration, etc., forces previously seen as less relevant and too ephemeral to undermine the 'realist' view of states[12]. The questions about modern political community, democracy, ethnicity etc. are left wide open to rethinking[13], as is the extent of the control that the nation-state can or should cover, by which I mean that the external boundaries of the state's competence might be fixed, but the barriers of internal competencies are blurred and might even transgress the external boundaries.

This last option is the one, I wish to argue, is the realistic picture of globalisation - the state, still a part of an anarchical system of states remains the bearer of sovereignty and autonomy, but faces political constraints from the international system, therefore its sovereignty and autonomy are redefined, but only to a degree that the state chooses to be constrained. We see the difficulties the international community has in constraining some rogue states, e.g. Iraq, or Serbia in the recent past, when only the politics of 'other means', that is the threat of force are effective.

*Further perspectives on the 'global'*

If democracy is to become a truly global ideology, the task is to pursue it in such a way that the national and international and their mutual penetration are interconnected. This is not new; Kant already saw the state in the context of the 'society of states'. The first half of this century and the ensuing Cold War confirmed the 'realist' view of international relations[14], but if international relations theory is to account for the interconnectedness of states, it has to seek out the 'liberal idealist' tradition[15], which involves sensibility and compromise to external developments. Simply stated, it means that there cannot be an account of a democratic state without an examination of its functioning in the international community, as there cannot be an account of a global system without a consideration for a democratic state. Democracy and the international system have become intimately connected and the distinction between internal and external affairs is being increasingly eroded.

This erosion emerged firstly, from the inability of states to control the economic, political, cultural and security interconnectedness of the global system; secondly, from regional organisations which change the nature and dynamics of national politics; and thirdly, from different cultural groups, movements and nationalisms which question the state's legitimacy as the sole representative of their interests. Democracy has to come to terms with this unfolding process and that has led some scholars to seek a new framework of democratic institutions and procedures, such as, for example, a model of cosmopolitan democracy[16]. This is not the place to discuss potential or workability of this paradigm, which would require, in the first place, an establishment of an international democratic polity, thus the possibility of political participation across borders and across political communities, as well as the creation of effective mechanisms to enact and enforce these different procedures and legal arrangements stemming from them. One of the conditions for such a process to emerge would include political parties capable of inspiring a debate which would address and synchronise 'interests that transcend the borders'[17]. The European Union is pioneering a new, less national form of governance and the European Parliament could possibly serve as an example from which to begin the inquiry into such mechanisms.

The most intractable obstacle to the realisation of cosmopolitan community comes from identity, ethnic or national, and its increasingly important role in politics, parallel to the globalisation of the idea of self-determination and democracy (and that is the other side of the 'global' coin). The interpretation of political and civil rights leads to a different interpretation of identity; any community based on a global identity would expect ethnic and national identity to become very immediate and subordinate to the more important identity, that of a citizen of a 'universal state of mankind' (Kant). Building on Kant's thought and complementing the idea of cosmopolitan democracy is the concept of cosmopolitan citizenship[18]. This is a different citizenship from what we know: it is divorced from the territorially based nation-state, it is abstract and not rooted in rights and duties attached to national self-determination, but attached to the larger moral community - the world. It aspires to higher moral considerations and obligations to the rest of humanity, something that the nation-state with its emphasis on its own citizens often neglects. Both theoretical concepts are an attempt to conceptualise democracy in such a way that it reflects the new global order and the evidently changed role of nation-states.

I am aware that my doubts about the establishment of international polity are premised on what someone aptly described as 'methodological nationalism' which views states and their national governments as 'the basic units of political analysis'[19]. However, the subject of my deliberation here is to convey the challenges of new 'state democracies' in the world that is beginning to question this historical orthodoxy, but the response, thus far, must not be overstated.

*Fragmentation of cultures*

We live in the world of two 'imagined communities' - the nation and the 'imagined community' of the 'global village', brought nearer by the globalising effect of modern communications, thus producing cultural globalisation, similarly to the 'print capitalism'[20] in the 18th century which drew people together despite the spatial separation and assisted in the formation of national identity. Such a process, by offering access to information about places which may not otherwise be accessed or experienced by individuals or groups, will, so the theory goes, erode the traditional, ethnic and national identities in favour of an even larger identity - belonging to the world. Such claims are, however, premature, despite some issues, such as human rights and the environment, which do support a new 'global perspective'.

National and ethnic identities are deeply rooted in myths and history imagined, told, construed and real (ethnohistories); they are hardly going to be stamped out by the global culture, should such a thing come into existence and even then it would take such a long time that the relevance for contemporary politics is doubtful. As the situation is, the bringing of peoples and nations together, their cooperation and development may enhance mutual understanding, possibly respect, but at the same time it leads to the accentuation of differences - which equally may not have happened otherwise. Being confronted daily with the difference and mostly conflicts (for such is the way of reporting the news) in far away places does not necessarily remove distance, on the contrary it could make 'the local' seem more endangered, therefore in need of more protection. Confrontation leads to relativisation of one's values, which on the whole is civilising, but does not necessarily inspire the breaking down of cultural barriers - in fact it appears to contribute to the fragmentation of cultures[21]. These cultures are a result of memories, local ways of thinking, customs and norms that grew out of the necessities of local struggles, or out of reinterpreted histories and retold stories. No such culture has or can easily emerge from universal history, even if it was in the making. What seems more apparent is that the plurality of meanings and references persists and global awareness struggles to grow out of the soil made thick with such deep roots.

This is by no means a defence of the primordialist approach to nationalism, but rather an attempt to concede that no matter how 'constructed', 'imagined' and 'false' national and ethnic identities might be, we have no others with which to make comparisons. By this I mean that there is a limit to this argument about the 'falsity' of national identity, and ironically it is actually an argument that nationalists are partial to. Our formative experiences, our childhood and everything that frames our initial memories are wrapped up with the language, tradition and customs of the place of our initial active experience of belonging. That does not mean that our allegiance is unshakable or that ethnic identity is written in blood and is not an artifact, but its importance should not be dismissed. All experience with nationalism shows that a disregard for ethnic identity, and usually it is the identity of others, on the basis that it is not a real thing, has led to an increase in nationalist mobilisation, not to its decrease.

Of course, identity invented once can be reinvented, in fact identity is prone to reinvention and the nation is a constant production of such inventions[22]; ideas and symbols are produced and reproduced as circumstances require. The 'reinvention' that takes place, particularly in new states, is usually an answer to the pursuit of recognition in need of reassertion, the process of a self-searching nature, reaching into the past in order to explain the present and show a way forward, thus a process given to self-possession and self-glorification, rather than self-criticism and enlarged horizons. The aspiration to universal principles is problematic not because we cannot agree on the principles, but because the application faces idiosyncratic problems, thus we live in a world of universal principles and idiosyncratic conflicts.

## Reconciling Sovereignty and Transnationality

Nationalist mobilisation in Eastern/Central Europe is a result of the reconfiguration of states on the basis of nationalism in pursuit of self-determination. Viewed this way the process seems less archaic and more a part of European history[23], even if somewhat delayed and inconvenient.

Self-determination was not invented by the postcommunist leaders and not even by Wilson, but was an acknowledgment of a certain historical phenomenon bound up with principles of progress and justice. In that way the new states of ECE are truly 'returning' to Europe and as such, despite all the problems and setbacks, the process is a positive one.

There is however a crucial difference between the 'old' sovereignty-seeking nationalism and the 'new' nationalism in the region. The goal of nationalism has always been more recognition and more rights, leading to the assumption that the final goal of nationalism should be the establishment of a sovereign state. The situation has changed. Firstly, it is now universally acknowledged that a nation (culture) and the state (polity) do not have to be congruent[24]; moreover, with a universal recognition of diversity, nearly all states are 'multicultural' to a greater or a lesser degree. Nationalism is not always state-seeking, the interplay of various nationalisms, the homogenising pressure of a new state, the minority nationalisms seeking various forms of autonomy and regional cooperation all take place post-independence and are a part of domestic politics. The international community faces a difficult task to balance the support for legitimate claims of minorities, whilst on the other hand, it has to condemn aggressive nationalism of the majority, all in the name of democratisation.

Secondly, the newly gained national sovereignty has to be given up, partially, but almost immediately in the name of the ultimate national recognition - European integration. Exchanging absolute sovereignty for transnationality has become an integral part of democratisation. This gives rise to the paradox that sovereignty, crucial as it is in nationalist discourse, has become a necessary stage on the way to integration. This is difficult for all countries, but it pays to keep in mind that the newly independent postcommunist states have just liberated themselves from one integration, that of the Soviet Empire and the enforced internationalism of communism where they were also expected to give up sovereignty, and in some cases more than partially (Warsaw Pact). This indicates why the notion of integration is often not acted upon as enthusiastically as it is proclaimed by political elites and why it is accompanied by exaggerated national rhetoric often in order to reaffirm the newly achieved status.

*International Recognition*

Nationalism cannot be understood, nor can we come to grips with its assumed opposition to the 'international' dimension, if we are preoccupied with the identity it creates, instead of understanding the specific 'identity of nationalism'[25]. Nationalism is not like any other historical or contemporary form of collective allegiance. It is not its 'ethnic' or 'civic' character, it is not its future mission, or its traditionalism - it is all of those at once - and nowhere is it as evident as in the new states in the transition to democracy. The nation and its state have to review the strategies adopted through nationalism, because the externally imposed criticism is impartial and nationalism has to live up to demands of the world where approval by the international community is crucial. The question is not just about limits to sovereignty, but about the international arena in which states are attributed a place depending on how they behave. International isolation is a poor reward for the stubborn insistence on national sovereignty (e.g. Serbia and less dramatically Slovakia). The legal recognition of the state might be a necessary condition for the state's existence (not for its creation), but for the further development what matters is another type of recognition, less legalistic, less national and more rooted in international approval, which is what guarantees the investment from abroad, the educational, technological and cultural exchanges and successful diplomatic relations.

Nationalism offers little by way of this kind of recognition and I would argue that in the contemporary world nationalism's influence over the matters of the state should be limited to the time of the state's creation. So, nationalist sentiments bruised by the erosion of their control over the state, might become very defensive and protective of culture - its last remaining bastion. This might be the reason why nationalisms of our time are so culturally rooted, generally and in ECE particularly. One way to look at it is that culture is not divorced from social and political institutions, that institutions bring different arrangements, different cost-and-benefit calculations, different values which legitimise different attitudes. In the long term, institutions change the context within which politics take place and the political salience of nationalism can diminish. I emphasise long term, because if developing political culture is not divorced from institutions, the establishment of those institutions is also in response to the context of the society in which the process takes place. Simply stated, if democratisation and nationalism are tied together, they both contribute to the international position of their state, but not in equal measures - too much national assertion can become an obstacle to the international aspect of democratisation.

Post-independence Slovakia is a good example of this. By 1992 the civic Czechoslovak identity no longer answered the demands for 'recognition' of Slovakia, and the latest redefinition of Slovak national identity became much narrower, not only in geographic terms. The motivation was not democracy, but the recognition of Slovakia as a 'nation' and a compensation for perceived injustices of the past. Discontent goaded by the political elite with all to gain and little to lose in both republics, led to independence which was an unexpected, but by no means a tragic result.

There was nevertheless a price to pay - the isolation of the country from its neighbours, the costs to the economy, and the loss of many years of democratic development. The political elites, in a society with a low reservoir of political arguments and a rather simplistic vision of how to conduct politics, and who conducts it, managed to convince a large majority of the population that nationalism was democratisation and thus, the quest for international recognition turned out to lead to less recognition in the end.

## National Identity and Foreign Policy -Making

The above discussion indicates that national identity translates into international relations, thus that national identity affects the making of foreign policy[26] and those decisions bounce back and influence domestic politics. My contention is that there is a strong link between the ideological ambiance within the state, its foreign policy, the external reaction to it and the reflection of the latter inside the state. Foreign policy, it is said, is a highly pragmatic activity rooted in a rational assessment of clearly defined national interests; as such it is conducted by professionals and a small number of them at that.

However, that is only a part of the story. Were it true, Slovak leadership would not have chosen independence in 1992 and would not have lost 6 years of its independent existence alienating itself from Europe and the rest of the region. In order to understand the dynamics of foreign policy formation, it is important to understand how the identity of the polity has evolved, that is how the state perceives itself, its past and the future and its role in the international environment. An implicit argument here is that national identity constitutes a very important force behind the formation of foreign policy, because it is through national identity that 'the parameters of what a polity considers its national interests at home and abroad are defined'[27].

This is further dependent on who carries the responsibility for the ideological and intellectual reproduction of the 'story of the nation'. Even if there were a correlation between national identity and the resulting political leadership, it would be too simplistic to claim that 'the people' are the sole carriers of national identity. Objectivity is the aim of politics, but national identity is one side of politics that is susceptible to interpretation and thus manipulation of what is said to be a 'collective' memory. 'Memory of the nation' is highly selective and its emphasis shifts according to who selects and who draws conclusions. It should be no surprise that in new democracies, when one adds the fierce political struggle, the novelty of nationhood and the responsibility for a new sovereign state, national identity suffers from the worst misinterpretations, and leads to miscalculations in foreign policy. Mečiar's administration claimed a conspiracy of the Western powers and neighbouring states, namely Hungary, against Slovakia's entry into NATO and EU, thus exploiting the existing fears of a small nation never in control of its destiny. The Slovene elites on the basis of the same fear have pursued international and regional integration even prior to independence[28], whilst the post-1998 Slovak administration has immediately embarked on a 'salvage operation' to recover lost ground, if not for the purposes of NATO, than at least for an earlier reassessment[29] by the EU. The identity of a small newly-independent Central European nation with a similar history and similar fears can be told from many different angles.

All through this book it has been stressed that nationalism and the issues of national identity are not a particularity of new postcommunist states, but it has also been made clear that one of the characteristics of these states is the pervasiveness of nationalism in political life. The fact of a recent independence and thus the remnants of a particularly high levels of nationalist mobilisation aside, these societies' history is marked by continuous changes, political, geographical and ideological, whereby nothing remained constant for long enough to offer some binding tissue - except nationalism. Therefore, the nascent states' foreign policy formation involves a stronger element of national identity, mostly defined in ethnic terms, than foreign policy of established states.

However, observing the political dynamics in the EU, which at this point in history still consists only of established states, seems to contradict this claim. The most reluctant members appear to be Denmark (not other Scandinavian countries) and Britain (not Scotland) - a small state and what could be described as a middle power with a reputation of a great power. On the other hand there are enthusiastic small Benelux countries and other big states - France, Germany, Spain. We can see that the perception of national identity and in particular the articulation of dangers and national interests are subject to many factors, such as the fear of war, the fear of invasion, the notion of absolute and inalienable sovereignty, the economic benefits, the regional cooperation, the ethnic composition and the level of decentralisation, and not least the political elites and their involvement[30]. The union of established, developed and democratic states struggles with the national identities of its units and is not devoid of nationalist mobilisation. Nevertheless, two remarks about national identity are true for all states. Firstly, the identity of the polity is not dissimilar to the identity of an individual, it helps to define values and particularly the priority in which these are ranked. Secondly, the identity of the polity changes, usually inspired by crisis, external or internal[31], self image reacts to changed circumstances and aspirations reflect new needs.

## Europeanisation of Slovakia and Slovenia

> The commission concludes that: Slovenia presents the characteristics of a democracy, with stable institutions guaranteeing the rule of law, human rights and respect for the protection of minorities; Slovenia can be regarded as a functioning market economy and should be able to cope with competitive pressure and market within the Union... In the light of these considerations, the Commission recommends that negotiations for accession should be opened with Slovenia.

> In the light of these elements[32], although the institutional framework responds to the needs of parliamentary democracy, the situation is unsatisfactory both in terms of the stability of the institutions and of the extent to which they are rooted in political life. In the light of these considerations, the Commission concludes that Slovakia does not fulfil in a satisfying manner the political conditions set out by the European Council[33]...

'Europe' in the context of postcommunist integration carries a heavy political weight and is of enormous significance as a test of the stability and the success of the transition, and as a symbol of the state's acceptance among the world's developed nations. To put it simply, the question is not whether 'Europe' matters, but how it matters, to what degree, in what direction, and at what pace. The normative and political element of the integration is of course matched by the practical considerations, the economic benefits, and in the case of NATO membership, military security.

The above statements issued by the European Union show two countries, one aim and two results - Slovakia's integration, just as its democratisation process was waiting for a review. Europeanisation' connotes processes and mechanisms by which European institutions-building may cause changes at domestic level. The current Community legislation comprises of some 5000 Directives and Regulations, some of which impact directly on democratic forms and practices by which national groups integrate within the state, and directly on political traditions and the construction and interpretation of national identity.

The aim of the following section is to explore the link between nationalism, democratisation and integration generally whilst the focus of analysis will be on Slovakia as the more illustrative case of this relationship. I shall point out differences with Slovenia which led to what now appears to be a temporary disqualification of Slovakia from the

European integration. Slovenia to its great disappointment failed to secure the candidature in the first wave of NATO's eastern enlargement, just as Slovakia did, with a difference that Slovakia had not expected it, despite the pretence of Mečiar's government.

## Slovakia and Slovenia - Differences

Within Slovakia and Slovenia, the absence of independent statehood meant that all notions of identity and collective memory were related through literature and history, which is how political consensus has mostly been influenced and developed. In both countries this tradition is still detectable in the unusually high involvement of authors, historians and academics in political debates and all collective consciousness-forming platforms. It thus stands to reason that the change of political elite brings about a change in the intellectual elite which in turn brings subtle changes to how national identity and collective memories are articulated.

In Slovakia with its rather dramatic transition process, the official line concerning issues of the former Czechoslovakia and its disintegration, neighbouring Hungary, the importance, potentiality and most importantly, the mode of attainment of integration, all of which bear relevance to foreign policy formation, changes with each administration. Slovenia suffers less from shifts in foreign policy orientation having had a longer time to decide on the direction of its state and generally being less divided on the issues of collective memory, due to its longer nation-building process, and having established a better international reputation as a result. If both countries can date the beginning of their national aspirations to 1848, politically more autonomous Slovenia has always sought some form of statehood within a multinational entity (Austro-Hungarian Empire, first Yugoslavia 1918-1941; the second Yugoslavia 1945-1991), whilst Slovakia having always entertained aspirations of a fuller-bodied version of national autonomy (not necessarily independence) has been more resentful of its political status within Czechoslovakia[34].

In Slovenia the idea of independence from the very moment of its inception was in the name of democracy and European integration - that was the national project. Moreover, the strong Western orientation marked Slovenia's foreign policy for more than a decade and it is frequently stressed that Slovenia is not 'returning to Europe' - the borders have been open for decades. The willingness to cooperate in order to secure its political position in the European arena was not a part of domestic political struggle, but seen by all political actors as the only viable option for the country. The level of consensus among the political parties on the issues of integration and thus foreign policy decisions is almost paradoxical[35], considering the strong party competition in domestic affairs. Even the most nationalist SNS in its party programme mentions Slovenia (fully independent) in European structures as the first point[36]. The same applies to the general public. The majority of the population is in favour of the EU, though it is not true that the public is not critical, but it is pragmatic[37], which is not dissimilar to the public opinion in the member states - it is critical, but on the whole nobody wishes to abandon membership.

Some statistics[38] whilst contradicting the apparent openness of Slovenes, show this enthusiasm for the EU. The main identity appears to be overwhelmingly national and local (city, district, country 65.4%, the European identity 12.4%). Membership in the EU is considered beneficial for democracy by 74.3% of those surveyed, for security by 82.2%, economy by 72.4% (immigrants increase criminality 66.7%, the non-Slovenes should not have important positions in public life 50.5%), Slovenia would benefit by the membership in the EU 93.7%. Nationalism seems to have been conducive to the formation of independent Slovenia and the establishment of democracy, but Slovenes are susceptible to xenophobia as much as all other nations, whilst at the same time the inclusion in the larger community seems to be valued very highly. The most sensitive issue in Slovene integration was the liberalisation of real estate within the EU (see Europe Agreement 10 June 1996): 70.2% of the population agreed that foreigners should not be allowed to buy land in Slovenia. The reason being the size of the country and the fear of loss of control, exacerbated by the historical experience of the war - an issue from which some political parties (SDS and SNS) gained much political capital[39]. Since 1998 the Agreement has been ratified by the parliament, because there was 'no alternative', despite the issue of the liberalisation of real estate being still seen as 'too high a price' for integration[40]. A point worth noting is that these figures show how important official rhetoric is, because any encouragement of the existing latent anti-foreigners feelings can lead to an openly nationalistic rhetoric which in turn endangers the international reputation of the state and can reduce the chances of European integration.

In Slovakia, on the other hand, the simultaneous democratisation and independence processes highlighted the lack of consensus about the final conception of nationhood and statehood. Whilst Slovenes were able to co-opt nationalism and whatever degree of democratic tradition was inherited from self-management communism and a historically less repressed position into a positive force, Slovakia descended into 'solving the history'. The absence of democratic traditions, the resentments of the past, the lack of experience in dealing with the international community as an independent state and not in the least its communist legacy overwhelmed democratisation[41]. In contrast to Slovenia foreign policy became a prisoner of domestic politics, which apart from the difficulties that Slovakia encountered with postcommunist development, became submerged in personal conflicts among politicians and the preoccupation with 'Slovak' issues. All divisions in society were instrumentalised as part of the domestic political conflict, including the integration into European structures[42], as the following illustrates.

## Foreign Policy Failure: Slovakia

The first point to make about the international position of Slovakia is that it appears to be back where it started in 1993. The debate surrounding the process of independence in 1992/1993 could be divided into three strands and their validity depends on where Slovakia stands at the moment[43]. One position taken, mostly by intellectuals and some federalist politicians, argued that Slovak independence would endanger not only the geopolitical stability in Central Europe, but more importantly Slovak democracy and that these arguments outweighed the right to self-determination. Obviously, strongly nationalist politicians and intellectuals were vehemently opposed to such considerations and saw no danger that was great enough to outweigh the prestige and the logic of independence. The third and weighty argument, espoused by the majority of nationalists and more cynical democrats, admitted the dangers to democracy, but thought it a price worth paying for independence. Thus, Slovakia embarked on a six-year intensive course in political turmoil, and optimists can argue that precisely this experience is the best guarantee against future authoritarianism. It is an appealing argument to which I would like to add that a sympathetic and constructive approach from the EU, as observed of late[44], is more likely to ensure such desirable outcome.

If independence-seekers claimed that Slovakia could not miss the historical moment when Europe is prepared to respect the break up of states, as Slovaks, Croats and Slovenes can affirm, the federalists claimed that Slovakia could not miss the historical moment when Europe opened its arms and would embrace new democracies. Out of these two historical chances Slovakia chose the first one. Considering the delay in admitting even such success stories among new democracies as the Czech Republic, Hungary, Poland and Slovenia into the EU[45], the federalist position appears less persuasive now. Europe has changed - after the bloody disintegration of Yugoslavia, it no longer likes secession and the embrace is somewhat reluctant too[46]. If Slovakia manages to get into EU in the first wave[47], which is looking increasingly more realistic then all has ended well. If not, the big question about the price for independence will remain unanswered.

So, where did foreign policy fail during those intervening six years? The answer is - at home.

## Slovakia in Post-Cold War Central Europe

Czecho-Slovakia (which was the official name of the country in 1992) was the only multi-national state in postcommunist Europe, which was able to split in a civilised and peaceful way, and the Czech Republic and Slovakia received international recognition for this. The fact that Slovakia declared itself to be a successor of Czechoslovakia rather than the Slovak State was important for its relatively rapid international recognition. This was also helped by the Declaration of the National Council of the Slovak Republic that it would unambiguously accept the principles regulating international relations, to contribute to the process of disarmament and ensure the applications of human rights and the rights of minorities. Slovakia achieved the same international status and position as her immediate neighbours, the Czech Republic, Poland and Hungary, with a much longer tradition of foreign policy and independent statehood in the latter two cases.

Slovak elites try to compensate for the lack of statehood by claiming a thousand-year struggle for independence. Yet, even if the legality of the split cannot be doubted, the absence of a referendum, thus the will of citizens, will always put a question mark on the legitimacy of Czech and Slovak independence. It can be argued that the dissatisfaction with the federal state did not translate directly into the identification with a new one (as all opinion polls demonstrated) and that similarly to the democratisation process the new state lacked direction and inner conviction[48]. If there is one assumption about a precondition for successful foreign policy making, it must be a clear answer to 'who we are' and 'where do we want to belong'. It can be argued that the inability to answer these questions with sufficient conviction has hindered not only the Slovak democracy, but is also responsible for the foreign policy failures; the adherence to Western democracy and efforts to integrate into the Euro-Atlantic structures have been repeatedly declared, but if there was a serious intention the actions did not always support these claims.

The political decision about the enlargement of the EU was taken at the Copenhagen summit in 1993, in 1994 NATO adopted the programme Partnership for Peace and in 1997 Russia, by signing the Founding Act with NATO, de iure accepted the process of its former allies joining NATO - the bipolar world finally ended. The Treaty of Maastricht (February 1992, in force November 1993) committed all members of the EU to coordinate their foreign (and security) policies, whilst the majority of the EU member states are organised in the Western European Union (WEU), or in NATO, which effectively ties up all the countries of Europe into NATO, or EU[49], including neutral ones, as neutrality lost its economic and political justification.

Slovakia is a member of both the NATO's Partnership for Peace (February 1994) and the EU's associate member (October 1993). In addition, it participates in OSCE (January 1993) and is a member of the Council of Europe (June 1993). The basic conditions for EU enlargement (Essen 1994) are: stability of democratic institutions, recognition of human rights and the rights of minorities; a functioning market economy, including the ability to withstand the economic competition within the Union; the ability to undertake all duties (political, economic and monetary) resulting from the membership[50]. That means that perhaps never before in the history of Slovakia (and all new states in ECE) has foreign policy been the subject of the country's free will and choice and never before did it depend so much on internal politics.

*Conditions and limitations* There are some factors that contributed to the exclusion of Slovakia, which are not directly linked to governmental decisions, but as remnants of the past are a limiting factor in political development. The most important in this context are the absence of independent statehood and the nature of the previous regime. Many limitations to a successful conduct of international affairs derive precisely from these factors.

No tradition of statehood means a lack of well-trained diplomats, a handicap exacerbated by conflicts about who was suitable to represent the new Slovakia. Few of those Slovak diplomats who previously represented the Czecho-Slovak federation were deemed suitable to represent the new state, whose new elite based its legitimacy on 'purely' Slovak interests. In the tradition of the previous regime, diplomatic posts were given, often as a reward for favours rendered, to the people close to the government. The instability and weakness of the new state institutions in postcommunist countries is magnified by the attitude of the new elite, which considers itself in charge of the state and has as little respect for those institutions as the population has an understanding of them. Slovenia is exceptional in several respects: having been relatively free and advanced it had a pool of well-travelled politicians to chose from. The nature of the Yugoslav federation was such that Slovenia negotiated many bilateral treaties directly, which compensated for the lack of experience in independent statecraft; the orientation of the foreign policy was from the beginning of independent Slovenia unambiguously Western, so that the objectives were clearer.

Another limitation of a new statehood is the population which has no interest in international affairs and very little information about how these should be conducted. The lack of interest is a result of being previously deprived of opportunities to come into contact with foreign cultures, particularly the West. The number of people who travelled abroad and speak foreign languages is still very small in contrast to Slovenia, where English is a part of national curriculum from the age of ten. All research shows that the people with more active foreign experience are more interested in foreign affairs and have more confidence in the international integration of their country.

The general lack of 'foreign experience' does not mean that the international position of Slovakia is of no interest to the general public. On the contrary, 54% of respondents in 1997 expressed concern about Slovakia's failure to make the first 'Eastern' wave of the EU, and 47% felt embarrassed at their country's international position[51]. Nationalism here cuts both ways: embarrassment can lead to resentment as much as it can inspire a remedial action, providing the political leadership does not, in order to maintain its position, resort to a strategy of blaming others[52]. The most limiting factor to the successful integration for Slovakia has been the passivity of the public, which can be explained as a general postcommunist condition. In Slovakia this was exacerbated by an unclear vision about where the state was or should be heading, possibly best exemplified by another statement of Mečiar: 'if the West does not accept us, we will turn to the East'[53]. Initially, the symbol of communism's defeat in Slovakia and everywhere else became the integration into the developed democratic world, but very soon the path became littered with obstacles bequeathed by the past and gained in the present, and the ruling elites were claiming that Slovakia was 'making its own democracy, derived from the state's national past'[54], and therefore became an 'object of international conspiracy'[55]. Making its own democracy involved such undemocratic practices that in the period between November 1994 and October 1995 Slovakia received three diplomatic démarches[56]. Neither the EU, nor NATO did possibly expect that this would be the time when the Prime Minister would choose to visit Moscow and seek a customs union with Russia, because, as he put it, 'Slovakia will not stand in front of the EU or NATO as a pupil in front of a teacher'[57]. What one observes in those statements is a certain intransigence, a cheap flattery disguised as dignity, all designed to camouflage incompetence and unwillingness.

Judging by the 1997 and 1998 polls it is clear that the public, inspired by the vehement criticism from independent journalists, began to understand that Slovakia's exclusion was directly linked to the domestic scene and not to some anti-Slovak conspiracy as the government argued.

The government was seen as directly responsible by 55% of respondents, while 48% did not think that their country had met the criteria for integration and 43% (April 1998) did not know where the country was heading[58]. After six years of independence, during which the dominating force in Slovakia's politics was the populist HzDS assisted by the nationalist SNS, the faith that this was a government that would bring about the integration of Slovakia into the democratic West was diminishing rapidly. Whilst not wishing to argue that the foreign policy was the reason for Mečiar's government's defeat, it has most definitely contributed to the questioning of its true intentions and the direction Slovakia was taking.

*Challenges and Key Elements of Foreign Policy: Slovakia and Slovenia*

Slovenia has been for some time basking in the light of international approval, having emerged from the collapse of Yugoslavia as the most prosperous of the ECE states with an exceptionally good record on human rights and the political fast track reforms. The challenge now is twofold. The first concern is to remain on this track, whilst it is not the stability of democratic institutions that is an issue, but the completion of the institutional framework for an integrated market economy. The second challenge is the transformation of national identity from the one formed as a successful and separate part of a larger state to national identity of an independent small state, now comparing itself to other more developed states, not to the ex-Yugoslav republics. Connected to this is that the main achievements of Slovenia, its independence and the European integration were not achieved by the current opposition (since the gradual nature of the Slovene transition meant that there was hardly any change in political elites). Consequently their platform is more nationalist one, wrapped up with the blame of the leadership's negligence of national issues, thus Slovenia is not completely safe from the dangers of nationalism. The smallness of the country, which in the past was an advantage in creating consensus, can prove a disadvantage - it is vulnerable to any disturbance, whilst agitation can spread quickly.

Slovenia's only difficult neighbour is Italy which is however its second largest economic partner after Germany. The problems concern the protection of Slovene minority in Italy, which does not match the provisions guaranteed to the Italian minority in Slovenia, and the claims for compensation for expropriated Italian properties in territory ceded to Yugoslavia after the Second World War (similar to the Czech-German relations). The relations with the Southern neighbour, Croatia, are good despite some complications concerning unresolved issues of division of the property previously shared in the former Yugoslavia, a situation very similar to the Czech-Slovak 'who owes what to whom' after the split. Relations with Austria suffer slightly from historical resentments and a certain fear of 'Germanisation', whilst the relations with Hungary are excellent for there are no historical resentments between the two countries, or current minority issues to be resolved.

The challenge for Slovakia is much more encompassing, at home and abroad. With Poland, Hungary and the Czech Republic having entered NATO in February 1999 and being the first candidates for the EU, the definition of Central Europe will change and Slovakia, should it remain excluded, would be surrounded (94% of the borders) by members of the EU - Austria, Hungary, Poland and the Czech Republic. The key foreign policy partners for the future of Slovakia are Hungary and the Czech Republic, historically both a source of national resentment. The treatment of the Hungarian minority, particularly in view of the fact that Hungary enjoys a very favourable international status, becomes an important issue at home and abroad. The slightest escalation of conflict is unacceptable to NATO and the EU, whilst it must be said that the positive side of this is that Hungarian political elites will also be restrained in their concerns beyond their borders. Today the Czech Republic is the most important commercial partner of Slovakia (31% of exports). The Czecho - Slovak relations will have to overcome the historical animosities and the trauma of the disintegration of the common state, and it is up to Slovakia to somehow coordinate its political and economic development with that of the Czech Republic. In sum, the cooperation between Hungary, Slovakia and the Czech Republic needs significant improvement. The connection with internal Slovak politics gives these relations a complex character and requires a whole new interpretation of national interests far exceeding questions of national sentiments attached to the past.

The new government is facing a double challenge. It has to prove that Slovakia is safe from undemocratic practices whilst removing the political and economic debris of the last six years. To integrate into the EU in the late 1990s Europe is not an easy task - the union is battling with its own direction and the reluctance of some of its existing members, and therefore is less enthusiastic and more suspicious of new democracies. The domestic scene is impatient for quick results, the winners having removed the main obstacle - the previous administration - are faced with their own differences, whilst the defeated, still much in evidence, are waiting for an opportunity. Political elites are crucial for the interpretation of national identity and its translation into foreign policy making[59]. Therefore, the relationship between nationalism, national identity, democracy and foreign policy finds a true challenge in new democracies, such as Slovakia and Slovenia, if they are to qualify for European integration.

## Conclusion

As was argued throughout, the relationship between democracy and nationalism in the newly independent postcommunist states is something of a paradox; all challenges they pose to one another are matched by the inevitability and simultaneity of their coexistence. National self-determination, minority rights and national identity are juxtaposed to the creation of an all inclusive, culturally tolerant and politically united community and further compounded by the international environment.

This chapter portrayed the nation and the state in the highly interdependent world: the global world in which the distinction between internal and external affairs is being increasingly eroded. The process of democratisation is thus closely connected and synchronised with the processes of integration into the existing international structures. This challenge from the external environment, already compressed into a short time puts further pressure on nationalism - its ultimate achievement is not merely the recognition of its state's sovereignty, but the ability to relinquish, almost immediately, some of that sovereignty to transnational organisations.

The examination of the dynamic between national identity, democracy and nationalism in the newly independent democracies and their integrative efforts, sharpened the differences between them and emphasised the importance of consensus about international integration in domestic politics. In the contest between nationalism and democracy, nationalism easily becomes a challenge when the commitment to the latter is in any doubt - the same applies for international integration. I would like to assert that on balance, international integration by promoting transparency and compliance with democratic procedures and norms is conducive to the development of a more democratic political culture, which in the final analysis must reflect the state's international position. The process is not linear; the interference of the international context at times unleashes a backlash from the national, and the whole process resembles rather a two-step-forward-one-step-back dance than a slow march forward.

Despite clear evidence that some states, at times, perform below expectations, the overall assessment should be a positive one. It must take into account that the tasks facing the newly independent democracies of ECE were staggering, whilst expectations were too high and often not backed up by more than the rhetoric of good intent - something both sides tend to be guilty of.

# Notes

1 T.Niklasson 'The external dimension' in G. Pridham and T. Vanhanen *Democratisation in Eastern Europe* London, Routledge 1994 p.216.
2 The following paragraph was inspired by K.Booth 'Human Wrongs and International Relations' *International Affairs* 71:1 Winter 1995 pp.103-126.
3 V.Hribar 'The Slovenes and European Transnationality' *Nova Revija* Special edition July 1991.
4 V.Mečiar 1.January1993, cited in M.Leško 'Príbeh diskvalifikácie favorita' *Slovensko v Šedej Zóne* Bratislava, IVO 1998 p.16.
5 For example L.Diamond and M.Plattner: 'democracy has been left with no serious geopolitical or ideological rivals', in the introduction to *The Global Resurgence of Democracy* Baltimore, London, The Johns Hopkins University Press 1996.
6 A view particularly passionately defended by F.Fukuyama, see chapter 2.
7 S.Gill 'Gramsci, Modernity and Globalization' paper delivered at BISA Conference 15-17 December 1997 Leeds p.6.
8 A.Ágh *The Politics of Central Europe* London, Sage 1998 p.8.
9 'Globalization is the intractable fate of the world' in Z. Bauman *Globalization The Human Consequences* Cambridge, Polity, 1998 p.1.
10 L.Weiss 'Globalization and the Myth of the Powerless State' *New Left Review* 225 September/ October 1997 pp.3-26 p.4.
11 For this view see L.Weiss *The Myth of the Powerless State: Governing the Economy in a Global Era* Cambridge, Polity 1998.
12 This discussion is often the subject of a new concept in international relations referred to as 'societal security' (separate from state security, but parallel and broadening the agenda of security from the survival of the state to the survival of the society as equally relevant) see: O.Weawer, B.Buzan, M.Kelstrup and P.Lemaitre *Identity, Migration and the New Security Agenda in Europe* London, Pinter Publishers 1993.
13 For this more open-ended view see: A.McGrew 'A Global Society?' in S.Hall, D.Held and T.McGrew *Modernity and Its Futures* Oxford, Polity Press in Association with the Open University 1992.
14 For classic realist school of thought see H. Morgenthau (particularly *Politics Among Nations*), for a more updated neo-structuralist approach K.Waltz (*The Theory of International Politics* 1979).
15 See J.Rosenau (*Domestic Sources of Foreign Policy* 1967, *The Scientific Study of Foreign Policy* 1971).
16 D.Held *Democracy and the Global Order* Cambridge, Polity 1995.
17 See J.Habermas 'The European Nation-State and the Pressures of Globalization' *New Left Review* 235 May/June 1999 pp.46-59.
18 A.Linklater 'Cosmopolitan Citizenship' *Citizenship Studies* 2:1 February 1998 pp.23-43 p.24.
19 Cited in N.Walker 'The Idea of Constitutional Pluralism'. Paper prepared for a seminar 'Constitutionalism in Transition', University of Leeds, 5 July 2001.
20 See B.Anderson *Imagined Communities* London, Verso 1983.
21 S.Huntington in the following: 'The Clash of Civilizations?' and 'The West Unique, Not Universal' *Foreign Affairs*, 72:3 Summer 1993 pp.22-49 and 75:6 November/December 1996 pp.28-46 respectively.

[22] See: G.Hosking and G.Schöpflin ed. *Myths and Nationhood* London, Macmillan 1997; E. Hobsbawm and T. Ranger ed. *The Invention of Tradition* New York, Cambridge University Press 1983; For the relevance of myths in the politics of ECE see G.Gyáni 'Political Uses of Tradition in Postcommunist East Central Europe' *Social Research* 60:4 Winter 1993 pp.893-913.

[23] M.Hroch 'National Self-Determination from a Historic Perspective' in *Canadian Slavonic Papers* 37: 4 September/December 1995 pp.283-300.

[24] R.Brubaker 'Myths and Misconceptions in the Study of Nationalism' in J.Hall *The State of the Nation* Cambridge, Cambridge University Press 1998 p.294.

[25] U.Hedetoft 'The Nation-state meets the world: National Identities in the Context of Transnationality and Cultural Globalisation' paper prepared for BISA 15-17 December 1997 p.5.

[26] This is based on I.Prizel *National Identity and Foreign Policy* Cambridge, Cambridge University Press 1998, which is to my knowledge the only work of this kind.

[27] I. Prizel p.14.

[28] Slovene parliament adopted various Laws of Foreign Affairs to make signing of international treaties easier see B. Bučar 'Slovenia' H.Neuhold, P.Havlik and A.Suppan *Political and Economic Transformation in Eastern Central Europe* Boulder, Westview Press 1995.

[29] The Vienna summit (11-12 December 1998) decided to wait until December 1999 with a further reassessment of Slovakia's entry into the EU, but Prime Minister M.Dzurinda has announced that the new government will do what it can to get the reassessment moved to an earlier date in the spring 1999. See *The Slovak Spectator* 4:32.

[30] Drawn from D.Beetham and Ch.Lord *Legitimacy and the European Union* London, New York, Longman 1998 p. 47-55.

[31] I. Prizel p.2.

[32] The text under the heading 'Political Criteria' is preceded by 'problems in respect of the criteria defined by the European Council in Copenhagen, i.e.: government does not sufficiently respect powers devolved by the constitution to other bodies and disregards the opposition; the tension between the President and the government; the disregard for the Constitutional Court; the use made by government of police and the treatment of the Hungarian minority'.

[33] Agenda 2000 Summary and conclusions of the opinions of Commission concerning the Applications for Membership of the EU by the candidate countries Strasbourg 15 July 1997.

[34] 'Slovenia can manage federal Europe, for federal experience - we are used to it', said I.Bavčar, Slovene Minister for Europe. Slovene Study Day SSEES, London 21 April 1999.

[35] I.Brinar 'Slovenia: From Yugoslavia to the European Union' in K.Henderson *Back to Europe* London, UCL Press 1999 p.252.

[36] 'Povzetek Programa SNS' 1996.

[37] The government itself tries to lower the expectations, purposely, to avoid the backlash of disappointment. In conversation with S.Gaber, the Minister of Education 8 May 1998.

[38] These are results of surveys commissioned by the government to the University of Ljubljana N. Toš 'Informiranost in Stališča Ciljnih Skupin v Sloveniji o Evropski Uniji in Slovenskem Približevanju EU' 23 December 1997 pog.št. 121/97.

[39] *Financial Times* Survey Slovenia 28 April 1997.

[40] I.Bavčar 'Slovene Study Day'.

[41] For the discussion about how different historical experiences lead to different political institutions see M. Carpenter 'Slovakia and the Triumph of Nationalist Populism' *Communist and Post-Communist Studies* 30:2 1997 pp.205-220.

[42] For Slovakia's integration see also K.Henderson 'Slovakia and the Democratic Criteria for EU Accession' in K Henderson *Back to Europe* London, UCL Press 1999.

[43] M.Šimečka 'Cena za oneskorenú demokraciu' in *Domino* 7:51-52 p.2.

[44] Suspected embezzlement of European funds currently investigated in Slovakia has been treated surprisingly mildly by the Commission whose ambassador in Slovakia has ensured the government that the case will not affect Slovakia's chances of early integration and expressed hope that the investigation will be an opportunity to demonstrate the country's democratic credentials. *SME* 10 May 2001 and 23 July 2001.

[45] At the Amsterdam summit in June 1997 it was decided that the negotiations about the full membership of those four countries would begin in 1998.

[46] See for example the Irish referendum against the enlargement (June 2001). For the criticism of the EU and its lack of commitment to ECE entries see A.Hyde-Price *The International Politics of East Central Europe* Manchester, Manchester University Press 1996.

[47] The estimated date for the first entries could be as late as 2005, according to I.Bavčar.

[48] A.Duleba *Foreign Policy of the Slovak Republic Starting Points, Present situation and Prospects* Bratislava, Slovak Foreign Policy Association 1998 p.5. Henceforth, A. Duleba.

[49] For example: Norway is not a member of the EU, but a member of the NATO, Ireland is not a member of NATO, but the EU.

[50] A.Duleba p.19.

[51] M.Bútora and F.Šebej eds. *Slovensko v Sedej Zóne* Bratislava, IVO 1998 p.168.

[52] Mečiar in a meeting with an assistant to Madeleine Albright said that 'we will keep trying to get into NATO, but we know that we will not succeed, because the USA and Russia have agreed on this' *Slovenská Republika* 14 April 1997.

[53] *Slovensko v Šedej Zóne* p.179.

[54] *Slovenská Republika* 24 July 1997.

[55] *Slovenská Republika* 27 July 1997.

[56] The first one concerned with the removal of all opposition from the parliamentary posts and replacement of all media executives with government's supporters (November 1994), the second one concerning the government's actions against the President and the third one, from the USA, also concerned with 'the growing intolerance towards the opposition, the political atmosphere of fear and the opaqueness of privatisation'.

[57] *Slovensko v Šedej Zóne* p.39.

[58] *Slovensko v Šedej Zóne* p.181.

[59] It is interesting to note that the change of political elite in Slovakia and their commitment to the EU and NATO has already brought changes in perceptions about Europe and identity. According to a recent poll, Europe invokes a sense of pride among 67% of the population on the par with their locality (66%). IVO May 2001.

# 8 Reconciling Postcommunism, Nationalism and Democracy

That nationalism and democracy form a close but complicated relationship is a truism whose significance was nevertheless brought into a sharp focus in postcommunist transitions in Eastern Central Europe. The variation of patterns in which these transitions evolved, particularly in respect of choices given to national and minority issues was the starting point of this book. Among many possible approaches towards the explanation of these differences in the transition processes, I chose the 'nationalism-democracy' approach. Whilst I do not wish to claim that there is a direct correlation between the progress or stagnation of a particular transition to democracy and the corresponding nationalism, the journey through the postcommunist political landscape has shown the relevance of this approach.

The major themes running through this book were postcommunism, nationalism, democratisation and the link between them. My aim has been to generate an explanation of democratisation processes in the newly independent states that could be applicable to other countries in a similar situation. However, all conclusions drawn from the above cases are based on reflections on what has happened. Hence, modest suggestions projected from these conclusions cannot account for contingencies, such as a new crisis in the international environment, economic crisis or unexpected radical changes in the domestic scene.

The very nature of nationalism, underlying its political manifestations, is its rootedness in the psychological attachment to 'the nation', and thus, the capacity to influence group behaviour. If the events of the last decade can tell us anything important about the behaviour of states and nations in the turmoil of collapsing states and ideological frameworks, it is that nationalism is easily mobilised, for when it comes to emotional commitment, nationalism, at this point in history, does not seem to have many rivals as a form of collective allegiance. I have attempted to view nationalism objectively, given the evident legitimising, emancipating and energising role it has played in the liberation of ECE countries from communism. However, placing nationalism on a par with democracy, despite what at times appears to be an inexhaustible reservoir of political manoeuvre, is to give too much credence to its reliance on the exploitation of societal conflicts and obscure democracy's ability to resolve them.

*Disintegrating states and revived national identities*   Postcommunism is associated with a rapid economic and social transformation, based on the premise of democracy, human rights and European integration. The loss of lives over the last 10 years in the Balkans tarnished the promise of democracy and reduced the initial expectations of the 'revolutionary' year 1989 to more realistic proportions, by bringing to the fore one unexpected facet of these transformations - nationalism and its dangers. Yet the former Yugoslavia is not a characterisation of postcommunism, but a sign of a disintegrating federation whose ideological basis for existence was removed and replaced by different aims sought by its various constituent units. Nationalism on its own cannot cause wars, regardless of how strong the sense of national identity or injured pride may be; violence needs many other ingredients for it to be activated and critical among them are: insecurity and resistance to change, personal ambitions of politicians, or attempts to inflate political legitimacy through the exploitation of ethnic allegiances. In that sense Serbian nationalism, despite the human catastrophe caused by its emergence, is not too different from any other nationalism whose goal is to halt the change at any cost and deprive others of aspirations deemed righteous for one's own nation. Nationalism has a double-edged quality - it can be an instrument of change as much as it can be an impediment to change.

The second point worth noting in connection to postcommunism is that nationalism was not its cause, but sprung into action once it became clear that communism had exhausted its power by which it imposed its legitimacy. This is not to argue the rights or wrongs of communist ideology, but to assert that communism as a system operating in the ECE countries camouflaged the lack of legitimacy by rhetoric and coercion, a method eventually proved to have been of limited duration.

Hence the question here was not why postcommunism and why democracy, but firstly what makes postcommunism such a fertile ground for nationalism and secondly, on a more theoretical level, what makes democracy and nationalism both complementary and conflicting and thirdly, given that this is the case, how can the conflictual side of this relationship be minimised so that the more complementary facets become more enhanced. This last point was the subject of this book and remains a continuing problem for all democratisation processes.

The first chapter proposed five factors considered relevant to the question why nationalism became a logical conclusion to the fall of communism and a feature of postcommunism. These were: the 'ancient hatred' theory; the inadvertent and deformed nation-building under communism; nationalism as a 'replacement' ideology; the role of elites in postcommunism; and conflicts between minorities and majorities intensified by the role of 'external' homelands. It appeared that all of those propositions bore relevance to the salience of nationalism in varying degrees.

The underlying argument however was that it is a certain type of nationalism which concerned us here and the type of politics that it engenders. The challenge to democracy comes from ethnic politics, which involves necessarily the promotion and seeking of preferential treatment for the dominant ethnic group within the state, or a pursuit of more recognition by a minority, characteristically in response to the former. Ethnic politics are usually a response to some external challenge. It can be a reaction of a nation that perceives itself neglected by history or by another nation and is now in a position to rectify the past, it can be a minority responding to aggressive nation-building policies of the majority, or pre-empting such a process, it could be a nation in a multinational state attempting to redistribute control over the state, it could be an ethnically homogenous society looking for an imaginary enemy - or any other variation of the above. The root of ethnic politics is always attached to ethnic or national identity and its (re)assertion, in order to assert or readjust the national position, whether for reasons of insecurity or superiority (cultural, numerical, economic, political), of which Slovakia and Slovenia were good examples.

**Table 8.1  Assessment of 'salience of nationalism' hypotheses**

| Proposition | Czecho-Slovak split | Slovak-Hungarian relationship | Slovene independence |
|---|---|---|---|
| 1. 'ancient hatreds' | partially | Yes | |
| 2. Nation-building under communism | Yes | | Yes |
| 3. Nationalism as a 'replacement' ideology | Yes | Yes | |
| 4. Elite competition | Yes | Yes | |
| 5. Mutually reinforcing majority and minority nationalism | | Yes | |

Looking at table above and the three national issues discussed throughout, the Czecho-Slovak split, the Slovak-Hungarian relationship and Slovene independence, it could be argued that the higher the number of propositions applicable to the Slovak case, in comparison to Slovenia, explains the higher prominence of ethnic politics in Slovakia. This however does not say which of those hypotheses has a stronger potential and under which circumstances (in itself a worthwhile project for further investigation, with an aim to contribute to theories for the prevention of ethnic conflicts). The nationalist phenomenon is inspired by a multiplicity of factors, which also suggests the large range of possibilities towards the reduction of some of these factors.

Given that history cannot be undone and that reflection of the past and conclusions drawn from that past are an integral part of national myths, the 'ancient hatred' hypothesis is potent, but only to the extent to which it is exploited and, as I have argued, the success of ethnic mobilisation on the historical issues depends more on contemporary factors than on 'ancient ones'. Postcommunism affected societies in such an all-encompassing way that no identity, whether the state, the individual or the nation remained intact; hence the issue of identity and its redefinition in accordance with new aspirations, aims and traumas became a logical accompaniment of postcommunism. The manipulation by elites which can and did substantially increase the levels of conflict is based on the premise that there is a level of discontent about national position which is felt or recognised by the majority of its members. That then suggests that the influence of political elites can operate also in the opposite direction, towards the minimising of ethnic politics, as was indicated by the change of political scene in Slovakia after the last general elections.

In the context of contemporary politics in the region the interplay between minorities and majorities exercises a considerable influence on domestic and foreign politics and is potentially an explosive issue. However, the perception of the minority vis-à-vis the majority and the state and vice-versa is not fixed, but changes in response to the political developments within the state; more precisely, according to how the state and its dominant nation views the minority(ies).

The true nature of democratic politics is a mutual accommodation (the emphasis is on 'mutual', which means that the responsibility does not rest exclusively with the majority, but equally with the minority) within a multiethnic state, whilst the aim should be the establishment of a political community with a collective identity attached to the state. Evidently the construction of such identity in culturally diverse societies is not easily achieved; ultimately it requires a redefinition of national identity in such a way that certain elements of the identity formation become attached to the common political (co)existence within the state, in order to bridge culturally related differences. I hope I have conveyed sufficiently the inadequacy of the civic versus ethnic distinction of nationalism in our times, but in the context of this concluding chapter, I want to stress again that the establishment of an united political community does not necessarily mean a replacement of ethnic identity by a civic one, but the removal of ethnicity as a conflict-generating issue from the top of the domestic political agenda. Slovakia (and prior Czechoslovakia) have repeatedly failed this test of democracy which proved damaging to Slovakia's transition and integration process.

*Between the 'old' and 'new' nationalism* If none of the above propositions is conclusive, but merely contributory, there must be one overwhelming reason for the manifest prominence of nationalism in postcommunist societies. I argued that it is democratisation itself. For all the complexity surrounding the relationship between nationalism and democracy, the connection between them is rather easily summed up. Democracy needs the state, for a clearly defined political unit is a prerequisite for the exercise of democracy; the nation also needs a state in order to secure its recognition and exert control over the destiny of the nation, thus inevitably it seeks to appropriate as much control over the state as it can muster - thus, statehood and nationhood come together and the link is even tighter when the new state is forming and democracy is being established.

The well known dictum that 'nationalism is primarily a political principle, which holds that the political and the national unit should be congruent' (Gellner) applies as much as other definitions of nationalism as a movement for unity, autonomy and identity of the national group (Smith), to name but two of the most used ones. These however are definitions of classical nationalism and tell only a part of the story which is now being played out. One reason is obvious, the political unit is usually not 'national', in the sense that in most cases not one nation can call it its own, despite the nationalist leaders' pretensions to the contrary. Consequently, more than one unity and more than one identity are seeking autonomy.

So, what is the nature of postcommunist nationalism, implying nationalism during the period of communism's collapse and the initial transition to democracy. My suggestion is that it is a specific type of nationalism which combines all elements of classical 19th century nationalism with entirely new features, previously not associated with nationalism, but rather with internationalism.

The systemic change which produced the transformation of the political, social and economic spheres has also produced a need for a deeper legitimacy than a new political order. The change challenged not only the regimes, but the states, their foundations and their boundaries, the challenge that the existing multinational states could not withstand. Democracy came with new national aspirations and those aspirations questioned not only the boundaries, but the very contents of those boundaries and a kind of second round of nationalist endeavour took hold; the first round was national liberation from communism in which ethnic identity was secondary to democracy, but this pro-democracy solidarity did not last to the second round.

Once the main obstacle, the old communist regime was dismantled, the flow of changes gathered momentum to bring up another force - national identity. Nations in possession of states were re-stating their relationships with neighbours and minorities, nations that lost their states were reclaiming them, whilst nations that were 'half way' through with a limited sovereignty of a federal republic saw an opportunity to as it were finish 'the job' history has deprived them of. The calculation of costs and benefits, and the historical ties, were pushed aside in the name of a democracy that had hardly been born. What was born were new sovereign states, in which democracy, state and the nation were all establishing themselves and seeking to legitimise their existence via each other; minorities, also in the process of reassessing their new identity, were left fighting not to get forgotten in the great battle for the nation-state and its legitimacy.

Postcommunist transitions of the newly independent states should, from another point of view, less absorbed in the economy and the establishment of the democratic procedures, be defined as synchronisation of two major historical processes, nation-building and state-building which became in an unprecedented way compressed into one process - the democratisation process. Clearly, seeking a comparison with other democratisation processes from other authoritarian regimes does not do justice to the enormity of this task, whose specificity is a twin project - political transformation accompanied by national independence under the conditions of double insecurity. Nationalism lies at the junction where these processes meet and its role is defined by the levels of political and national development at that moment.

Postcommunist nationalism is linked to democracy in an almost old-fashioned 'revolutionary' way, similar to the year 1848, which is a paradox, considering the often used adjective 'new'. Another 'old' element of this contemporary postcommunist nationalism is the ethnic thrust of it, the reason for which is to be found on two levels. First, the novelty of the ethnic nation establishing the state and second, the abandonment of the previous civic identity in favour of the ethnic one.

There is however a crucial difference with the 'old' nationalism. A truly new trait in postcommunist nationalism is that it moved its goal posts

- from national sovereignty to international integration. The recognition of the nation has since the 19th century assumed a new dimension in the form of the acceptance among the developed democratic nations who are secure enough in their democracy and nationhood to relinquish some of their sovereignty in the name of the larger community, in this case Europe. If the synchronisation of the nation-building and state-building appeared a difficult task, this added dimension puts the whole process into another realm altogether. To secure nationhood in the conditions of having just achieved it, to secure democracy when there was very little time for it to sink its roots into the society deep enough not to be swayed by various challenges, at the same time as complying with rules and regulations put into practice by long established states and democracies seems almost an unfair proposition. Yet, at the time of writing 10 postcommunist Eastern and Central European states, among them such difficult cases of transition as Slovakia and Rumania have been accepted for the negotiations about the admission to the European Union, which can only be described as an achievement.

*The final reflection on the role of nationalism in the democratisation process* This contradicts the accusations of regression and anachronism addressed to postcommunist nationalism and asks another important question about the future of nationalism. If Slovak nationalism can wane and turn the corner towards European integration, then perhaps all nationalisms can. It has brought my argument a full circle, from stating its dangers to the main argument of this book that nationalism does not operate independently and hence its role in the democratisation process depends on the evolving dynamics between many variables within the state.

The case studies concentrated mainly on the following factors: the level of national consciousness and satisfaction, the historical factors, the ethnic composition and harmony, the political, economic and cultural development prior to independence, but more importantly the political development during the transition and the formation of elites, equally importantly the mode of attainment of independence and lastly, the international environment. All of those factors have been dealt with at length in the previous chapters.

The omission of the mode of transition from this list is worth a comment and possibly criticism. However, as much as the gradual transition in Slovenia has been the main argument for the success of the Slovene transition in comparison to the less successful Slovak case, the mode of transition shared by the Czech Republic and Slovakia produced nevertheless contrasting transition processes, with the Czech case resembling Slovenia rather than Slovakia. This says something about the level of national confidence, the political tradition and the conviction about democracy rather than about the mode of transition and the severity of the previous regime. It also says a great deal about different conclusions the nation and its leaders draw from the past.

It appears that the further one moves away from postcommunism, the more the other facets of that society's existence come to the fore. The importance of the gradualism of the Slovene transition does not lie in the actual moment of the collapse of the previous regime, but in the length of time it allowed for the negotiations about the future direction of the state prior to the final departure from communism and the federation. In fact Slovenia, in terms of political development, had left the federation long before the question of independence became a paramount issue - in Slovenia democratisation took precedence and national independence followed from it.

Slovakia, on the other hand illustrated the accumulation of negative conditions for the process of democratisation: injured and halted nation-building prior to communism leading to a fascist regime during the Second World War, the pitfalls of the communist modernisation and ultimately a sudden democratisation bestowed on the nation unprepared for it and undecided about its future direction. The consequent independence and problems with the Hungarian minority were a reflection of a society insecure in both democracy and nationhood. Nationalism in Slovakia illustrated all the hallmarks of postcommunist nationalism in the early stages of democratisation, including its close, but contradictory connection to democracy. If the democratisation process manages to sustain its current progress, nationalism will have been of a temporary nature. If that is the case (and the final judgment on the Slovak democracy and hence the integration into Europe is still out), it can be argued that nationalism has played out its role in that democratisation process, it did provide a political unit, it redressed some historical injustice, clearly important to a large part of the population and now has little else to offer.

Whichever way, nationalism is a device, it relies on a legitimacy it enjoys by virtue of a psychological attachment to the nation it claims to serve and protect and thus is an accompaniment to great changes, which it can speed-up or obstruct, depending on its nation's aspirations. It is those aspirations that change, depending on the politics of the time and so does the role of nationalism. As much as it can be mobilised, it can be reduced, possibly even eliminated and this is where democracy - its sometimes partner, sometimes challenger - comes to play an even a larger role.

Paradoxically, the undisputed global belief in democracy and in the 'imagined community of the world' has so far failed to diminish the relevance of the 'imagined community' of the nation, which leads me to conclude that firstly, nationalism for the foreseeable future has to be accepted as a permanent feature of our world, because democracy and identity are intimately linked, and secondly that the remedy for the 'narrowness', thus the exclusiveness and defiance of nationalism, has to be sought in democracy and the extension of imagination and compassion beyond one's own nation.

# Appendices

## Appendix 1

### Party programmes:

*Slovakia*

Program Slovenskej Národnej Strany (Pracovný návrh), 1994.
Volebný Program Združenia robotníkov Slovenska, 1994.
"HzDS do toho" Bratislava, 1994.
Magyar Kereszténydemokrata Mozgalom, Program MKDH.
'Pokoj a istota' Maďarská Občianská Strana, 1994.
Koalícia Spoločná Voľba, 9 September 1994.
'Ide o veľa. Ide o Slovensko.' Demokratická Únia Slovenska, 1994.
Volebný program politického hnutia Spolužitia, Voľby 1994.
Memorandum Slovenskej Demokratickej Koalície, 30 Augusta 1997 v Martine.

*Slovenia*

Commandments of the Associated List, 1996.
Slovenija 2000 Volilni Program Liberalne Demokracije Slovenije.
SDSS Politični Program Socialdemokratska Stranka Slovenije, Maj 1995.
Program SKD 1994.
SNS Za Tiste, Ki Imamo Slovenijo Radi, 1996.
Program Slovenska Ljudska Stranka ,1996.
Socialdemokratski Program za Slovenijo, Združena Lista, 1996 .

## Appendix 2

### Interviews in Slovakia: August - October 1997 and May 1999

Bajánik, S.,Vicepresident of Matica Slovenská, Bratislava.
Bútorová, Z., Political analyst, Institute for Public Question, Bratislava.
Duleba, A., Political analyst, Research Centre of the Slovak Foreign Policy Association, Prešov.
Fogáš, Ľ., MP and the Vice Chairman of The Party of Democratic Left.

Gajdoš, M., Historian, Slovak Academy of Sciences, Košice.

Hóka, L., Hungarian Christian Democratic Movement, Secretary of the Central Committee, Bratislava.

Hunčík, P., psychiatrist, Sándor Marai Foundation, Bratislava.

Jurová, A., Historian, Slovak Academy of Sciences, Košice.

Kováč, D., Director of the Institute of History, Slovak Academy of Sciences, Bratislava.

Mesežnikov, G., Director of the Institute for Public Questions, Bratislava.

Miháliková, S., Professor at the Department of Politics, Comenius University, Bratislava.

Novosád, F., Senior editor of Parlamentný Kuriér, Bratislava.

Pálko, V., MP, spokesman for Christian Democratic Movement.

Pichler, T., Director of the Institute of Philosophy, Slovak Academy of Sciences, Bratislava.

Podoba, J., Institute of Ethnology, Slovak Academy of Sciences, Bratislava.

Slobodník, D., MP, Movement for Democratic Slovakia, chairman of the government committee for Foreign Affairs 1994-1998, Bratislava.

Weiss, P., MP, The Party of Democratic Left, chairman of the government committee for Foreign Affairs since 1998, Bratslava.

Zajac, P., Publicist, Bratislava.

Zemko, M., Presidential Office (President M.Kováč), Director Domestic Policy Department, Bratislava.


**Interviews in Slovenia: April-May 1998**

Adam, F., Faculty of Social Sciences (Sociology), University of Ljubljana.

Bernik, I., Faculty of Social Sciences (Sociology), University of Ljubljana.

Fink-Hafner, D., Faculty of Social Sciences (Politics), University of Ljubljana.

Gaber, S., Minister of Education, Liberal Democratic Party, Ljubljana.

Hafner-Fink, M., Faculty of Social Sciences (Centre for Public Opinion), University of Ljubljana.

Lukšič, I., Vice-Chairman of the Associated List of Social Democrats, Ljubljana.

Krašovec, A., Faculty of Social Sciences (Politics), University of Ljubljana.

Kreft, L., Faculty of Philosophy, University of Ljubljana, Vice-President of the National Assembly 1991-1994.

Kuzmanić, T., Peace Institute, Ljubljana.

Rizman, R., Faculty of Philosophy, University of Ljubljana.

Toš, N., Director of the Centre for Public Opinion at the University of Ljubljana.

Ule, M., Faculty of Social Sciences (Sociology), University ofLjubljana .

Žagar, M., Institute for Ethnic Studies, Ljubljana.

Zajc, D., Faculty of Social Sciences (Politics), University of Ljubljana.

Zver, M., Vice-President of the Committee for Local Self-Government (Social Democratic Party), The National Council, Secretary of the City Council of Ljubljana.

# Bibliography

Adam, F. ed. (1993), *Volitve in Politika po Slovensko*, Založnik, Ljubljana.

Adam, F. and Tomc, G. (eds) (1994), *Small Societies in Transition: The Case of Slovenia*, Faculty of Social Sciences, Ljubljana.

Agenda 2000, The Opinions of the European Commission on the Applications for Accession, European Commission, Strasbourg, July 1997.

Agenda 2000, Vol. 1: For a Stronger and Wider Union, Doc/97/6, European Commission, Strasbourg, July 1997.

Agenda 2000, Vol. 2: The Challenge of Enlargement, Doc/97/6, European Commission, Brussels, July 1997.

Ágh, A. (1998), *The Politics of Central Europe*, Sage, London.

Alter, P. (1994), *Nationalism*, Edward Arnold, London.

Anderson, B. (1983), *Imagined Communities*, Verso, London.

Asmus, R. and Larrabee, F. (1996), 'Nato and Have-Nots', *Foreign Affairs*, Vol. 75, pp.13-21.

Bačová, V. (1996), *Historická Pamäť a Identita*, Spoločenskovedný Ústav SAV, Košice.

Banać, I. (1992), 'The Fearful Asymmetry of the War: The Causes and Consequences of Yugoslavia's Demise', *Daedalus* 121, pp.141-173.

Batt, J. (1966), *New Slovakia*, Discussion Paper, The Royal Institute of International Affairs.

Bauman, Z. (1998), *Globalization The Human Consequences*, Polity, Cambridge.

Baylis, J. and Rengger, N. (1992), *Dilemmas of World Politics: International Issues in Changing World*, Clarendon, Oxford.

Beetham, D. (1991), *The Legitimation of Power*, Macmillan, London.

Beetham, D. (1994), 'Conditions for Democratic Consolidation', *Review of African Political Economy* 60, pp.157-172.

Beetham, D. and Boyle, K. (1995), *Introducing Democracy: 80 Questions and Answers*, Polity, Cambridge.

Beetham, D. and Lord CH. (1998), *Legitimacy and the European Union*, Longman, London.

Beissinger, M. (1996), 'How Nationalism Spread: Eastern Europe Adrift the Tides and Cycles of Nationalist Contention', *Social Research*, Vol. 63, pp.97-146.

Benderly, J. and Kraft, E. (1997), *Independent Slovenia Origins, Movements Prospects*, Macmillan, London.

Benhke, A. (1997), 'Citizenship, Nationhood and the Production of Political Space', *Citizenship Studies*, Vol.1, pp. 243-265.

Bennett, Ch. (1995), *Yugoslavia's Bloody Collapse Causes, Course and Consequences*, Hurst & Company, London .

Berlin, I. (1972), 'The Bent Twig: A Note on Nationalism', *Foreign Affairs*, Vol. 51, pp.11-31.

Bernik, I. and Molnar, B. (1997), 'Ethism, Nationalism and State-Building: The case of Slovenia', Congress of the International Political Association, Seoul.

Beyme von, K.(1996), *Transitions to Democracy in Eastern Europe*, Macmillan, London.

Bibič, A. and Graziano, G. (1994), *Civil Society, Political Society, Democracy*, Political Science Association, Ljubljana.

Bicanić, I. (1950), 'The Economic Causes of New State Formation During Transition', *East European Politics and Societies*, Vol. 9, pp 2-21.

Blackburn, R. (1991), *After the Fall*, Verso, London.

Bollerup, S. and Christensen, Ch. (1997), *Nationalism in Eastern Europe*, Macmillan, London.

Booth, K. (1995), 'Human Wrongs and International Relations', *International Affairs*, Vol. 71, pp. 103-126.

Bowen, J. (1996), 'The Myth of Global Ethnic Conflict', *Journal of Democracy*, Vol.7, pp. 3-15.

Bözóki, A. (1999), *Intellectuals and Politics in Central Europe*, Central European University Press, Budapest.

Breuilly, J. (1982), *Nationalism and the State*, Manchester University Press, Manchester.

Brown, A. (2000), 'Transnational influences in the transition from communism', *Post-Soviet Affairs*, Vol.16, pp.177-200.

Brubaker, R. (1992), 'National Minorities, Nationalizing States, and External Homelands in the New Europe', *Daedalus* 121, pp. 107-132.

Brubaker, R. (1996), *Nationalism Reframed Nationhood and the National question in the New Europe*, Cambridge University Press, Cambridge.

Bučar, B. and Kuhle, S. (1994), *Small States Compared: Politics of Norway and Slovenia*, Alma Mater, Bergen (Norway).

Bugajski, J. (1995), *Ethnic Politics in Eastern Europe*, M.E.Sharpe, London.

Bunce, V. (1995), 'Comparing East and South', *Journal of Democracy*, Vol. 6, pp. 87-99.

Bunce, V. (1995), 'Should Transitologists be Grounded?', *Slavic Review*, Vol. 54, pp.111- 127.

Bútora, M. and Bútorová, Z. (1993), 'Slovakia: The identity Challenges of the Newly Born State', *Social Research*, Vol. 60, pp.705-736.

Bútora, M. and Hunčík, P. (1996), *Slovensko 1995*, Nadácia Sándora Máraiho, Bratislava.

Bútora, M. and Šebej, F. (1998), *Slovensko v Šedej Zóne*, Inštitút pre verejné otázky, Bratislava.

Bútorová, Z. (1993), 'Premyslené "áno" Zániku ČSFR', *Sociologický Časopis* XXIX, pp.88-103.

Bútorová, Z. (1997), *Slovensko 1996*, Inštitút pre Verejné Otázky, Bratislava.

Caplan, R. and Feffer, J. (1996), *Europe's New Nationalism States and Minorities in Conflict*, Oxford University Press, Oxford.

Carpenter, M. (1997), 'Slovakia and the Triumph of National Populism', *Communist and Post-Communist Studies*, Vol.30, pp.205-220.

Chan, S. (1997), 'In Search of Democratic Peace: Problems and Promise', *Mershon International Studies Review*, Vol. 41, pp.59-91.

Chmel, R. (1997), *Slovenská Otázka v 20.storočí*, Kalligram, Bratislava.

Cohen, L.J. (1993), *Broken Bonds*, Westview Press, Boulder, Oxford.

Cohen, S. (1999), *Politics Without a Past*, Duke University Press, Durham.

Connor, W. (1972), 'Nation-Building or Nation-Destroying?', *World Politics*, Vol. 24, pp. 319-355.

Connor, W. (1984), *The National Question in Marxist-Leninist Theory and Strategy*, Princeton University Press, Princeton.

Connor, W. (1993), 'Beyond Reason: the Nature of the Ethnonational Bond', *Ethnic and Racial Studies*, Vol.16, pp.373 - 388.

Connor, W. (1994), *Ethnonationalism*, Princeton University Press, Princeton.

'Constitution of the Republike Slovenije', (1993), Časopisni zavod, Uradni List Republike Slovenije, Ljubljana.

Dahl, R. (1982), *Dilemmas of Pluralist Democracy*, Yale University Press, New Haven.

Dallin, A. and Lapidus, L. (1991), *The Soviet System in Crisis*, Westview, Oxford.

Dawisha, K. and Parrot, B. (1997), *Politics, Power and the Struggle for Democracy in South-East Europe*, Cambridge University Press, Cambridge.

*Delo*, daily newspaper, Slovenia.

Denitch, B. (1976), *The Legitimation of a Revolution: The Yugoslav Case*, Yale University Press, New Haven, London.

Devetak, S. (1993), *Kleine Nationen und Ethnische Minderheiten im Umbruch Europas*, Slavica Verlag Dr.Anton Kovac, München.

Diamond, L. (1993), *Political Culture and Democracy in Developing Countries*, Lynne Rienner Publishers, London.

Diamond, L. and Plattner, M.F. (1994), *Nationalism, Ethnic Conflict, and Democracy*, The Johns Hopkins University Press, Baltimore.

Djilas, M. (1958), *The New Class,* Thames and Hudson, London.

*Domino Forum*, weekly magazine, Slovakia.

Druckner, D. (1994), 'Nationalism, Patriotism, and the Group Loyalty', *Mershon International Studies Review*, Vol. 38, pp.43-68.

Dunn, J. (1992), *Democracy the Unfinished Journey*, Oxford University Press, Oxford.

Duleba, A. (1998), *Foreign Policy of the Slovak Republic*, Slovak Foreign Policy Association, Bratislava.

Duleba, A.(1998), 'Program Strany Maďarskej Koalície 1998', and 'Program Slovenskej Národnej Strany (1994 and 1998)', Výskumné Centrum Slovenskej Spoločnosti pre Zahraničnú Politiku, Prešov.

Elster, J., Offe, C. and Preuss, U. (1998), *Institutional Design in Post-communist Societies*, Cambridge University Press, Cambridge.

'Ethnic Minorities in Slovenia' (1994), Institute for Ethnic Studies Information, Bureau Government, Ljubljana.

Evans, G. and Whitefield, S. (1995), 'Social and Ideological Cleavage Formation in Post-Communist Hungary', *Europe- Asia Studies*, Vol. 7, pp.1177-1204.

Evans, G. and Whitefield, S. (1998), 'The Structuring of Political Cleavages in Post-communist Societies: the Case of the Czech Republic and Slovakia', *Political Studies*, Vol. XLVI., pp.115-139.

Fink-Hafner, D and Cox, T. (ed) (1996), *Into Europe? Perspectives from Britain and Slovenia*, Scientific Library of Faculty of Social Sciences, Ljubljana.

Fink-Hafner, D. and Robbins, J. (1997), *Making a New Nation: The Formation of Slovenia*, Dartmouth, Aldershot.

Fink-Hafner, D. (1995), 'The Disintegration of Yugoslavia', *Canadian Slavonic Papers*, Vol. XXXVII, pp.339-352.

Fukuyama, F. (1989), 'The end of History?', *National Interest*, pp.3-18.

Fukuyama, F. (1992), *The End of History and the Last Man*, Free Press, New York.

Gaddis, J. (1986), 'The Long Peace', *International Security*, Vol.10, pp.99-142.

Gál, F., Frič, P., Hunčík, P. and Lord, C.(1993), *Maďarská Menšina na Slovensku*, National Endowment for Democracy in Washington & Nadácia Sándor Márai, Bratislava.

Garton Ash ,T. (1990), *The Magic Lantern*, Random House, New York.

Garton Ash, T. (1990), *The Uses of Adeversity*, Vintage, New York.

Garton Ash, T. (1999),'Cry the Dismembered Country', *New York Times Review*, January 14, pp.29-33.

Gaubatz, K.T. (1996),'Kant, Democracy and History', *Journal of Democracy*,Vol.7, pp.136-151.

Gellner, E. (1983), *Nations and Nationalism*, Blackwell, Oxford.

Gellner, E. (1992), *Postmodernism, Reason and Religion*, Routledge, London.

Gellner, E. and Ionescu, G. (1969), *Populism its Meanings and National Characteristics*, Weidenfeld and Nicholson, London.

Gill, S. (1997), 'Gramsci, Modernity and Globalization', paper given at BISA Conference, Leeds.

Glenny, M. (1990), *The Rebirth of History*, Penguin Books, London.

Glenny, M. (1999), *The Balkans 1804-1999*, Granta Books, London.

Goode, P. and Bottomore, T. (1978), *Austro-Marxism*, Clarendon, Oxford.

Gordon Skilling, H. (1997-8) 'Czechs and Slovaks', *International Journal*, Vol. LIII, pp.73-94.

Greenfeld, L. (1992), *Nationalism Five Roads to Modernity*, Harvard University Press, Cambridge London.

Greenfeld, L. (1996), 'Nationalism and Modernity', *Social Research*, Vol. 63, pp.4-40.

Guiberneau, M. (1996), *Nationalisms*, Polity, Cambridge.

Gyáni, G. (1993), 'Political Uses of Tradition in Post-Commnunist Eastern and Central Europe', *Social Research*, Vol. 60, pp.893-913.

Habermas, J. (1999), The European Nation-State and the Pressures of Globalization', *New Left Review* 235, pp. 46-58.

Halliday, F. (1999), *Revolutions and World Politics*, Macmillan, London.

Hall, J. (ed) (1998), *The State of the Nation*, Cambridge University Press, Cambridge.

Hall, S., Held, D. and McGrew, T.(1996), *Modernity and its Futures*, Polity Press in Association with The Open University, Cambridge.

Haller, M. and Richter, R. (1994), *Toward a European Nation?*, M.E. Sharpe, New York.

Hafner-Fink, M. (1997), 'Changing Social Structure in the Process of Transition from Socialism: The case of Slovenia', paper prepared for the 68th Annual Pacific Sociological Association meeting, San Diego, California.

Hafner-Fink, M. (1996) '(Trans)formation of the Idea of Self-management: Slovenian Perspectives', paper prepared for the 5th Conference of the International Society for the Study of European ideas, Utrecht

Harris, E. (1998), 'The Slovak Question at the End of the Twentieth Century: National Identity, Political Culture and Democratisation' in *Čarnijev Zbornik*, Faculty of Arts, Ljubljana.

Harris, E.(1999), 'Nacionalizmus a Demokratizačný Proces', *OS* 11, pp.42-47.

Harris, E. (1999), 'Assessing the Compatibility Between Nationalism and Democracy in Postcommunist Societies: Some Perspectives from Slovakia and Slovenia', *Slovak Sociological Review*, Vol.31, pp.587-602.

Hasner, P. (1993)'Beyond Nationalism and Internationalism', *Survival*, Vol. 35, pp.49-65.

Havel, V. (1989), *Living in Truth*, Faber and Faber, London.

Hedetoft, U. (1997), 'The Nation-State Meets the World: National Identities in the Context of Transnationality and Cultural Globalisation', paper prepared for BISA Conference, Leeds University.

Held, D. (eds) (1993), *Prospects for Democracy*, Polity, Cambridge.

Held, D. (1997), *Democracy and the Global Order*, Polity, Cambridge.

Henderson, K. (1999), *Back to Europe*, UCL Press, London.

Herb, G. and Kaplan, D. (1998), *Nested Identities*, Rowman and Littlefield Publishers, Boulder, New York.

Hobsbawm, E. (1996), 'Language, Culture and National Identity', *Social Research*, Vol. 63, pp.1065-1079.

Hockenos, P. (1993), *Free to Hate*, Routledge, London.

Holmes, S. (1994), 'Liberalism for the World of Ethnic Passions and Decaying States', *Social Research*, Vol. 61, pp.599-611.

Horowitz, D. (1985), *Ethnic Groups in Conflict*, University of California Press, Berkeley.

Hribar, T. (1987), 'Slovenska Državnost', *Nova Revija* VI, special issue Prispevki za Slovenski Nacionalni program, pp.3-29, and 'The Slovenes and European Transnationality' in the same issue, pp.33-36.

Hroch, M. (1985), *The Social Preconditions of National Revival in Europe*, Cambridge University Press, Cambridge.

Hroch, M. (1993), 'From National Movements to the Fully-Formed Nation', *New Left Review* 198, pp.3-20.

Hroch, M. (1995), 'National Self-Determination from a Historic Perspective', *Canadian Slavonic Papers*, Vol. 37, pp.283-300.

Huntington, S. (1993), *The Third Wave*, University of Oklahoma Press, Norman OK.

Huntington, S. (1993), 'The Clash of Civilizations?', *Foreign Affairs*, Vol. 72, pp.22-49.

Huntington, S. (1996), 'The West Unique, Not Universal', *Foreign Affairs*, Vol. 75, pp.28-46.

Hutchinson, J. (1994), *Modern Nationalism*, Fontana Press, London.

Hutchinson J. and Smith, A.D. (1994), *Nationalism*, Oxford University Press, Oxford.

Hutchinson J. and Smith, A.D. (1996), *Ethnicity*, Oxford University Press, Oxford.

Hyde-Pryce, A. (1999), *The International Politics of East Central Europe*, Sage, London.

Ignatieff, M. (1994), *Blood and Belonging*, Vintage, London.

Isaac, C. (1996), 'The Meanings of 1989', *Social Research*, Vol. 63, pp.291-344.

Joo, R. (1991), 'Slovenes in Hungary and Hungarians in Slovenia: Ethnic and State Identity', *Ethnic and Racial Studies*, Vol. 14, pp.100-106.

Joppke, Ch. (1999), *Immigration and the Nation-State*, Oxford University Press, Oxford.

Judah, T.(1997), 'The Serbs: The Sweet and Rotten Smell of History', *Daedalus* 126, pp.23-45.

Jurová, A. (1993), *Vývoj Rómskej Problematiky na Slovensku po Roku 1945*, Goldpress Publishers, Košice.

Kaldor, M. and Vejvoda, I. (1997), 'Democratization in East Central European Countries', *International Affairs*, Vol. 73, pp.59-83.

Kamenec, I. (1998), *Tragédia Politika, Kňaza a Človeka*, Bratislava, Archa.

Kant, I. (1991), *Political Writings*, Cambridge University Press, Cambridge.

Keohane, R., Nye, J. and Hoffmann, S.(1993), *After the Cold War*, Harvard University Press, Cambridge, London.

Khan, M. (1995), 'Bosnia-Herzegovina and the Crisis of the Post-Cold War International System', *East European Politics and Societies*, Vol. 9, pp.459-498.

Kiss, J. (1995), 'Beyond the Nation State', *Social Research*, Vol. 63, pp.191-245.

Kováč, D. (1997), *Slováci a Češi*, AEP, Bratislava.

Kováč, D. (1997), 'Nacionalizmus 19. a 20. Storočia', *Historický Časopis*, Vol. 45, pp.77-90.

Kovač, M. (1988), 'The Slovene Spring', *New Left Review* 171, pp.115-128.

Krašovec, A. (2000), *Moč v Političnih Strankah*, Profesija, Ljubljana.

Krivý, V. (1996), *Slovensko a Jeho Regióny*, Nadácia Média, Bratislava.

Kučan, M. (1998), 'Narod je Zgodovinska Tvorba in ne Izmislek', *Kolaps* 5, pp. 34-39.

Kupchan, Ch. (1995), *Nationalism and Nationalities in the New Europe*, Cornell University Press, Ithaca.

Kuzio, T. (2001), ''Nationalizing states', or nation-building? A critical review of the theoretical literature and empirical evidence', *Nations and Nationalism*, Vol.7, pp.135-154.

Latawski, P. (eds) (1995), *Contemporary Nationalism in East Central Europe*, Macmillan, London.

Layne, C. (1994), 'Kant or Cant: The Myth of the Democratic Peace', *International Security*, Vol.19, pp.5-49.

Leibich, A. (1995), 'Nations, States, Minorities: Why is Eastern Europe Different?', Dissent,Vol.42, pp.307-313.

Linklater, A. (1998), 'Cosmopolitan Citizenship', *Citizenship Studies*, Vol. 2, pp.23-43.

Linz, J. (1990), 'Transitions to Democracy', *The Washington Quarterly*, Vol. 13, pp.143-164.

Linz, J.J. and Stepan, A. (1996), *Problems of Democratic Transition and Consolidation*, The Johns Hopkins University Press, Baltimore.

Lipták, L. (1997), 'Okrúhlý stôl: Phenomén Ďurica', *Kritika a Kontext*, Vol. 2, pp. 4-23.

Lipták, L. (1998), *Slovensko v 2O.storoččí*, Kalligram, Bratislava.

Maier, C.S. (1994), 'Democracy and its Discontents', *Foreign Affairs*, Vol.73, pp. 48-65.

Mair, P. (1997), 'E.E. Schattschneider's The Semisovereign People', *Political Studies*, Vol. XLV.pp.947-954.

Mandelbaum, M. (ed.) (1996), *Postcommunism*, Council on Foreign Relations Books, New York.

Mann, M. (1999), 'The Dark Side of Democracy: The Modern Tradition of Ethnic and Political Cleansing', *New Left Review* 235, pp.18-45.

Mannová, E. (ed.) (1998), *Meštianstvo a Občianská Spoločnosť na Slovensku 1900-1989*, AEP, Bratislava

Mastný V. (2000), 'The historical experience of federalism in East Central Europe', *East European politics and Societies*, Vol. 14, pp.64-97.

McLellan, D. (1988), *Marxism*, Oxford University Press, Oxford.

Mearsheimer, J. (1990), 'Back to the Future', *International Security*, Vol.15, pp. 5-56.

Mearsheimer, J. (1994/1995), 'The False Promise of International Institutions', *International Security*, Vol.19, pp.5-49.

Medved, F. (1994-5), 'A Path Towards Carthography of Slovene National Identity', *Razprave in Gradivo*, Vol. 29, Inštitut za Narodnostna Vprašanja, Ljubljana, pp.177-210.

Meiklejohn Terry, S. (1993), 'Thinking About Post-Communist Transitions: How Different Are They?', *Slavic Review*, Vol. 52, pp.333-337.

Mesežnikov, G. (ed.) (1995), *Slovakia Parliamentary elections 1994*, Slovak Political Science Association, Bratislava.

Mesežnikov, G. and Kollár, M. (2001), 'O výrobe coca coly z vody: pozitívné hodnotenie situacie dnes nie je v móde', *Kultúrny život,* verzia pre tlačiareň, 5.5.2001, www.ivo.sk.

Michnik, A. (1991), 'Nationalism', *Social Research,* Vol. 58, pp.757-763.

Miháliková, S. (1996), 'Národné Symboly Slovenskej Štátnosti', *Political Review*, Vol.2, pp.53-70.

Mill J.S. (1991), *On Liberty and Other Essays*, Oxford University Press, Oxford.

Miller, D. (1995), *On Nationality*, Clarendon Press, Oxford.

Motyl, A. (ed.) (1992), *The Post-Soviet Nations*, Columbia Press, New York.

Mudde, C. and Kopecký, P. (2000), 'Explaining Different paths of Democratization: the Czech and Slovak Republics', *Journal of Communist Studies and Transition Politics*, Vol.16, pp.63-84.

Musil, J. (1992), 'Czechoslovakia in the Middle of Transition', *Daedalus* 121, pp.175-195.

Musil, J. (ed) (1995), *The End of Czechoslovakia*, Central European University Press, Budapest.

Nairn, T. (1975), 'The Modern Janus', *New Left Review* 94, pp.3-31.

*Národná Obroda*, daily newspaper, Slovakia.

Nedelsky, N. (2001), 'The wartime Slovak State: a case study in the relationship between ethnic nationalism and authoritarian patterns of governance', *Nations and Nationalism*, Vol. 7, pp.215-234.

Nelson, D. (1993), 'Democracy, Markets and Security in Eastern Europe', *Survival*, Vol. 3, pp.156-171

Neuhold, H., Havlik, P. and Suppan, A. (1995), *Political and Economic Transformation in East Central Europe*, Westview Press, Boulder.

Nodia, G. (1996), 'How Different Are Postcommunist Transitions?', *Journal of Democracy*,Vol.7, pp.15-29.

Offe, C. (1991), 'Capitalism by Democratic Design?', *Social Research*, Vol. 58, pp. 865-892.

Offe, C. (1996), *Modernity and the State*, Polity, Cambridge.

Pavlowitch, S. (1988), *The Improbable Survivor*, C. Hurst & Company, London.

Periwal, S. (1995), *Notions of Nationalism*, Central European University Press, Budapest.

Pithart, P. (1993), 'Intellectuals in Politics: Double Dissent in the Past Double Disappointment Today', *Social Research*, Vol. 60, pp.751-761.

Pithart, P. (1995), 'The Division of Czechoslovakia: A Preliminary Balance Sheet for the End of a Respectable Country', *Canadian Slavonic Papers*, Vol. 37, pp.321-338.

Plasser, F. and Pribersky, A. (1996), *Political Culture in East Central Europe*, Ashgate Publishing, Aldershot.

Posen, B. (1993), 'The Security Dilemma and Ethnic Conflict', *Survival*, Vol. 35, pp.27-47.

Pridham, G. and Vanhanen, T. (1994), *Democratization in Eastern Europe*, Routledge, London.

Prizel, J. (1998) *National Identity and Foreign Policy*, Cambridge University Press, Cambridge.

Prunk, J. (1996), *A Brief History of Slovenia*, Založba Grad, Ljubljana.

Przeworski, A. (1995), *Sustainable Democracy*, Cambridge University Press, Cambridge.

Przeworski, A., Alvarez, M., Cheibub, J. and Limongi, L. (1996), 'What Makes Democracies Endure', *Journal of Democracy* Vol. 7, pp.39-55.

Ramet, S. (1992), *Nationalism and Federalism in Yugoslavia 1962-1991*, Indiana University Press, Indianopolis.

Ramet, S. and Adamovich, L. (1995), *Beyond Yugoslavia*, Westview Press, Boulder.

Rizman, R. (1991), *Studies on Ethnonationalism*, Krt, Ljubljana

Rizman, R. (1997), *Izzivi Odprte Družbe*, Liberalna Akademija, Ljubljana.

Rothschild, J. (1981), *Ethnopolitics: A Conceptual Framework*, Columbia University Press, New York.

Ruggie, J.G. (1993), 'Territoriality and Beyond: Problematizing Modernity in International Relations', *International Organizations*, Vol. 47, pp.139-174.

Rupel, D. (ed.) (1996), *Slovenska Smer*, Čankarjeva Založba, Ljubljana.

Rupnik, J. (1996), 'The Reawakening of European Nationalism', *Social Research*, Vol. 63, pp.41-75.

Rupnik, J. (1999), 'The Postcommunist Divide', *Journal of Democracy*, Vol. 10, pp.57- 63.

Rupnik, J. (2000), 'Eastern Europe: the International Context', *Journal of Democracy*, Vol.11, pp.115-129.

Rustow, D. (1970), 'Transition to Democracy', *Comparative Politics*, Vol. 2, pp. 337-363.

Saideman, S. (1996), 'The Dual Dynamics of Disintegration: Ethnic Politics and Security Dilemmas in Eastern Europe', *Nationalism and Ethnic Politics*, Vol. 2, pp.18-43.

Sartori, G. (1995), 'How Far Can Free Government Travel?', *Journal of Democracy*, Vol. 6, pp.101-111.

Schedler, A. (1998), 'What is Democratic Consolidation', *Journal of Democracy*, Vol. 9, pp.91-103.

Schmitter, P. (1994), 'Dangers and Dilemmas of Democracy', *Journal of Democracy*, Vol. 5, pp.57-74.

Schnapper, D. (1996/97),'Beyond the opposition: 'civic' nation versus 'ethnic' nation', *The ASEN Bulletin* 12, pp.4-8.

Schöpflin, G. (1994), 'The Problems of Democratic Construction', *Daedalus* 123, pp.127-141.

Schwarzmantel, J.J. (1997), *The Age of Ideology*, Macmillan, London.

Schwarzmantel, J.J. (1991), *Socialism and the Idea of the Nation*, Harvester Wheatsheaf, Hemel Hempstead.

Seroka, J. (1992), 'The Political Future of Yugoslavia: Nationalism and the Critical Years 1989-1991', *Canadian Review of Studies in Nationalism*, Vol. XIX, pp. 151-160.

Skalnik Leff, C. (1988), *National Conflict in Czechoslovakia*, Princeton University Press, Princeton.

Skalnik Leff, C. (1997), *The Czech and Slovak Republics*, Westview Press, Boulder.

*Slovak Spectator*, December 1998.

Slovene Writers Association Special (1991), 'The Case of Slovenia', *Nova Revija*, July edition.

*Slovenská Republika*, daily newspaper, Slovakia.

*Sme*, spravodajský denník, Slovakia and www.sme.sk.

Smith, A.D. (1971), *Theories of Nationalism*, Duckworth, London.

Smolar, A. (1996), 'Revolutionary Spectacle and Peaceful Transition', *Social Research*, Vol. 63, pp.439-449.

Snyder, J. (1993), 'Nationalism and the Crisis of the Post-Soviet State', *Survival*, Vol. 35, pp.5-27.

*Socialism in Yugoslav Theory and Practice*, (1974), Collection of Conferences, University of Beograd, Beograd.

Sørensen, L. and Eliason, L. (ed.) (1997), *Forward to the Past?*, Aarhus University Press, Aarhus.

Sugar, P. (ed.) (1995), *Eastern European Nationalism in the 20th Century*, The American University Press, Washington.

Szomolányi, S. (ed.) (1997), *Slovensko:Problémy Konsolidácie Demokracie*, Slovenské Združenie pre Politické Vedy, Nadácia Friedricha Eberta, Bratislava.

Šiklová, J. (1996), 'What Did We Lose', *Social Research*, Vol. 63, pp.531-564.

Šubrt, P. and Toš, N. (1995), *Crossroads of Transition*, Faculty of Charles University, Praha.

Švob Dokić, N. (1994), *Medunarodni Položaj Novih Europskih Zemalja*, IRMO, Zagreb.

Taguieff, P. (1995), 'Political Science confronts Populism: From a Conceptual Mirage to a Real Problem', *Telos* 103, pp.9-45.

Tambini, D. (2001), 'Post-national Citizenship', *Ethnic and Racial Studies*, Vol.24, pp.195-217.

Tismaneanu, V. (1999), 'Reassessing the Revolutions of 1989', *Journal of Democracy*, Vol. 10, pp.69-73.

Tocqueville de, A. (1969), *Democracy in America*, Anchor Books, New York.

Toš, N. (1997),'Informiranost in Stališča Ciljnih Skupin v Sloveniji o Evropski Unii in Slovenskem Približenanju EU', pog.št.121/97, University of Ljubljana, Ljubljana.

Thornberry, P. (1993), *"UN Declaration on the Rights of Persons Belonging to National or Ethnic, Religious and Linguistic Minorities"*, Minority Rights Group, London.

Tulchin, J. and Romero, B. (1995), *The Consolidation of Democracy in Latin America*, Lynne Rienner, London.

Urban, M. (1994), 'The politics of Identity in Russia's Postcommunist Transition: The nation Against Itself', *Slavic Review*, Vol. 53, pp.733-765.

'Ustava Slovenskej Republiky' (1992), NVK International, Bratislava.

Verdery, K. (1993), 'Nationalism and National Sentiments in Post-socialist Romania', *Slavic Review*, Vol.5, pp.179-203.

Verdery, K. (1996), 'Nationalism, Postsocialism and Space in Eastern Europe', *Social Research*, Vol. 63, pp.77-95.

'Verejný Audit Volebných Programov Politických Strán', (1998), Nadácia F.A. Hayeka, Bratislava.

Vreg, F. (2001), 'Volitve 2000 in Predvolilna Kampanja', *Teorija in Praksa*, Vol.38, pp.181-200.

Waever, O., Buzan, B., Kelstrup, M. and Lamaitre, P. (1993), *Identity, Migration and the New Security Agenda in Europe*, Pinter Publishers, London.

Waltz, K. (1979), *Theory of International Politics*, Adison Wesley, Reading.

Walzer, M. (1992), 'The New Tribalism', *Dissent* 39, pp.164-171.

Weber, E. (1976), *Peasants into Frenchmen: The modernization of Rural France 1870-1914*, Stanford University Press, Stanford.

Weiss, L. (1998), *The Myth of the Powerless State,* Polity, Cambridge.

Weiss, L. (1997), 'Globalization and the Myth of the Powerless State', *New Left Review* 222, pp.3-26.

'White Paper on Education in the Republic of Slovenia' (1996), Ministry of Education and Sport, Ljubljana.

Yiftachel,O. (1997), 'Nation-building or Ethnic Fragmentation? Frontier Settlement and Collective Identities in Israel', *Space & Polity*, Vol.1, pp.149-169.

Yiftachel, O. (1998), 'Nation-Building and Social Division of Space', *Nationalism and Ethnic Politics*, Vol.4, pp.33-58.

Zajc, D., Kropivnik, S. and Lukšič, I. (1996), *Conflict and Consensus*, Political Science Association, Ljubljana.

Zajc, D. (2000), 'The Role of National Parliament in the Process of Accession to European Union – The Case of Slovenia', paper presented at the XVIIIth IPSA World Congress, Quebec.

Zaslavsky, V. (1992), 'Nationalism and Democratic Transition in Postcommunist Societies', *Daedalus* 121, pp.97-121.

Zver, M. (1996), *100 Let Social-Demokracije*, Veda, Ljubljana.

Žagar, M. (1995), 'Nationality, Protection of Minorities and Transition to Democracy: the Case of Slovenia', I and II, *Teorija in Praksa*, Vol.32, pp.88-95 and pp.243-254.

Žižek, S. (1997), 'Multiculturalism, or, the Cultural Logic of Multinational Capitalism', *New Left Review* 225, pp.28-52.

# Index